Cultural Reciprocity
in Special Education

Cultural Reciprocity
in Special Education

Building Family–Professional Relationships

by

Maya Kalyanpur, Ph.D.
Ministry of Education, Youth and Sports
Phnom Penh, Cambodia

and

Beth Harry, Ph.D.
University of Miami
Florida

with invited contributors

·P·A·U·L·H·
BROOKES
PUBLISHING C.º ®

Baltimore • London • Sydney

Paul H. Brookes Publishing Co.
Post Office Box 10624
Baltimore, Maryland 21285-0624
USA

www.brookespublishing.com

"Paul H. Brookes Publishing Co." is a registered trademark of
Paul H. Brookes Publishing Co., Inc.

Typeset by Integrated Publishing Solutions, Grand Rapids, Michigan.
Manufactured in the United States of America by
Sheridan Books, Inc., Chelsea, Michigan.

Case examples are based on the authors' experiences and are used by permission as applicable.
Names have been changed to protect confidentiality.

Cover photos © istockphoto.com.

Library of Congress Cataloging-in-Publication Data

Kalyanpur, Maya.
   Cultural reciprocity in special education : building family–professional
relationships / by Maya Kalyanpur and Beth Harry.
      p.   cm.
   Includes bibliographical references and index.
   ISBN 978-1-59857-231-5 — ISBN 1-59857-231-8   1. Special
education—Social aspects—United States.   2. Special education—Parent
participation—United States.   3. Minority people with
disabilities—Education—United States   4. Intercultural
communication—United States.   I. Harry, Beth.   II. Title.

   LC3981.K33 2012
   371.0—dc23   2012013386

British Library Cataloguing in Publication data are available from the British Library.

2016   2015   2014   2013   2012

10   9   8   7   6   5   4   3   2   1

Contents

About the Authors

Maya Kalyanpur, Ph.D., Inclusive Education Advisor, Education Sector Support Scale Up Program (ESSSUAP) – Global Partnership for Education (GPE), Ministry of Education, Youth and Sports, 27 St. 606 Beoung Kok 2, Toul Kork, Phnom Penh 12302, Cambodia

Maya Kalyanpur started her career as a teacher of children with intellectual disabilities in India in 1981. She received her doctoral degree in special education from Syracuse University in 1994 and taught at Towson University for 14 years, retiring as Professor. She authored books and numerous articles on special education policy and families from culturally diverse backgrounds in the United States and India. Since 2006, she has been a consultant in Cambodia on projects relating to inclusive education.

Beth Harry, Ph.D., Professor, Special Education, School of Education, University of Miami, Merrick Building Room 222, Coral Gables, Florida 33124

Beth Harry, a native of Jamaica, received her bachelor's and master's degrees from the University of Toronto and her doctoral degree from Syracuse University. She entered the field of special education as a parent of a child with cerebral palsy, an experience that she has chronicled in the memoir *Melanie, Bird with a Broken Wing: A Mother's Story* (Paul H. Brookes Publishing Co., 2010). An author of several books and articles, her teaching and research focus on issues related to the intersection of disability and diversity, with a particular concern for their impact on families. In 2002, she served on the National Academy of Sciences panel on ethnic disproportionality in special education.

About the Contributors

Monimalika Day, Ph.D., Consultant, Ambedkar University, India; Assistant Professor, College of Education and Human Development, George Mason University, Prince William Campus, Bull Run Hall, Room 220, 10900 University Boulevard, Manassas, Virginia 20110

Monimalika Day is a visiting associate professor at the Center for Early Childhood Education and Development at Ambedkar University in Delhi, India, where she is currently engaged in an extensive research project on quality indicators for early childhood programs. Prior to her work in India, she was an assistant professor at George Mason University and worked jointly with the Early Childhood Education Program and the Initiative for Educational Transformation, a graduate program for public school teachers. She has a doctoral degree from the University of Maryland. Her research and publications focus on preparing educators to work effectively with culturally, linguistically, and ability-diverse children and their families.

Shernaz García, Ph.D., Associate Professor, Multicultural/Bilingual Special Education, Department of Special Education, The University of Texas at Austin, 1 University Station, D5300, Austin, Texas 78712

Shernaz García's research and teaching interests are centered on the intercultural nature of teaching and learning and the impact of this interplay of difference on students and families from nondominant cultural and linguistic communities. She has been integrally involved in redesigning her department's teacher education program to foster special educators' ability to provide culturally responsive services and to build collaborative relationships with families as well as general educators. A native of India, her work continues to be informed by her cultural identity status in a predominantly white university.

Davenia Lea, Ph.D., Associate Director, Early Childhood Education, Office of Education, North American Division of the Seventh-Day Adventist Church, 12501 Old Columbia Pike, Silver Spring, Maryland 20904

Davenia Lea has worked in the field of early childhood special education for nearly 20 years. She has served as an early interventionist (birth to 3) for 10 years in Prince Georges County Public Schools in Maryland. She has also served as an assistant professor at Bowie State University and Towson University and as an associate professor and a department chair at Washington Adventist University.

Eva Thorp, Ed.D., Associate Professor, College of Education and Human Development, George Mason University, MS4C2, Thompson 1252, 4400 University Drive, Fairfax, Virginia 22030

Eva Thorp began her career as a teacher of young children with disabilities. Her research and publications focus on preparing early educators to work effectively with culturally, linguistically, and ability-diverse young children and their families. She has been the recipient of multiple federal grants that have enabled her to cultivate professional development materials; design in-service, preservice, and doctoral programs that embed coursework on issues of culture, language, equity, and social justice; and develop and evaluate strategies for recruiting and supporting a more diverse pool of early educators.

Preface

This book reflects the incredible response we have had over the years to our original book, *Culture in Special Education: Building Reciprocal Family–Professional Relationships* (Kalyanpur & Harry, 1999), and its companion volume, *Building Cultural Reciprocity with Families: Case Studies in Special Education* (Harry, Kalyanpur, & Day, 1999). Students and professionals alike have expressed their excitement at the novelty of the concept that our cultural values guide our professional behavior and at the recommendations we make to parents. The basic premise of our argument remains unchanged. If anything, the argument is more relevant than ever in today's world, even though so much has changed.

For one, Maya isn't in Kansas anymore! Whereas the first book was written when Maya was a postdoctoral fellow at the Beach Center for Families at the University of Kansas, she now lives and works in Cambodia. On the one hand, Maya has tried to bring to this book the duality of her experiences of being in a culture that is familiar to her as a fellow Asian even as she remains an outsider and becomes increasingly aware of how American she is. On the other hand, living halfway across the world from the United States has created in her a sense of being an outsider looking in on America and has increased her awareness of America's global impact on the rest of the world, particularly with regard to models and theories in the field of disability and inclusive education. (By the way, because this book is all about identifying values, if you caught the literary allusion in the first sentence of this paragraph to L. Frank Baum's *The Wizard of Oz*, you share a value, a common literary heritage, with mainstream America!)

A much more drastic and sobering change in the last decade is the economic downturn that has affected millions of ordinary families. Now here is an interesting fact about the United States, using Cambodia as a point of reference: Economists measure the wealth of nations through the gross national income (GNI) per capita or wealth level by population. In 2009, the United States' GNI was $43,360, whereas Cambodia's was just $650 (World Bank, 2010). Looking at this statistic, one would agree that Cambodia is a poor country in comparison to the United States. However, economists also calculate the distribution of this wealth using an inequality measure—the Gini coefficient or index—of a nation's richest 20% to the poorest 20%. In 2009, the United States' score on this index was 41, whereas Cambodia's score was 42, just 1 point below (United Nations Educational, Scientific and Cultural Organization [UNESCO], 2010). In other words, although the United States may be one of the richest countries—indeed, it was ranked 6th in the world in 2009—it also has extremes in how this wealth is distributed. With the top 10% of the population in the United States garnering 48.5% of all reported income in 2010 (Noah, 2010), it is hardly surprising that more and more people in the United States are living in poverty. Furthermore, whereas 15% of white children in the United States lived below poverty levels in 2008, 30% of Hispanic and 34% of African American children did so (U.S. Census Bureau, 2011). The current crisis of home foreclosures has hit families of color the hardest. As of 2010, an estimated 17% of Latino homeowners and 11% of African American homeowners already have lost their homes to foreclosure as compared to

4.5% of non-Hispanic whites (Bocian, Li, & Ernst, 2010). As professionals, it behooves us to understand the impact of these economic changes on the families we may serve and be sensitive to the likelihood that the communication gap between families and professionals is widening along with the economic gap.

Of equal significance is the fact that, as a nation, we are living under the shadow cast by the horrific events of 9/11. Maya remembers vividly an incident that occurred when, as a graduate assistant in 1986, she gave the class of students an exercise to get them to think about how as individuals we tend to make snap judgments about people. The students were given a list of people all based on stereotypes (e.g., hippie, banker, mother-of-three) and were asked—in the event of an end-of-the-world situation in which one uncontaminated nuclear fallout shelter remained—to select who they perceived as the "right" people to accompany them into the shelter and "save the world." It is interesting that one of the students, glancing quickly through the list, asked in all sincerity, "What's a fundamentalist Muslim?" There is no doubt that following the events of 9/11 we have lost some of that innocence. We may assume that many more people in the United States now know what a fundamentalist Muslim is, but the common accompanying idea that a Muslim, fundamentalist or not, is a terrorist is extremely disturbing; after all, the Oklahoma City bombing of 1995 and the Oslo mass murder in the summer of 2011 also were acts of terrorism committed by nominal Christians. And, this sense of "otherness" still exists, even as the United States receives more immigrants than ever and it is expected that by 2025 the immigrant or foreign-born share of the population will surpass the peak reached during the last great wave of immigration between 1890 and 1920 (Passel & Cohn, 2008). The United States may have moved from the model of the melting pot in which all cultures mixed and everyone emerged thinking alike, but we still hope new immigrants will "hybridize" by adapting to the mainstream culture without losing all aspects of their own culture in a process of selective acculturation (Portes & Rumbaut, 2006). Many of the families served by professionals are immigrants to the United States. In 2008, the U.S. immigrant or foreign-born population neared 38 million, constituting 12% of the total U.S. population. In some states, the growth of immigrants has been explosive; for instance, Arizona has experienced a 235% increase in its immigrant population since 1990. It is very likely that a sense of "otherness" has contributed to the recent enactment of a law in Arizona that, among other mandates, makes the failure to carry immigration documents a crime—a law that many have criticized as "an open invitation for harassment and discrimination against Hispanics" (Archibold, 2010). It is troubling to note that this divisive sentiment is being expressed in other countries as well, most particularly in European nations such as Denmark, Sweden, and Switzerland, long regarded as the most racially tolerant of nations.

In the international arena, the impact of globalization and American influence cannot be underestimated. As countries that have tended to lag behind in economic development scurry to catch up, the American or Western model of development continues to predominate. As part of this model of development, inclusive and special education policies and practices in the Western world and in the United States in particular have been and are being introduced, sometimes adapted for greater cultural relevance, and implemented in many developing countries (Armstrong, Armstrong, & Spandagou, 2010). For instance, Korea adopted a policy identical to the United States of providing services to children with disabilities only after they have undergone a process of identification and labeling. However, the persisting social stigma against children with intellectual or learning disabilities within the Korean culture, in which education and academic success are highly prized, has contributed to an underrepresentation of children with learning disabilities in inclusive schools because many parents prefer to arrange private tutoring services rather than have their child publicly labeled (Dr. Seung-Hee Park, Professor, Department of Special Education, Ewha Womans University, Seoul, personal communication, March 8, 2010). Similarly, international consultants in disability, in an effort to introduce to Cambodia the concept of the rights-based or social model of disability, have presented it as an alternative to the medical model; ironically, the medical model is a historical legacy of institutionalization in their own countries and not in Cambodia (Last, 2010).

The issues we have raised may seem too sweeping and beyond the scope of most professionals working on an individual basis with families of children with disabilities. Like many high school students, it seems natural to ask "How does this relate to me?" The fact is that what happens in the rest of the world relates as much to an individual as what happens in one's own environment and especially relates to families from culturally and linguistically diverse backgrounds. Ten years after we published our first book, we still live in a world where families from culturally and linguistically diverse backgrounds are disadvantaged. The disadvantage may be economic because of restricted access to quality education, health and housing, and, in the ultimate analysis, wealth, or it may be sociopolitical through a racially based national and global policy agenda. This is true both for native minorities as well as immigrant groups. Overall, families from culturally and linguistically diverse backgrounds continue to be more likely to need social services while being served by professionals who, in the majority, are Anglo-American, not poor, and not immigrant, and who, by virtue of their training, may be unaware of the implications of these differences and may take for granted that their professional expertise allows them to practice this anywhere in the world.

The first purpose of this book, then, is to revisit these taken for granted assumptions and, by including more anecdotes based either on our personal experiences or from recent research, illustrate the currency of the concept of and the need for cultural reciprocity. The second purpose is to respond to the question "How can we 'do' cultural reciprocity?" that has been raised time and again. At the risk of presenting cultural reciprocity within the clichéd formula of contrasting traditions seen as discrete stances, we suggest that cultural reciprocity is not something to "do" but rather to "be"—a frame of mind rather than a plan of action. Most important, we wish to emphasize that the process is not a linear, step-by-step approach. Our four-step guidelines are intended to facilitate a process of introspection that does not necessarily have to occur in a specific sequence. The ultimate intention is the empowerment of *both* parties by gaining a better understanding of each other's cultural values that allows them to make *informed* choices or decisions. Toward this, we have invited contributors who have applied the principles of cultural reciprocity in their own practice to describe these experiences in the second part of the book. We believe that these three chapters will illustrate the range of personalized interpretations that can be stimulated by immersion in the cultural reciprocity process.

REFERENCES

Archibold, R. (2010, April 23). Arizona enacts stringent law on immigration. *The New York Times.* Retrieved from http://www.nytimes.com/2010/04/24/us/politics/24immig.html

Armstrong, A.C., Armstrong, D., & Spandagou, I. (2010). *Inclusive education: International policy and practice.* Thousand Oaks, CA: Sage Publications.

Baum, L. F. (1900). *The wonderful wizard of Oz.* Chicago, IL: George M. Hill Company.

Bocian, D.G., Li, W., & Ernst, K.S. (2010). *Foreclosures by race and ethnicity: The demographics of a crisis.* Durham, NC: Center for Responsible Lending.

Harry, B., Kalyanpur, M., & Day, M. (1999). *Building cultural reciprocity with families: Case studies in special education.* Baltimore, MD: Paul H. Brookes Publishing Co.

Kalyanpur, M., & Harry, B. (1999). *Culture in special education: Building reciprocal family–professional relationhips.* Baltimore, MD: Paul H. Brookes Publishing Co.

Last, U. (2010). Mainstreaming disability: Approach and observations from a development practitioner in Cambodia. *Disability and International Development, 2,* 4–11.

Noah, T. (2010, September 3). The United States of inequality: Introducing the great divergence. *Slate.* Retrieved from http://www.slate.com/id/2266025/entry/2266026

Passel, J.S., & Cohn, D. (2008). *U.S. Population Projections: 2005–2050.* Washington, DC: Pew Research Center.

Portes, A., & Rumbaut, R. (2006). *Immigrant America: A portrait* (3rd ed.). Berkeley: University of California Press.

United Nations Educational, Scientific and Cultural Organization (UNESCO). (2010). *Education for all global monitoring report 2010: Reaching the marginalized.* Oxford, United Kingdom: Oxford University Press.

U.S. Census Bureau. (2011). *Statistical abstract of the United States: 2011.* Retrieved from http://www.census.gov/compendia/statab/2011/tables/11s0711.pdf

World Bank. (2010). *World development report: Development and climate change.* Washington, DC: Author.

Acknowledgment

Special thanks to Andrea Adelman, doctoral student at the University of Miami, for her invaluable assistance with our literature search and reference list.

In memory of Renuka Wanchoo, Sarah Rao,
Bhaskar Kalyanpurkar, and Leela Rao Kalyanpurkar,
four fewer stars in my firmament

—Maya

With thanks to Ben and Mark for their continuing support

—Beth

Cultural Reciprocity

Working with Families

In this section, we present the process of cultural reciprocity as a means to facilitate a process of introspection that ultimately results in the empowerment of professionals and families alike by gaining a better understanding of each other's cultural values. This process allows both sides to collaborate in making informed choices or decisions. We do this by examining taken-for-granted assumptions in the legal and epistemological underpinnings of definitions of disability and in the way in which professional expertise and language are conceptualized. We also analyze these cultural assumptions embedded in professionals' recommendations to parents regarding parenting styles and in professional interactions with parents around issues of goal setting for students. We introduce each chapter with a personal anecdote that highlights the impact that unstated cultural assumptions can have on people who do not share those assumptions.

Chapter 1

Cultural Underpinnings of Special Education

Beth's Story

On a trip to Albuquerque in the middle of winter, I had the disconcerting experience of boarding a plane at the Baltimore/Washington International Airport and, within minutes, being asked to deplane. Back at the departure gate, I waited with other anxious passengers for some information regarding the status of the flight. After about a half an hour's wait came the following announcement: "Passengers on the flight to Albuquerque—please be advised that we will be boarding in about an hour's time since a new piece of equipment will soon be arriving from Philadelphia."

Being a very phobic air traveler and knowing nothing about the mechanics of any kind of vehicle, I reacted to this announcement with some consternation. I thought, "A new piece of equipment? What could it be? A wrench? A new steering wheel? Some new radar equipment? Does this mean that we'll have to wait while they fix it or replace some part? Shouldn't they just give us a new plane?" I went to the desk and asked the attendant what the announcement meant. The attendant replied, "It said they're sending a new plane."

This was about 12 years ago, and I still remember vividly my annoyance at what seemed to me the use of language as a subterfuge. Since then, I have repeated this story to many people, asking for their impression of the meaning of this language event. Although many people are now more accustomed to hearing the term *equipment* used in this way in airports, everyone agrees that it is a prime example of jargon, in which a group of people who belong to a particular field of work use language in a way that differs from the way that it would be used by the population at large. It also is an example of how people use jargon that is specific to their field without even being aware that they are doing so.

My main concern is the effect that such language might have on the uninitiated. This depends on the perspective that any individual has regarding airplane travel. For me, connotations of the word *equipment* compared with the word *airplane* reflect my fear of flying; therefore, the following associations with the word *equipment* come to mind readily: a tool, a large class of technical items, something neutral, or something made and manipulated by human beings. Associations for the word *airplane* rush in just as quickly: something that takes you up into the sky, defying the laws of gravity; something huge and powerful that carries large numbers of people at once; or something that can come crashing down to earth and kill those large numbers of people. Thus, to refer to an airplane as a "piece of equipment" is to minimize, neutralize, and mitigate the features that, for me, are dominant: its power and its danger. A piece of equipment is, after all, within human control—simply a tool at our disposal; an airplane, however, in its totality, somehow seems more than the sum of its parts. Someone who finds flying safe and exhilarating might have interpreted this kind of communication quite differently. My point is that language is more than denotative. It is connotative, and connotations evoke emotions that are beyond rationalization.

In the departure lounge at the Baltimore/Washington International Airport, the language of the announcement reflected a technological culture with which the airplane experts probably identified. Within that culture, such use of the word *equipment* is probably commonplace and not thought of as having any particular effect. As an anxious passenger, however, I was a total outsider to that culture.

In much the same way that the language of airplanes was "foreign" to Beth in this story, we, the authors of this book, have felt like outsiders to the culture of special education in the United States. We had not, of course, expected to feel this way. In our home countries, Jamaica and India, we had assumed that disabilities were factual phenomena and that special education for people with disabilities would somehow reflect a universality of meaning, of affect, or, at the very least, of value. That is not to say that we thought that we already knew the answers or even all of the questions. Certainly, we expected to be introduced to new theories and new instructional approaches, but neither of us had conceived of the coming experience as a cultural event, the underpinnings of which would take several years for us to "unpack."

CULTURAL IDENTITY AND THE ACCULTURATION PROCESS

What do we mean by the *culture of special education?* In its larger meaning, the term *culture* denotes the shared implicit and explicit rules and traditions that express the beliefs, values, and goals of a group of people. Consider, first, the meaning of *cultural identity* and *acculturation*.

Children are raised within a cultural framework that imposes rewards and sanctions for efficient learning of the group's norms and expectations. According to the traditional view of culture, most individuals have been brought up within one such framework. The process of acculturation involves being introduced to a new system and gradually accommodating to it. Berry, Phinney, Sam, and Vedder defined acculturation as the following:

> The process of cultural and psychological change that follows intercultural contact.... Cultural changes include alterations in a group's customs and in their economic and political life. Psychological changes include alterations in individuals' attitudes toward the acculturation process, their cultural identities…and their social behaviors in relation to the groups in contact. (2006, p. 305)

Various versions of the acculturation process have been offered that view acculturation on a spectrum. For example, Ramírez and Castañeda (1974) described acculturation as a series of stages ranging from traditional to dualistic to atraditional. Leung (1988) specified *marginality* as the transition between traditionalism and biculturalism and conceived of the fourth stage as *overacculturation,* whereby the elements of one's original culture have been totally rejected. Going further, Red Horse (1980) added a fifth stage, which he called "pan-renaissance," in which a group seeks a revitalization or revival of the traditional culture, such as that sought by African Americans in the 1960s or by some North American Indian tribes in the United States and Canada.

The foregoing spectrum or stage theories suggest that cultures are somehow discrete, that acculturation is a process of change over time, and that an individual can be no more than *bicultural*—a state that often is metaphorically described as "walking in two worlds" (Henze & Vanett, 1993, p. 116). Rather than identifying points on a spectrum, Berry and colleagues conceptualized the outcomes of acculturation as representing "the degree to which people wish to maintain their heritage culture and identity; and the degree to which people seek involvement with the larger society" (2006, p. 306). In a study of data on immigrant youth from 26 different cultural backgrounds living in 13 different countries, Berry and colleagues identified four predominant acculturation patterns: *assimilation* (little maintenance of the original culture), *separation* (some cultural maintenance with avoidance of involvement with the mainstream), *marginalization* (neither cultural maintenance nor involvement with the larger society), and *integration* (a balance of both cultural maintenance and involvement with the larger society).

More akin to the view of Berry and colleagues (2006) is the perspective offered by Banks and McGee Banks (2010), who described a more fluid and less discrete way of thinking about cultural identity. Banks and McGee Banks's view is applicable to multicultural societies such as the United States that consist of "a shared culture as well as many subcultures" (p. 7). They described a complex picture of macro- and microlevels of culture in which the macrocultural framework is an overarching national frame that includes many microcultural groups, each of which participates to varying extents in the macroculture while simultaneously retaining varying amounts of its original cultural traditions. Thus, the cultural identity of any individual may reflect features of the macroculture, of one's original microculture, and of any other microcultural groups within the society. Factors such as race, ethnicity, nationality, language, social status, and geographical location are key ingredients in the pattern of identity that emerges.

The challenge of responding to the need to acculturate also applies to other aspects of identity besides ethnic and national identity. Individuals may develop affiliations with professional or personal interest groups that have their own norms and rules; these features also feed into cultural identity. As Banks and McGee Banks (2010) noted, each individual belongs to several groups at the same time and may experience stronger or weaker identification with the tenets of one group as compared with another based on the extent of socialization that is experienced within each group. It is also interesting to note that a group may be identified explicitly as such by means of well-defined beliefs and practices such as a particular religion, but it also may be a group by virtue of a particular experience such as being the parent of a child with a disability. Cultural identity, then, is multifaceted and highly individualized.

Both of us, the authors of this book, can cite readily affiliations with several microcultural groups while simultaneously participating in the American macroculture. These affiliations are strong enough to require sometimes separate, sometimes overlapping, and sometimes conflicting sets of rules for conduct. Both of us identify with the academic community, with women, and with other parents; however, Beth, in particular, feels affiliated to other parents who have children with disabilities. Beth's primary ethnic affiliation is Caribbean and also black in a broader sense, whereas Maya identifies herself as Indian and Hindu.

SPECIAL EDUCATION AS A CULTURAL INSTITUTION

What does it mean, then, to say that an individual shares membership in the culture of special education? We begin by viewing the special education system as a subsystem within the social institution of education. Bullivant (1993) explained the powerful relationship between the larger macroculture and the social institutions that carry out the cultural program of a society. First, he identified such institutions as "major interrelated systems of social roles and norms (rules) organized to satisfy important social and human needs" (p. 31). These institutions include the nuclear family, the education system, the legal system, and so forth. Bullivant explained the following:

> The distinctive pattern or style of an institutional agency's operation is determined by its charter or ideology. A charter consists of a collection of beliefs, values, and ideas about what the institutional agency aims at (its ends) and how it will arrange its structure and organization (the means) to carry out its aims. (p. 32)

> Much as a computer is programmed by software containing instructions, so an institutional agency's ideology, organization, structure, and operation are programmed by instructions and information that enable it to function properly. They also provide people in the agency with the necessary knowledge and ideas about which behaviors are appropriate and which are not, together with the rules and routines to follow. All these instructions, knowledge, and information are selected from the society's culture. (p. 33)

According to this analysis of social institutions, it would be expected that the special education system will reflect the "beliefs, values, and ideas" regarding both the ends and the means of education, which in turn reflect those of the national macroculture. Several powerful analyses of the historical development of U.S. public schools have emphasized that the education system's main charge has been transmission of the essential cultural tenets of U.S. society. Spindler and Spindler's (1990) classic analysis asserted that all American cultural dialogue, whether it be public speech such as editorials, public policy, campaign speeches, and classroom discussions or private speech such as parent–child interactions, is facilitated by a tacit understanding of core American values. They identified five such core values, all of which refer most directly to individual rights:

> Freedom of speech (and other forms of personal freedom); the rights of an individual (to be an individual and act on his or her own behalf); equality (as equality of opportunity and including sexual equality); the desirability of achievement attained by hard work (and the belief that anyone can achieve success if he or she works hard enough); and social mobility (the assumption that anyone can improve social status because the social structure is open and hard work will get you there. (p. 23)

On a more political level, Banks and McGee Banks added to this list expansionism, manifest destiny, and capitalism, which they describe as revealing "the less positive side of U.S. national values" (2010, p. 10).

In their analysis of the historical development of public schooling in America, Tyack and Hansot (1982) placed the Protestant ethic and capitalism at the core of that history. These authors described the early 19th-century efforts to establish a common school system as a "crusade" whose charge was to combine the Christian virtues of a "generalized Protestantism," such as hard work, literacy, temperance, and frugality, with "a work ethic and ideology favoring the development of capitalism" (p. 28). Along with this was the ideal of *equity*, one of the cornerstones of American democracy.

The latter half of the 19th century saw two powerful movements that further influenced the direction of the public school vision. The first movement was *industrialization*, as a result of which the vision became increasingly secular and, driven by a growing faith in science and scientific management, incorporated the Protestant ethic into what Tyack and Hansot referred to as "the gospel of efficiency" (1982, p. 121). The second force directing the charge of education was the vastly increasing and changing nature of the immigrant population. Concerns about the socialization of non–Anglo-Saxon immigrants resulted in the drive to "Americanization," which by the 1930s and 1940s was considered essential to combat the evils of urbanization, poverty, and cultural differences that were consistently interpreted as deficits of character and capability (Fass, 1989). As many scholars (e.g., Fass, 1989; Gould, 1981) have shown, beliefs about cultural and racial inferiority were fueled by the development of "mental testing" and were applied both to immigrants and to native-born minorities.

As Skrtic (1991) pointed out, equity is a difficult goal to achieve because of a conflict between the rapidly increasing heterogeneity of the school population and the drive for a bureaucratic uniformity in schools. As school leaders turned more and more to the IQ test as a means of sorting students into the manageable units required by the gospel of efficiency, the concept of individual impairment became institutionalized. This was the cornerstone on which the special education system was built, and the fact that this system still serves a disproportionately high percentage of minorities ought not be surprising. In summarizing and extending his analysis of this relationship, Skrtic described the constructs of student disability and special education as follows:

> Institutional categories created by a perfect storm in the historical development of public education—the fateful convergence of a dramatic increase in student diversity and the extensive bureaucratization of schools in the first half of the 20th century...a legitimating device, an institutional practice that, in effect, shifts the blame for school failure to students through medicalizing and objectifying discourses, while reducing the uncertainty of diversity by containing it through exclusionary practices." (2005, pp. 149–150)

Beyond a historical analysis, structural analysis also reveals the cultural charge given to the institution of education. Skrtic (1991) and Skrtic and McCall (2010) offered a detailed explication of how the epistemological and organizational bases of general education became interpreted and institutionalized within the professional culture of special education and subsequently became increasingly resistant to change. In essence, Skrtic and Skrtic and McCall argued that the field of education has been dominated by the positivist tradition of *knowledge,* which, with its assumption that reality is objective and unchangeable, has led to a mechanistic model of services ("a machine bureaucracy") and to a view of teaching that is based on a model of technical rationality (see also Schön, 1983). Special education, Skrtic argued, has been expressed as a "more extreme version" (1991, p. 105) of that model, and the special education teacher, "even more so than the general education teacher, is conceptualized as a technician" (1991, p. 106).

Hall's (1981) now famous classification of "low-context" and "high-context" cultures is helpful in understanding the cultural basis of the positivist tradition. Hall asserted that the emphasis on objectivity occurs most frequently in what he termed "low-context" cultures, in which "bureaucratic ranking systems" are based on the belief that when both action and agent are stripped of their contexts, or "decontextualized," the action can be conducted by anyone anywhere and, conversely, still have the same meaning in all contexts. He gave the example of the American legal system, which, in allowing "only established facts, stripped of all contextual background data, as admissible as evidence," is, he stated, "the epitome of low-context systems" (p. 107). A caveat to Hall's classic analysis was offered by Kittler, Rygal, and McKinnon (2011), who warned that the low- and/or high-context concept has been applied with too broad a brush to many societies, not taking into account the nuances of within-group variability in any society. Nevertheless, special education law, in its requirement for categorical classification of children's disabilities, reflects exactly this kind of abstracted, low-context language as contrasted with a more "high-context" approach that would accept or even encourage conclusions that tolerate greater ambiguity.

According to Skrtic (1995b), the low-context culture of technical rationalism results in an uncritical approach to the underpinnings of special education. Skrtic's answer to this is "critical pragmatism," which does the following:

> Approaches decision making in a way that recognizes and treats as problematic the assumptions, theories, and metatheories behind professional models, practices, and tools; it accepts the fact that our assumptions, theories, and metatheories themselves require evaluation and reappraisal. (p. 44)

FOCUS OF THIS BOOK

In this book, epistemological and organizational aspects of professional culture as they relate to parent–professional relationships and Skrtic's point about an uncritical approach are essential to our own arguments. We use a critical pragmatist approach to examine the underpinnings that form the value base of special education—in particular, the core American values of equity, individualism, personal choice, and hard work (Banks & McGee Banks, 2010; Spindler & Spindler, 1990). Furthermore, we place our concern within the context of the inevitably multicultural nature of the United States and the challenge that special education professionals face in collaborating with families and individuals whose implicit and explicit values base may be radically different from their own. Thus, the bulk of this book addresses the issue of how the ideals of the U.S. macroculture are represented in special education and the resulting implications for cross-cultural communication.

At this point, however, it is important to specify the book's central argument: Professional knowledge is largely acquired by an implicit process that needs to be made explicit and conscious if school personnel are to become effective collaborators in a multicultural society. Critical pragmatism makes that process explicit (Skrtic, 1995a). Our "process of cultural reciprocity," which is outlined in Chapter 2, facilitates professionals' engagement in this process to bring about effective parent–professional collaboration.

BECOMING A MEMBER:
THE IMPORTANCE OF EMBEDDED BELIEFS

How does an individual gain membership into the institution of special education? First, each individual brings his or her own complex of macro and microcultural frameworks and the belief systems that he or she espouses. The process that prepares the individual for membership in this particular institution, however, draws most heavily on the macrocultural belief systems on which the field is built. Because most professionals who come into this field have demonstrated through their success in the education system considerable mastery of the belief systems of the overarching macroculture, it is clear that the implicit and explicit beliefs of the macroculture are not new to them. Induction into special education, then, is accomplished by building on the implicit knowledge base of the macroculture through formal instruction in the theoretical and applied knowledge of the field and, finally, through practical experience in schools (Skrtic, 1991).

Our central point is that new members often learn the approved goals—and means of attaining those goals—without having to specify explicitly their cultural basis. In most situations, the rules of a cultural institution may never be taught explicitly to the inductee precisely because the insiders themselves may not be aware of the rules. Indeed, Apple (2003) argued that the teaching of social and economic norms and expectations to students in school is a covert or tacit process that creates the valued canon of knowledge based on the society's values and commitments. In considering the effect of such hegemony, Bowles and Gintis (1976, 2002) argued that it is not only that the knowledge being transmitted succeeds in reproducing the societal status quo but also that schools are structured so as to replicate different levels of workplace environments, which in turn socialize students into behaviors that will prepare them for levels similar to those of their families of origin. Giroux (2006) called for schools to counter these hegemonic processes by creating curricula that build on students' cultural resources.

Illich (1971) became famous for his analysis of educational practices that increasingly engaged in the "deskilling" of teachers, leaving them with little choice but to perpetuate the kind of indoctrination previously described. Since that time, criticisms of this approach have continued, yet many believe that the trend has only intensified with the advent of high-stakes testing under the No Child Left Behind Act of 2001 (PL 107-110; Provenzo, Renaud, & Provenzo, 2008), resulting in more and more scripted programs that encourage fragmented and decontextualized learning that disempowers teachers and reduces their ability to be critical consumers or engage in critical pedagogy.

This kind of professional preparation appears to have two unfortunate consequences. First, the fact that school professionals are not made aware of the cultural underpinnings of their fields and the implicit values and beliefs that are specific to the dominant macroculture means that they can operate only as technicians. Second, students who belong to a minority group may lack access to the "cultural capital," or the tools for success in the mainstream, and may need to be taught those rules and strategies explicitly, in a way that students who have grown up in the mainstream do not need to be taught (Delpit, 1995).

In special education, personnel preparation programs explicitly teach the policies and practices of the field, explications of which can be found in any textbook or any course outlines used by teachers' colleges. As Skrtic pointed out, this process of socialization is a vital part of professional induction:

> When students can demonstrate that they have internalized the profession's knowledge, skills, norms, and values—how to think and act as professionals—they are duly certified as professionally competent by the professional school, admitted to the professional community by the relevant professional association, and licensed by the state to practice the profession. (1995b, p. 11)

However, the beliefs that underlie these policies and practices often are not made explicit and are conveyed to the initiate in forms that are so embedded as to be unacknowledged, even unrecognized, by those who teach them. Bowers (1984, 1995) referred to this knowledge as the "taken-for-granted" beliefs that are experienced as "the natural order of things" (1984, p. 36) rather than as a set of values that have been explicitly learned. Special education is full of such embedded beliefs.

REIFICATION OF DISABILITY CATEGORIES

An embedded belief that has received considerable attention is the way that the concept of disability becomes reified—or made into a "thing" that an individual has (Bogdan & Knoll, 1995; Stein, 2002). According to this belief, the disability is a feature of the individual's constitution and exists as objective reality.

The reification perspective is particularly controversial regarding specific learning disability (SLD), which, Mercer (1997) argued, reflects a factual phenomenon that exists within the brain of an individual and may be caused by a particular structural anomaly of the brain. A line of continuing research by Shaywitz and Shaywitz (2004, 2009) has extended this explanation by using brain scan technology to study brain activity during the process of reading. This research indicates that there are different patterns of brain activity and differential usage of areas of the brain by struggling readers compared with accomplished readers; it also indicates that with effective instruction the struggling readers' patterns can change. Although the authors of that research argue that these differential patterns reflect built-in neurological differences between struggling and accomplished readers, this explanation is debatable because, as Hruby and Hynd observed, the poor readers' brain activity patterns could reflect "not neurophysiological destiny, but a lack of literacy preparation in optimal contextual circumstances" (2006, p. 550). In other words, the correlation between reading efficiency and brain activity does not indicate the direction of the effect. It is not appropriate to assume that brain activity patterns result in efficient or inefficient reading. Rather, it is possible that efficient preparation and practice result in one kind of pattern while inefficient reading behaviors result in a different pattern.

In contrast to the biological interpretations, social constructionists counter that a learning difficulty is a disability only when it is in an area of learning that is so valued by the society that its absence places the individual at a significant disadvantage. Sleeter (1986, 1998, 2010), for example, argued that after the launching of Sputnik in

1957, the growing demands of a technological economy led to a raising of reading standards, which contributed to the establishment of the learning disability category; this was supported by parents of white students, who wanted their children's academic difficulties to be distinguished from the difficulties of minorities and children from low-income families. Similarly, Stanovich and Stanovich (1996) and Skrtic (2005) interpreted the development and reification of this category as a political solution to student diversity.

The traditional approach in special education has been to assume the reification perspective. Skrtic (1991), in his analysis of the epistemological source of this perspective, pointed out that special education knowledge is grounded in the "functionalist paradigm," in which reality is viewed as objective and independent of the human perspective. He argued that in the social sciences, the manifestation of functionalism that has most directly influenced the accepted special education knowledge base is *functionalist psychology*—in particular, psychological behaviorism and experimental psychology. Thus, in considering a spectrum of epistemological approaches from subjectivist to objectivist, Skrtic located the special education knowledge tradition "in the most extreme objectivist region of the functionalist paradigm" (p. 106).

What are the implications of this view of knowledge for teacher preparation? As Skrtic (1991) observed, because objectivists consider this way of viewing the world as the only way, the teacher preparation process, especially in special education, typically does not require students to acknowledge other theories of knowledge. Skrtic proposed that professions are guided by a hierarchy of presuppositions, from the most abstract to the most applied, as follows: metatheories, theories, assumptions, models, practices, and tools. He argued that in special education, only the more practical rather than the theoretical levels of this hierarchy are acknowledged; that is, any criticism of special education historically has centered only on "the ethics and efficacy of its models, practices, and tools, but not on its assumptions, theories, and metatheories" (pp. 55–56). So, for example, prospective teachers may be asked to examine the efficacy of a tool, such as a psychometric test, for identifying a disability but are not asked to examine the underlying belief that disabilities are objective phenomena that can be objectively and accurately diagnosed by such a test (Bogdan & Knoll, 1995). By not addressing this issue, teacher preparation programs inculcate an important principle of the field at the deepest level of belief—what Bowers (1995) called the taken-for-granted level—whereby the belief represents a premise that is so embedded as to be invisible to the learner.

There are important implications of the reification perspective's going unexamined. First, this perspective reflects the medical model of disease that has been transported into the field of special education (Mercer, 1973; Sleeter, 2010). Society's implicit faith in the medical model leads professionals to believe that what is really a very subjective process is objective and scientific. This is particularly problematic for high-incidence categories such as SLD, emotional and/or behavior disorder (EBD), and intellectual disability (ID) in the mild range, for which such misplaced faith can have paradoxical results. On the one hand, the subjectivity inherent in the classification process can lead to the overrepresentation of low-performing groups in these disability categories (Harry & Klingner, 2006; McCall & Skrtic, 2009). On the other hand, in the case of SLD, this actually can work the other way around; in its certainty that this disability represents an intrinsic impairment, the field offers an official definition that explicitly rules out the influence of environmental factors as an explanation for the student's learning difficulties. Yet, it is virtually impossible to know whether the academic difficulties of a young student who shows no signs of developmental delay are a result of experience or of intrinsic impairment, and it has long been argued that the assessment instruments available do not convincingly distinguish between low-achieving students and students with a "learning disability" (Ysseldyke, Algozzine, & Thurlow, 1992). Further, as Collins and Camblin (1983) argued and Sleeter (2010) continued to corroborate, the exclusion of environmental effects in the classification of learning disability actually discriminates against children from low socioeconomic or potentially detrimental social backgrounds.

As a result of the foregoing debates, challenges to the field's traditional reliance on a discrepancy between IQ score and an academic achievement score as the main indicator of SLD have resulted in the development of the response to intervention (RTI) model. This multitiered approach aims to ensure that children receive "evidence-based" instruction tailored to their needs while providing consistent monitoring of their response to this instruction. This model does not exclude the notion of SLD; rather, it attempts to withhold application of the label until a child's achievement scores indicate a lack of response to the instruction. The absence of response is then taken as an indicator of a within-child impairment. Thus, critical scholars such as Ferri have argued that the reification assumption is still at the heart of the model, continuing the "foundational assumption that there are two distinct student types, one disabled and one 'typical' or 'normal'" (2011, p. 1).

THE REIFICATION PERSPECTIVE AND CULTURALLY VARIABLE PARAMETERS OF NORMALCY

We, the authors, offer the issue of reification to illustrate the tremendously complex belief systems that surround the concept of disability and to argue that such complexity demands an approach to professional preparation that will ensure a critical awareness of the entrenched beliefs that underlie special education practice. For us, this awareness has been an essential requirement of becoming members of the institution of special education as it is practiced in the United States. Being required to understand special education practices in a new society forced us to become aware of the taken-for-granted beliefs of our native institutions of education. For example, on the reification issue outlined previously, we did not differ, initially, from the traditional U.S. perspective. We also assumed that a disability was a factual phenomenon that someone has—until we noticed that people designated as having a disability in U.S. society often did not match our understanding of disabilities.

We came to see that the parameters that we used to define a disability were much broader than those being used by the U.S. school system. This was particularly true for the high-incidence disabilities such as SLD, EBD, and mild ID. For example, because both of our native societies operated education systems that offered advanced education only to a minority of the population, the many children who did not show an aptitude for academic skills would not be perceived as having disabilities; rather, it would simply be accepted that they should pursue career goals that are not based on advanced academic skills. Thus, difficulties in learning such skills would not be perceived as outside the norm. In our native societies, a child's difficulties would have to be quite severe before he or she would be seen as atypical. In fact, the notion of disability tended to be tied most often to physical anomalies or readily discernible impediments that interfere, in relatively gross ways, with interpersonal communication, social interaction, or basic academic skills.

We came to see that if we could change our view of who had a disability simply by changing the parameters of *normalcy,* then a disability could not be a universally recognizable or factual phenomenon. It became important to understand that the criteria for determining disability in the United States reflected a narrower view of normalcy than that to which we were accustomed. Two questions became important to us: 1) How were these parameters established? 2) What values did they represent?

As Bowers cogently stated, "The authority that culture exercises over us...is internalized in such a way that the person under its sway experiences it as part of the natural order of things" (1984, p. 36). The reason why we think it is important for professionals to examine their taken-for-granted beliefs is that the United States is rapidly becoming the most multicultural society in the world. Although the process of acculturation is a given within such a society, it is almost always the newcomer or outsider who is required to acculturate to the ways of the mainstream.

In special education, the result of such ethnocentric practice is that families who do not share or value the principles on which special education policies and practices are built are all too often alienated and excluded from collaboration in the treatment of their children's difficulties (for a comprehensive review, see Harry, 2008). When families are excluded, children suffer, and professionals' attempts at remediation and support result in minimal progress for children and in frustration for the professionals and families alike. The principle of family-centered practice now espoused by early interventionists points the way that is needed. Without cultural reciprocity, however, the ideal of parent–professional collaboration will continue to elude those who work with families from diverse cultures and belief systems.

The purpose of this book is to deconstruct the natural order of things—the values base on which the policies and practices of special education in the United States are built. The goal of such deconstruction is not to promote a laissez-faire attitude of "anything goes" as professionals work with people from diverse cultures but rather to advocate for a level of cultural awareness that can radically alter the ethnocentricity with which professionals usually approach families and communities that diverge significantly from the culture of special education. With this level of awareness, professionals can begin to develop what we the authors describe as *cultural reciprocity.*

TOWARD A PROCESS OF CULTURAL RECIPROCITY

Certain key concepts form the substance of this book; we delineate these throughout Section I of the text. As outlined in this chapter, we consider these concepts to be the underpinnings on which disability policy and practice in the United States are based. In Chapter 2, we describe and give examples of the process of cultural reciprocity, which we recommend not as a cookbook approach or a strategy but rather as a framework for transforming communication between professionals and family members. In Chapter 3, we show that these concepts are both explicit and implicit in the law itself by examining the legal and epistemological underpinnings of definitions of disability. Chapter 4 illustrates how these underpinnings have an impact on the way in which professional expertise and language are conceptualized. Chapter 5 analyzes the cultural underpinnings of professionals' recommendations to parents regarding parenting styles, and Chapter 6 applies this analysis to professional interactions with parents around issues of goal setting for students.

Section II presents three quite different applications of cultural reciprocity as practiced and modified by three colleagues who have used our previous book *Culture in Special Education: Building Reciprocal Family–Professional Relationships* (Kalyanpur & Harry, 1999) over many years. First, Davenia Lea presents an intriguing portrait of her own journey of self-discovery as an African American researcher negotiating relationships with a group of African American teenage mothers whose identities diverged widely from her own. Next, Eva Thorp and Monimalika Day offer vivid portraits of their use of "cultural dilemmas" as a lens for helping graduate students develop a reciprocal understanding of the cultural differences between themselves and families. The book closes with a thoughtful analysis by Shernaz García of the meaning of cultural reciprocity as she worked to bridge the distance between her American students and herself—the multifaceted, multicultural "other."

    Overall, we recommend the process of cultural reciprocity as a way of being that will inevitably be crafted and modified to suit individual personalities and complex social contexts as professionals attempt to provide services to the wide range of families that constitute the very diverse composition of U.S. society.

REVIEW QUESTIONS

1. Beyond the four main values of individualism, independence, choice, and equity identified in the chapter, are there other core values of the mainstream culture that you can identify? Think of an everyday situation or event in your life such as driving your own car to work or university instead of carpooling or eating with a friend but not sharing your lunches and reflect on the embedded values in your actions. Could they be considered mainstream values?

2. What do you think of the chapter's assertion that most professional training programs present technical information as universal truths and do not offer trainees the opportunity to question the assumptions underlying these so-called truths? Do you think professionals should question the beliefs and values of their field? What suggestions would you have for professionals trained in the United States who might also want to work in their field outside of the United States?

3. Work with a partner to identify any processes that are considered essential practices in the field (e.g., intelligence testing, achievement testing, behavioral interventions, lesson planning). Discuss whether you have learned about the reason for these practices and the theories that underlie them or have engaged in any critical examination of the practices. Develop a list of questions about these practices that you think would help you understand them more fully.

Chapter **2**

Cultural Reciprocity as an Approach Toward Building Parent–Professional Relationships

Beth's Story

My daughter, Melanie, was diagnosed as having cerebral palsy soon after her birth. The most crucial problems were her inability to swallow or suck at birth; when she did begin to swallow, she would regurgitate most of her fluids. When she was 1 year old, she weighed only 9 pounds, and this continuing "failure to thrive" culminated in a critical state of electrolyte imbalance complicated by an aspiration pneumonia. This crisis led to a month's stay in the leading children's hospital in Toronto, Canada, where we were living at the time. After approximately 1 week in intensive care, her lungs were clear and her electrolytes were back in balance, but the doctors decided to keep her longer to find a solution to her vomiting.

For 3 weeks, the professional team at the hospital tried a variety of thickened formulas, methods of feeding, and medications intended to mitigate the vomiting. Quantitative measures of how much she was fed and how much she regurgitated were kept, the latter by the use of an absorbent bib that was weighed before and after regurgitation. The medications did not work because they mostly came up as she vomited. Thicker or thinner fluids made no difference. Spoon feeding was quickly replaced by a nasogastric tube because she did seem to retain a bit more by this method. All details of her feeding were carefully documented and shared with me by a caring and meticulous professional team of doctors, nurses, and a nutritionist.

After about 3 weeks of minimal progress, the team and my family discussed but rejected a couple of more radical approaches: giving Melanie intramuscular injections of the medication and even inserting a stomach tube. We all agreed that these were too invasive. Finally, the doctors concluded that there was nothing more that they could do; they had tried all reasonable approaches, and, unfortunately, I would simply have to take Melanie home and keep trying.

The day before she was to be discharged, I sat at Melanie's bedside, talking anxiously with one of her nurses. I told her that I was puzzled about the fact that despite Melanie's continued vomiting she had actually gained 8 ounces in her month in the hospital. This was a much greater rate of weight gain than she had ever shown. Together, the nurse and I wondered what the explanation could be. Suddenly, a thought occurred to her: "Wait a minute! You know, we give her tube feeds while she's sleeping at night, and I don't think I've ever seen her vomit during her night feeds." She went over to the other nurse and asked whether she had noticed this. The other nurse concurred: "No, I don't believe I've ever seen her wake during those feeds."

In amazement, I saw that the solution was before us. I exclaimed, "Well, then, that's what I'll do! I'll just feed her most of her fluids while she sleeps!" The next steps were simple: A nurse in the outpatient department taught me all I needed to know about inserting the nasal tube, the pediatrician prescribed a minimal dose of a nonnarcotic sedative, and the occupational therapist suggested that I pin a small mitten to Melanie's pajama shirt into which the feeding end of the tube could be tucked at night. We would leave her free of the tube during the days. I left the hospital armed with these materials and began a regimen of giving Melanie three feeds of sugared water per night. During the days, she ate semisolids and no more than a couple of teaspoons of juice or water. The nurses were right: Melanie never woke during her night feeds, and as the months went by I watched my frail little girl gain pound after pound. As she gained weight, she vomited less in the daytime. Eight months later, just before the birth of her baby brother, Mark, I was able to stop tube feeding Melanie altogether. During the days, she drank juice or small amounts of water from a bottle and never again needed to have the hated tube inserted in her nose.

I have never forgotten my amazement that this professional team, in its attempt to quantify and measure the effects of its efforts, had failed to note a simple fact that had not been anticipated in its interventions. The nurses, who would have been the ones to observe the pattern directly, had been instructed to weigh and measure Melanie's vomiting but had not been asked whether differential patterns existed between day and night feedings or to consider the treatment implications of such patterns.

I can interpret this only as an example of professionalism that had been reduced to technicianism—the following of instructions without making an effort to engage in individual problem solving or hypothesis testing. Apart from the nurses, the rest of the members of the professional team, who might have noted that their failure-to-thrive patient was thriving better than usual, did not think to ask whether this improvement might represent a meaningful pattern. I suspect that the emphasis on categorical recording of an intervention and on what Hall (1983) referred to as "low-context" communication reduced the likelihood that these professionals would note the unanticipated event or ask the unanticipated question. I believe that truly reflective practitioners would have done so.

Finally, the story teaches a crucial lesson about parent–professional communication: The everyday knowledge of a parent can be as important as the scientific measures and theories of a professional. As a parent, I had intimate knowledge of my child's usual rate of weight gain, I had an overwhelming need to solve the problem, and I had the will to seek and implement solutions that never may have been suggested in a textbook. (For a closer look at my experience with Melanie, see *Melanie, Bird with a Broken Wing: A Mother's Story* [Harry, 2010]).

This chapter presents cultural reciprocity as a method of inquiry for professionals to reflect on their practices and question the assumptions of the field. The process of cultural reciprocity consists of the following four steps:

1. Identify the cultural values that are embedded in your interpretation of a student's difficulties or in the recommendation for service.

2. Find out whether the family being served recognizes and values these assumptions and, if not, how its view differs from yours.

3. Acknowledge and give explicit respect to any cultural differences identified and fully explain the cultural basis of your assumptions.

4. Through discussion and collaboration, set about determining the most effective way of adapting your professional interpretations or recommendations to the value system of the family.

This chapter consists of three parts. The first section explains why cultural reciprocity is necessary, the second part identifies the key features of cultural reciprocity, and the third section describes the process of cultural reciprocity, using an example of transition planning as an illustration.

The Need for Cultural Reciprocity

Rani is a 21-year-old Native American woman with intellectual impairments. Her mother cannot understand why the professionals who work with Rani are recommending, even insisting, that Rani should move into an apartment off of the reservation with another woman who has intellectual impairments and look after herself with intermittent support from professional caregivers. Rani's married sisters live on the reservation, and Rani's mother believes that Rani herself—because of her intellectual impairment—would best be looked after by Rani's mother and father and, later, Rani's siblings. The professionals, however, cannot understand why Rani's mother would want Rani to continue to live with her and the family now that Rani has turned 21. Situations such as Rani's present themselves to service providers quite often, not merely in terms of a lack of awareness that a difference with potential for misunderstanding exists in the first place but that the difference is related to differing worldviews.

Culture is what provides most individuals with their worldview. It is what helps people make sense of what they know. Culture is so embedded in an individual's perspective, in fact, that, like fish in water, it is easy to be unaware of the degree of its influence. Awareness of cultural differences, then, is the recognition that the way that individuals act and what they believe can be different from the way that other people act or what they believe. When talking about an issue such as disability, however, which is so open to varying interpretations, cultural awareness needs to go beyond the mere acknowledgment of stereotypical characteristics about particular communities. As Skrtic and McCall (2010) suggested, professionals need to go through a process of introspection and inquiry that questions the assumptions that are made in the field of special education and forces professionals to confront the contradictions between their values and practices.

Using the framework that was developed by Delpit (1995) to describe levels of racial discrimination, we, the authors, propose that there are three levels of cultural awareness: *overt*, *covert*, and *subtle*. The overt level is the awareness of obvious differences such as language or manner of dress. These differences often are external and therefore expected; in fact, their very expectedness makes it easier to accommodate them. When dealing with families from culturally diverse backgrounds, most mainstream professionals are aware of the more explicit aspects of cultural differences and the need for sensitivity to those differences. Indeed, the provision of an interpreter for non–English-speaking families is the most common adaptive practice. Other culturally sensitive practices include arranging for child care, arranging for transportation, and holding the meetings at a place and a time that are convenient to the participants.

Because these universal strategies are based on certain stereotypical assumptions about families' needs, however, they may neither respond to families' varying levels of acculturation or need nor change the power dynamics of the interaction in favor of the family (Skinner & Weisner, 2007). For instance, in the early 1980s, Brazilian immigrants to Boston must have been surprised when they were provided with Spanish-speaking interpreters by local social services agencies, who had quite overlooked the fact that Brazilians speak Portuguese (Guerreiro, 1987).

The covert level of cultural awareness goes a little deeper and involves an awareness of differences that cannot be recognized by outward signs—what Philips (1983) referred to as aspects of "invisible culture," such as parameters of status or interpersonal communication styles that require sustained contact or observation before becoming apparent. Although covert levels of awareness can help professionals achieve greater sensitivity and acceptance of differences, the effect is still limited because professionals either may not seek an explanation for the behavior or may find an explanation that makes sense to them but does not make sense to the families. For instance, varying cultural concepts of time can present major barriers to effective parent–professional interaction if not understood or respected. In Kalyanpur's (1998) study of a Native American parent support group, the organizer, who was Anglo-American, noticed that the meetings never started until at least 30 minutes after the members arrived. Acknowledging the need for flexibility, she adjusted her schedule accordingly and applied her concept of time and punctuality to explain that the meetings were starting late. To her, this explanation made sense, but she did not really understand the Native American mothers' perception of time. They did not think that the meetings were starting late. As they saw it, the support group meetings were an occasion for them to get together, and the informal interactions among them were part of the meetings.

The limitations of both overt and covert levels of awareness are obvious. In the case of the Brazilians, prior assumptions and stereotypes on the part of the professionals brought all communication to a halt. In the case of the Native Americans, had the organizer of the support group meetings sought to understand the mothers' perspectives on the purpose of the meetings, she might have come to see the first 30 minutes not as a waste of time but as an invaluable opportunity for her to get to know the participants and learn their needs. In both cases, what was needed was a deeper level of cultural awareness: the subtle level, examined next.

The subtle level of cultural awareness involves the recognition of embedded values and beliefs that underlie people's actions and the awareness that these beliefs that, to this point, have been taken for granted and assumed to be universal are, in fact, beliefs and values that are specific to one's culture. This effort is the most challenging because identifying these features is difficult not only in the culture of others but even more so in one's own culture. For instance, for years, the Wechsler Intelligence Scale for Children (WISC-5; Wechsler, 1991, 2004) continued to ask questions such as "Who discovered America?" and "Why is a brick house better than a wooden house?" in the belief that, as a universal truth, there was only one correct answer. In the effort to measure IQ scientifically and objectively, there was no room for those students who might think that Vespucci, not Columbus, discovered America (and even that America was never "discovered") or that in an earthquake zone, a wooden house would be safer to live in.

To reach the subtle level of cultural awareness, professionals must ask themselves, "Why?" "Why do I want 21-year-old Rani to move out on her own into a supported apartment?" "Why do I want 4-year-old Mira to feed herself?" "Why do I want Tommy to learn to read?" For instance, Skinner and Weisner (2007) assert that standardized assessments of family characteristics and quality of life, although useful, may not capture the individual nuances of family and child well-being because they fail to ask the question "why?" By reflecting on what and why service providers do what they do, individuals come to understand what their personal and/or professional values are; that is, service providers can open their eyes to the fact that many of what are assumed to be universal truths are in fact specific to one's culture. At this point, one can begin to recognize the embedded values or, in other words, the cultural underpinnings of one's professional knowledge. This is what scholars have referred to as *critical pragmatism* (Frattura & Topinka, 2006; Skrtic & McCall, 2010).

Service providers typically are aware that potential avenues for miscommunication in parent–professional interactions are legion. The situation rarely improves when the two parties come from culturally diverse groups. It is imperative that professionals recognize that much of special education policy and practice emerges from the prevailing values and ideals of the dominant mainstream—values that may not always be held by minority cultures—so that they may decrease the potential for cross-cultural dissonance.

Awareness of cultural differences provides merely the scaffolding for building collaborative relationships. Knowledge of the underlying belief and value that bring about the difference in perspective provides the reinforcing strength to the relationship. It is toward this end that we, the authors, have developed the approach of cultural reciprocity. We suggest that professionals adopt an approach in which they engage in explicit discussions with families regarding differences in cultural values and practices, bringing to the interactions an openness of mind, the ability to be reflective in their practice, and the ability to listen to the other perspective. Furthermore, they must respect the new body of knowledge that emerges from these discussions and make allowances for differences in perspective when responding to the family's needs.

KEY FEATURES OF CULTURAL RECIPROCITY

Cultural reciprocity has five key features that make it eminently suited to the purpose of building effective parent–professional collaboration: It 1) goes beyond awareness of differences to self-awareness, 2) aims for subtle levels of awareness of differences, 3) has universal applicability, 4) avoids stereotyping, and 5) ensures that both parents and professionals are empowered.

Cultural Reciprocity Goes Beyond Awareness of Differences to Self-Awareness

Developing collaborative relationships is not only a question of implementing some steps toward understanding each other when the potential for misunderstanding arises but also a constant awareness of self and others (Harry, 1992a). Furthermore, acknowledgment of a difference in perspective is insufficient without the nonjudgmental acceptance and knowledge of the worldview behind it.

In his seminal study, Schön (1983) wrote of the need for professionals to be reflective practitioners who recognize their fallibility and the knowledge that being experts in their respective fields does not mean that they have all of the answers. He suggested that relationships between practitioners and their clients be interactive so that practitioners become aware not only of themselves and what he refers to as their "appreciative systems" (i.e., religious, moral, political, and social ideals; social and cultural environment; and professional socialization) but also of that of others. Cultural reciprocity is informed by Schön's model of the reflective practitioner.

Cultural Reciprocity Aims for Subtle Levels of Awareness of Differences

Cultural reciprocity goes beyond recognizing overt differences to understanding cultural values that underlie professional assumptions and families' responses. As mentioned previously, culturally sensitive strategies that respond to stereotypes, although useful, are insufficient. So, too, are strategies that are based on more specific knowledge of the family's values but without an understanding of the family's point of view. The following is an example from Maya's experience:

A preschool teacher scheduled a meeting with the parents of her Afghani student. She knew that many Muslims believe that women should be modest and not show their legs or arms, so she wore a long skirt and a long-sleeved blouse for the occasion. Even though her decision was based on a stereotype about Muslims, it was a courteous and thoughtful gesture; as expected, it earned her goodwill and started things off well.

The teacher told the Afghani mother that her son refused to help clean up after play and meals. The mother's response was, "Yes, after all, he is a boy. And we don't ask boys to do that." The teacher responded politely, "Well, I understand that, but in my class each student has to do his or her share and helping to clean up is part of that." When the mother said nothing to this, the teacher believed that the matter was resolved. Weeks later, however, the boy still refused to clean up.

The story may have had a different ending had the teacher sought to understand the cultural values underlying her professional assumptions and the mother's response and asked herself "why?" Why does she expect all of the children to do their share? Maybe it is because she shares the values of most Americans and believes in equality and wants to treat everyone equally. Maybe she also believes in another cherished American value, that of independence, and wants all of the children to become independent and do things such as cleanup after meals or play for themselves.

Why, then, does the mother from Afghanistan not ask her son to clean up? Maybe it is because she shares the values of *her* culture. Perhaps she believes in a social hierarchy in which each individual's role and status is predetermined by community norms and cleaning up traditionally has been something that women do. Perhaps, in addition, she cherishes the value of interdependence and cooperation, whereby having to depend on somebody to do something for you is not devaluing. By asking "why," professionals can better understand themselves and the families they serve and be in a better position to develop mutually acceptable interventions. Perhaps if the preschool teacher had clarified these embedded assumptions, the mother might have been persuaded to allow her son to acquire skills for success in the mainstream preschool environment while maintaining his own traditions at home.

Cultural Reciprocity Has Universal Applicability

Our presentation at the beginning of the chapter of cultural reciprocity as a four-step process is in itself a deconstruction of a subconscious, almost intuitive, approach to facilitate easier understanding of the process. Breaking down the process into discrete components does not imply that it is a linear process and that these steps or guidelines must be followed in strict succession. In particular, we do not wish to present it as a toolkit or simply another approach in a teacher's repertoire of strategies that can be pulled out magically at the right moment for just the right result (Kalyanpur, 2005). Culture is messy and insidious, so much so that many of Kalyanpur's and Harry's Caucasian or Anglo-American university students, when asked to identify their cultural roots or traditions, often claimed to have "no culture." Culture is also fluid. Just as two siblings with the same upbringing often will develop very different personalities in response to their experiences within the family, two families from the same cultural background may not subscribe to all the same values. The guidelines for cultural reciprocity are intended to respond to this fluidity and the uniqueness of each family. Once internalized, these guidelines become an intuitive process by which professionals engage in dialogue with families. Indeed, the basic construct from which cultural reciprocity emerges—that communication involves listening to and respecting both perspectives—has universal applicability. We advocate the need for professionals to internalize the values of reciprocity, respect, and collaboration. To paraphrase Schön (1983), reflective practice should become a way of life for professionals and not be just an 8-hour syndrome.

Cultural Reciprocity Avoids Stereotyping

Through the internalization of the values of reciprocity, respect, and collaboration, cultural reciprocity avoids the trap of stereotypical solutions by investigating each situation as unique. Families may have differing reasons for exhibiting the same behavior. For instance, parents' silence at individualized education program (IEP) meetings and similar forms of nonparticipation of minority families in decision-making processes for their child occur for various reasons, including mistrust, discomfort with direct questioning regarding sensitive topics, fear of appearing incompetent and ignorant, deference to authority, and feelings of defiance and frustration at being silenced (Harry & Kalyanpur, 1994). Cultural reciprocity enables professionals to understand each family's reasons for its silence or other specific behaviors.

Cultural Reciprocity Ensures that Both Parents and Professionals Are Empowered

Cultural reciprocity enables both parties to engage in a dialogue in which each learns from the other. For instance, in the process of learning to manage a class of 4-year-old Haitian children, Ballenger (1994, 1999) learned about Haitian cultural ways and to query the assumptions that shaped her own experience as a North American teacher. Ballenger, a middle-income Anglo-American, noticed that her students would not respond when she told them, "If you don't clean up, you won't get a snack." In addition, when she told a child whose mother had left him that she understood that he missed his mother but that he still needed to share his toys, it made not the slightest difference in his behavior.

Reflecting on her practice of asking the students to become responsible for their own behavior and to make their own moral choices, Ballenger became aware of the powerful individualism, typical of many North American teachers, underlying her approach. Through several conversations with the parents of the children and the Haitian teachers at the school, Ballenger discovered that, to make a child behave, they would tell a child, "We don't do that," and make the child accountable to his family, even the entire community, for his behavior. She began to recognize the strong Haitian understanding that an entire extended family, as well as many members of the community, are involved in a child's upbringing and that moral choices such as showing respect for parents and other adults and obedience to God are predetermined by communal norms.

Ballenger then presented her interpretations to the Haitian teachers and families of the children and asked them to reflect on the two cultures. Many said that although they wanted to maintain the Haitian emphasis on family unity and accountability, they thought that their children would benefit from learning the values of the North American culture by being allowed to make their own moral choices. For example, one mother stated that although she continued to see respect as a value that she needed to impart to her children, she realized that there might be other ways to teach respect. In response, Ballenger developed what she referred to as "a mélange of styles," combining the Haitian teachers' and parents' form of verbal disciplining to emphasize communal accountability with mainstream methods that offered children opportunities to make their own choices; using both methods, Ballenger found that she could effectively manage the children's behavior. We, the authors, contend that professionals in disability-related fields can be similarly effective as they not only learn more about the culture of the families whom they serve but also understand more about their own culture.

In Jamaica Kincaid's book (1990), Lucy, a young Caribbean girl, wakes up on her first morning in New York to a sunny day and puts on a cotton dress she would have worn at home to step out into the sun. Growing up in the Caribbean, that a sunny day meant a warm, even hot, day was something she had known and taken for granted all her life. In New York, however, it is the middle of January. Imagine her shock when she discovers that even though the sun is shining, the day is bitterly cold and that something she had taken for granted all her life was no longer the case. We use this anecdote to illustrate how the culture of special education can seem foreign and unfamiliar to families from culturally and linguistically diverse backgrounds. We encourage professionals to "step into the shoes" of the families they serve to begin to understand why the culture of special education might seem so foreign. The first half of the next section explains the process of cultural reciprocity. The second half of the section presents Beth's application of the process of cultural reciprocity.

THE PROCESS OF CULTURAL RECIPROCITY

Many of you have had an experience similar to that of Lucy, in which something that has been taken for granted suddenly is just not right. This type of experience makes you aware of what you have taken for granted until that point in time. The experience may be a visit to a foreign country, in which overt cultural differences—for example, another language—are expected.

During the course of the trip, however, you may begin to notice other unexpected differences. For instance, perhaps the people in this country stand much closer to each other when speaking than is typical in your own country. Or, maybe parents and children and grandparents talk to each other in a different manner than you are used to. How might these experiences make you feel? Uncomfortable? Irritated? Threatened? Bewildered? Curious? Fortunate for the learning experience? Would it have helped if somebody had been available to explain what was happening to put you at ease?

As explained in Chapter 1, all of the factors mentioned here as well as many others contribute to *culture*. People who have lived all of their lives within the dominant group of a society often think that they have no culture; they tend to think that culture is something that belongs to minority groups. The reason for this thinking is that people who belong to the group that holds power in a society usually do not have to define, explain, or contrast themselves to anyone because they belong to the group whose ways and rules are the given in the society. If you find yourself thinking this way, then the easiest way to become aware you really do have a culture is to visit another society or community. Another, though more abstract, way to become more aware is to question yourself carefully about what you value most in life and then ask from where those beliefs were derived. For example, a quick look at a famous phrase from the U.S. Constitution reveals a great deal about American culture: U.S. citizens have the right to "life, liberty, and the pursuit of happiness." These values are so deeply embedded in U.S. society that it may be hard to imagine that they are not necessarily universal values. Yet, these values are not the cornerstones of many societies. For instance, in China, Confucian values within the economic-political context of socialist modernization emphasize the protection of social rights, or "harmonized cooperation," over the rights of individual citizens (Killion, 2005).

Discovering your cultural stance and how it affects your interaction with families is what this chapter is about. It will give you opportunities to learn about yourself and to develop an awareness of cultural identity, to learn to recognize the taken-for-granted values and beliefs that you hold and that make you think and act the way you do, and to use this understanding about yourself to understand others. You may ask, "What does this have to do with special education?" Everything, we, the authors, believe.

For many families of children with disabilities, entering the culture of special education is like going to a foreign country. Just as each country has a dominant culture, so does each profession. The culture of a professional group may have several markers: language, style of dress, personal interaction patterns, status differentiation, laws and regulations, and, certainly, values and beliefs. To a great extent, these cultural markers are expressions of the various aspects of the national culture.

As explained in Chapter 1, special education in the United States is a product of American culture. There are certain core American values that have contributed to the way in which the field of special education has developed over the years, and they continue to be the underpinnings for policy and practice. For instance, in the Individuals with Disabilities Education Improvement Act (IDEA) of 2004 (PL 108-446; U.S. Department of Education, 2007), the principle of parent participation is based on the value of equality and the expectation that parents and service providers should develop partnerships in the education decision-making process of students with disabilities. The principle of due process of law is based on the value of individualism: the understanding that, in a culture in which individuality is highly prized, people have rights to ensure that their individual interests are protected. Conversely, when families believe in social hierarchies rather than in social equality and consider professionals to be the experts and the holders of authority, the expectation that the family should partner with professionals can be bewildering. When families do not value individual rights because they believe that society is more important than the individual, the expectation that the family members will advocate for their children and assert their rights can make them quite uncomfortable. If they do not have someone to explain what is happening and make them feel a little less out of place, then they can end up becoming alienated from the process. As a result, the services that their children receive will be less effective and nobody will benefit.

As a professional in the field of special education, you know the current recommended professional practices and you possess the skills to implement them. This is what is learned in professional training programs. You may even have taken a course on working with families of children with disabilities and learned that collaborating with families is a recommended professional practice—even a legal requirement. Perhaps you were taught the communication skills necessary for building relationships and collaborating with families. Chances are, however, that you probably did not have an opportunity to question why collaborating with families is considered recommended practice and is legally mandated. In fact, chances are that because of your beliefs in equality, you would accept without question, even take for granted, the premise that building partnerships with families is good professional practice. Yet the professional preparation program that you have undergone likely also has taught you another value: The knowledge you have received is highly specialized and is valued more highly than a layperson's knowledge. It is probable that you will not have been encouraged to note that the belief in equality and the belief in the superiority of expert knowledge are likely to come into conflict. In fact, if you have successfully undergone the process of becoming a professional, it is very likely that, although you share many of the values that are embedded in the culture of special education, you may never have explicitly acknowledged them.

The reason that many of your values may be common to those that are embedded in special education culture is that most of the values of special education are mainstream values, or what Banks and McGee Banks (2010) called the *values of the macroculture*. As explained in Chapter 1, this macroculture is a broad, overarching national culture that embodies core American values. By belonging to this national macroculture, you subscribe to all or some of these core values; they contribute to a part of who you are. But, as Figure 2.1 shows, subsumed under the macroculture are other, smaller, or *microcultural* groups to which you might also belong. These microcultures are likely to reflect the values of the particular ethnic group or groups in which you grew up. These microcultures may even overlap with each other. However, Banks and McGee Banks took the concept of culture to a more personal level by pointing out that other aspects of your identity, such as your ethnicity, your gender, your age, your religion, and your professional training, also combine to create a cultural identity that is uniquely yours. Culture, then, is a broad concept that reflects a wide range of beliefs, practices, and attitudes that make up each indi-

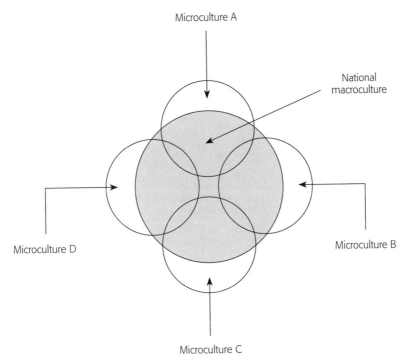

Microculture A

National
macroculture

Microculture D

Microculture B

Microculture C

Figure 2.1.   Microcultures and the national macroculture. (From *Multicultural Education: Issues and Perspectives* [3rd ed.], J.A. Banks & C.A. McGee Banks [Eds.]. Copyright © 1997 John Wiley & Sons. Reproduced with permission of John Wiley & Sons, Inc.)

vidual. Figure 2.2 gives you a picture of what the various microcultural affiliations might be. Look at each of these figures in turn, and think about how they may apply to you.

This unique combination of micro- and macrocultures that makes up your cultural identity is what you bring to any interaction with families in the special education system. It affects how you respond or react to them, what you recommend to them, and why you might feel comfortable working with some families and not with others. If you and the family both believe in equality, then you will find it easier to collaborate with family members because they are just as eager as you are to become partners. If, however, a family continues to defer to your authority or to avoid interactions with you, despite your best efforts to involve family members as partners, then you might begin to believe that it is impossible to collaborate. You may not understand why collaborating with this family is so difficult—unless you question the assumption, the taken-for-granted belief that is embedded in your asking the family to collaborate with you. To complicate matters further, you may not recognize that some of your own beliefs may be in conflict—that is, your belief in equality as well as your belief in expert knowledge. This conflict may be affecting your own attitude toward the importance of the family's input. In other words, you may want to see the family as equal to you, yet you may find it difficult to place as much value on its everyday knowledge as on your own specialized knowledge.

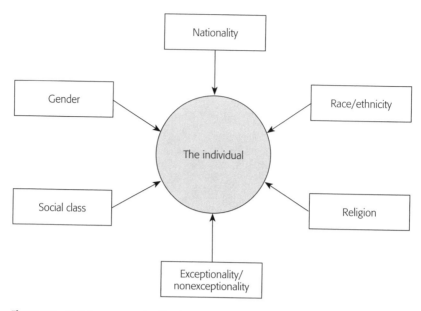

Figure 2.2. Multiple group membership. (From *Multicultural Education: Issues and Perspectives* [3rd ed.], J.A. Banks & C.A. McGee Banks [Eds.]. Copyright © 1997 John Wiley & Sons. Reproduced with permission of John Wiley & Sons, Inc.)

APPLYING THE PROCESS OF CULTURAL RECIPROCITY

The purpose of this chapter is to introduce you to an approach to learning more about yourself and the process of collaborative interaction with families of children with disabilities. Different cultural beliefs and practices have been noted as a frequent barrier to effective interaction; therefore, some movement toward mutual understanding usually is required before people can begin to work well together. However, many researchers have noted that it is most often the people from the minority group who are required to understand or become acculturated to the ways of the majority group. Overall, this is probably a reasonable expectation. However, the process of acculturation takes time, and professionals who are hoping to make a difference for children must be willing to take the initiative in building a bridge between the cultures of diverse families and the culture of schools. To do this, we advocate that professionals initiate a two-way process of information sharing and understanding—a process that can be truly reciprocal and lead to genuine mutual understanding and cooperation. Cultural reciprocity is a lifelong learning process. Banks' and McGee Banks' (2010) model of cultural identity allows a professional not only to define a nuanced composite of the various aspects of who he or she is but also allows one to redefine these composites over time.

Let us take the example of Silvia, a Salvadoran American young woman with cerebral palsy, and her family. Silvia's family was included in a research project Harry and her colleagues undertook to assist families in providing opportunities for social development for their children who had disabilities. The approach of the research team was to begin by finding out, through interviews and observations, what social goals the families held for these students and what opportunities the team could find or create for pursuing these goals in inclusive home or community environments. As it is beyond the scope of this chapter to present the details of the research project, the following is a thumbnail sketch of Silvia (for an extended description of this and other case studies, please see Harry, Kalyanpur, & Day, 1999):

Silvia was 17 when the team first met her. Her radiant smile and ready laughter, along with her frequently changing hairdos and attractive, light makeup, led her teachers to nickname her "Miss El Salvador." Owing to her cerebral palsy, Silvia used a wheelchair and had difficulties with her speech. When the team met her, her Spanish was more advanced than her English, but she could carry on a conversation in either language. She always worked very hard to articulate clearly, and she readily repeated words or phrases until her listener understood. In English, Silvia tended to speak in one- or two-word phrases, whereas her spoken Spanish was much more fluent and her understanding of Spanish seemed appropriate for her age. Silvia had good mobility in her upper body and, despite some spasticity in both hands, used her left hand for fine motor tasks such as writing, typing, or painting. Her mother, Rosa, described the youngest of her four children as *"una persona muy contenta"* (a very happy person). Silvia was in a self-contained special education class in a general high school, and her education program had a predominantly vocational emphasis with a job placement 4 days per week.

Silvia's father, Trinidad, had been the first in the family to leave his native El Salvador for the United States to pave the way for his family. Rosa followed him at a later date, leaving Silvia and her siblings in the care of their grandmother and aunt until they, too, could join their parents. Silvia came to the United States at the age of 11 years. Although she liked the United States, Silvia said she liked her native country better because she had many cousins there with whom she had a lot of fun. Growing up in a rural area of El Salvador, Rosa and Trinidad did not have the opportunity to attend school and learn to read and write. Both spoke Spanish, and although they understood some English, they did not speak it. These facts, however, did not deter the family from achieving its goals. The family purchased a small house that had been abandoned for some time and, according to Rosa, had snakes living in it but that now was undoubtedly the prettiest house on the street. Because the previous owners also had had a family member with a disability, they had built a ramp from the kitchen door out to the back garden. Unfortunately, throughout the 4 years of the team's project when members were in contact with Silvia and her family, Silvia's chair still had to be pushed up the slope from the street to the part of the garden where the ramp began. This daily effort took quite a toll on Rosa's petite frame; and when the team met her, she was having trouble with her back. Nevertheless, Rosa's smile was always cheerful, and her support of her daughter never wavered.

In the following sections, Harry describes the challenges faced with the team's beliefs about independence, choice, and advocacy as team members sought to examine and respond to Silvia's needs within the context of the expectations and hopes Silvia's parents, Rosa and Trinidad, had for Silvia. It must be noted that, although the steps of the process of cultural reciprocity have been made explicit to illustrate the approach, in actuality, the reciprocity developed instinctively as a part of the team gradually became more in tune with the family.

Step 1: Identify the Cultural Values that Are Embedded in the Interpretation of a Student's Difficulties or in the Recommendation for Service

Independence   When the team applied the process of cultural reciprocity in its interactions with Silvia's family, team members became aware that although all had agreed that independence was an important goal for Silvia, the research team had been focused primarily on its own interpretation of what that meant. What were the beliefs on which this focus was based? First was the belief that, as a young woman of almost 18, Silvia should be preparing for adulthood. What did adulthood mean? From the perspective of American society, it meant paid employment, social independence with freedom of choice of friendships, and the ability to pursue some social activities independent of her family. Where did these values come from? They most certainly came from the cultural norms of mainstream America.

Equity and Individual Rights   Where did the belief that Silvia should aim for the same kind of lifestyle as mainstream American youth come from? Was it from the team's belief in equity and individual rights? These were essential American values that were deeply inculcated in the team members' professional training as special educators. On what basis did the team set about identifying specific objectives that would represent the overall goal of independence? From the professional knowledge about transition planning for adulthood, the team knew that it was time to start employment planning, travel training, and social relationship building and that Silvia should make good progress in these areas before graduating from high school.

Thus, in the team's initial attempts to target the goal of independence and to provide Silvia with age-appropriate ways of attaining that goal, team members set about finding her a summer job and a job coach. Through this job, work skills, social skills, and use of public transportation became targeted goals. Socialization and having friends outside the family were equally appropriate goals toward independence for a teenager. The team envisioned assisting Silvia in attaining her expressed desire to extend her friendship with her classmate, Asha, into a typical teenage relationship in which they would meet outside school, hang out at the mall, and go to the movies together. This emphasis also reflected an individualistic focus for Silvia of having the option of using public transportation and increased opportunities to make friends that would enhance her self-esteem and sense of autonomy.

Both Rosa and Silvia responded eagerly to all of the team's suggestions regarding the aforementioned goals; however, there were two other goals that it took 1½ years to incorporate into the portfolio of action research for Silvia: learning to read and obtaining Social Security Disability Income (SSDI) benefits.

Literacy as Independence   On the issue of literacy, both Rosa and Silvia had told the team during the first encounter that this was something they wanted for Silvia. Although the team assisted Rosa in raising this issue at Silvia's annual IEP conference, members did not see it as an appropriate goal for the project because it was identified as an academic rather than a social goal. Team members also did not think of literacy development in terms of independence. In examining the team's slowness to revise its view of the importance of this issue, the team noted a couple of sources of its belief system: 1) professional education and 2) "social" charge. As special educators prepared for working with students with moderate to severe disabilities, team members were accustomed to focusing on community-based, functional curricula by the time students were 16 years old. Thus, the curriculum that the school was providing Silvia seemed appropriate. Part of the rationale for this is that the student has only a few years left in school and it is crucial to target skills that can be mastered in that time and that would be useful upon leaving school. Team members also interpreted social charge in terms of recreational socializing or friendship building and simply assumed that literacy was beyond the purview of the project. Rosa's expressed concerns about Silvia's eligibility for SSDI benefits, once more, was a goal with which the school was already assisting and that the team saw as having little to do with either social development or independence.

Step 2: Find Out Whether the Family Being Served Recognizes and Values These Assumptions and, If Not, How Its View Differs

The Meaning of Independence   In conversations with Silvia and Rosa, the team began to become aware of differences in its shared goal of independence for Silvia. Rosa's objection to the job coach's allowing Silvia to go part of the way to work using public transportation and her decision, in the third summer, that all of the trouble with public transportation just was not worth it sharpened the team's understanding of her point of view. Rosa viewed giving Silvia an opportunity to learn how to travel by herself on a bus as a good idea that she would readily support, but, as far as she was concerned, it was an opportunity and not a goal. Similarly, when efforts to extend Silvia and Asha's friendship did not materialize as team members had envisioned, Rosa seemed to accept it with resignation. Although she had enthusiastically endorsed the idea, she could accept the eventual outcome because 1) the friendship had not been a primary goal for her, 2) she quickly discerned that Asha's family members had been reluctant about the relationship and were unlikely to overlook the cultural differences between the two families, and 3) she knew that Silvia would continue to have friends within her family network.

Milestones to Adulthood   Team members knew that Rosa was just as concerned about increasing Silvia's independence. However, the team came to see that she approached this goal in terms of literacy acquisition. If Silvia learned to read, then she would not be dependent on family and friends to read for her when they went out together. In fact, by learning to read, she would have a skill that her parents did not have and that would be useful for the whole family. Rosa's concern for Silvia to obtain SSDI benefits was closely tied to independence—financial independence, which she hoped the SSDI allowance would enable. She hoped that, like her other children, Silvia would one day get married; however, regardless of whether she did, Rosa felt that Silvia should have a source of income that would contribute to her independence. Also, because Silvia's siblings were expected to—and would—look after their sister when the time came, Silvia's having her own money would lessen their economic burden. This goal, too, would help the whole family. In contrast to her attitude toward the travel and friendship plans, Rosa was much more persistent and assertive in reaction to any efforts toward Silvia's learning to read and obtaining SSDI benefits.

Step 3: Acknowledge and Give Explicit Respect to Any Cultural Differences Identified and Fully Explain the Cultural Basis of the Assumptions

Understandings of School   Step 3 was a gradual process that occurred through conversations with Rosa, Silvia, and Silvia's siblings, Doris and Oscar. In regard to SSDI, the team really could not say when it began involvement in these efforts. It seemed to creep up gradually as members became more and more aware of its importance to the family and of the fact that the school personnel simply could not do it all. In regard to the issue of literacy acquisition, however, the team changed its view very explicitly after listening to Rosa and Doris express their disbelief that Silvia was going to graduate from high school without learning to read. Suddenly, the team became aware that this was a cultural oxymoron. The parent's definition of school was a place where one learned to read, and, after all, the lack of this opportunity was why neither Rosa nor Trinidad could read. How could it be that their daughter was going to school and would graduate yet not be able to read? All of the other siblings had graduated from American high schools and were fully literate in English.

This was the point at which team members spent a good deal of time discussing with Rosa and Doris the different interpretations of what could and should constitute schooling. As the special education system and its goals were further explained, they understood that schooling that included students with disabilities had different goals than did traditional schooling and that Silvia's graduation certificate would not be a full diploma. They had been told this before, at the first annual IEP conference for Silvia, but like many new ideas, it took a while for them to absorb it. As Rosa and Doris came to see the reasoning behind the kind of schooling that Silvia was getting, the team became persuaded by their conviction that Silvia was capable of learning to read and that no stone should be left unturned until she had been offered all possible opportunities.

Step 4: Through Discussion and Collaboration, Set About Determining the Most Effective Way of Adapting Professional Interpretations or Recommendations to the Value System of the Family

Advocations for Silvia's Literacy   Through this discussion, the team's charge as action researchers became more clear. The research team came to see that literacy was, indeed, an aspect of independence for Silvia. In light of the importance of this decision, whether literacy was a social goal became immaterial. Team members would simply accept that a major focus of efforts for Silvia would have to be on literacy. This also meant a greater advocacy role for the team, either in trying to persuade the school to increase its emphasis on reading in Silvia's curriculum or, at least, to give the family members more support in advocating for themselves. Discussions with Silvia's family resulted in a commitment to providing tutoring for Silvia as well as assisting the family in presenting its case to school personnel.

CONCLUSION

Chapters 3–6 provide examples that illustrate how cultural reciprocity may be applied in interactions between parents and professionals of culturally diverse backgrounds. Examples that represent the core American values discussed in the first part of this book are examined in the context of cultural reciprocity to see how the outcome might change. However, interpretation of which and how many values are embedded in each vignette does not preclude the possibility of alternative explanations or interpretations.

Implementing cultural reciprocity is not easy. Perhaps the biggest barrier to implementation is time. As professionals battle to find time to send just a quick note home to parents every day or call on a regular basis to touch base with clients, it may seem unrealistic to expect anybody to take time to get to know each other, let alone engage in dialogue. To counter this argument, we refer to a point made previously. Cultural reciprocity cannot be seen as a bag of tricks to be pulled out during situations of conflict or in emergencies but rather as a value that is internalized and applied in all contexts. If you seek to understand yourself and the families whom you serve at every interaction, however small, then the task will seem less onerous. When you send a quick note or make a telephone call, if you reflect on the action and ask yourself why you are saying what you are saying, then you will be more likely to understand why families do not say what you want them to say and more likely to make the effort to learn why.

Another barrier is the mistaken belief that only professionals from minority cultures can work with families from minority cultures. There is no evidence that professionals who do belong to the same culture as their clients are any more successful at accomplishing collaborative relationships than those who do not. On the contrary, as studies (Harry, 1992a; Lea, 2006; Scarlett, 2005) have indicated, excellent examples of collaborative relationships can occur with professionals who have little or no affiliation with the culture of the families. The issue is not that you must have had the same experiences in terms of culture, ethnic background, race, socioeconomic status, or gender as the families you serve—because you cannot—but that you have the willingness to learn about and understand their experiences, that you are willing to understand how your own experiences have shaped you, and that you respect and accept these differences in your various experiences.

REVIEW QUESTIONS

1. Do you agree with this chapter's assertions that the responsibility of initiating and following through on the process of cultural reciprocity lies with professionals and that the professional's racial and/or ethnic or cultural identity does not necessarily help or hinder the relationship? Support your argument by giving an example from your own experience.

2. To begin this exercise introducing the process of cultural reciprocity, recollect an episode or an interaction that you have had with a parent of a child with a disability (or a child suspected to be at risk) in which you recommended a particular course of action or service. Briefly describe the incident. Now, respond to the following questions, which require you to work only on Step 1 of the process because you may not know enough about how the family really felt about the issues to imagine the rest of the process. If you think you do, however, then you might

be able to attempt a hypothetical analysis of how Steps 2, 3, and 4 might work. If you can do only Step 1, however, do not be concerned; the case study in Chapter 6 of the book will give you the opportunity to try the process in more depth.

- Why did you select the story you chose?
- What made you recommend that particular service?
- Does your recommendation reflect a value that comes from your culture? What do you think that value might be?
- Use your personal identity web to identify specific cultural affiliations that affected your recommendations and your interactions with this family.

3. Partner with a person in your class whom you do not know well or at all and spend some time getting to know him or her. Start with basic questions such as "Why are you in this class?" or, "Why did you choose this profession?" Then, ask more specific questions about his or her family and life; ask your partner to identify an incident during which he or she felt he or she didn't belong and why. Now, give your partner an opportunity to ask these same questions of you. What did you learn about yourself during this conversation? What did you learn about your partner? Were you able to relate to your partner's story, or to what extent was it different? Talk with your partner about the differences in your stories and the underlying values that caused the sense of difference.

Chapter **3**

Legal and Epistemological Underpinnings of the Construction of Disability

Maya's Story

I came to the United States for the first time as a graduate student after having taught in special schools in India for several years and began working with adults with developmental disabilities who lived in a group home. One of the first tasks that I was assigned was to teach them community living skills. My supervisor suggested taking the individual with whom I was working out to eat in a restaurant. I set off confidently to the nearest restaurant with my client, Gary, a young man with moderate intellectual disability; after all, I thought I knew what to expect. To me, a restaurant is a place where you go to eat. You wait to be seated, your waiter provides you with a menu, gives you time to choose, takes your order, and brings you your food. Then you eat your meal, pay the bill, leave a tip for the waiter, and leave.

Gary and I entered a fast-food restaurant. It was the first time in my life that I had entered a fast-food restaurant, and I realized, very quickly, that the rules here were very different from what I knew. As I hesitated, Gary sized up the situation. Taking my hand, he led me to the end of a line of people who, I realized with a start, were not waiters but customers waiting to place their orders. Gary pointed to the bewildering array of choices displayed on a sign above my head—bewildering because the menu did not read from top to bottom in traditional fashion but rather in blocks across the wall. I looked at the first block and began to make a choice when, as I came to the end of the list, I discovered that this block was for breakfast only and not available after 10 a.m. Then I looked at the second block and started to choose from the list when Gary directed my attention to the third block; I learned later that the second block was for specialty items. It seemed that despite the array of choices, our impecunious circumstances restricted us to a single option—the value meals in the third block.

By the time I had recognized the subtle differences between a Number 1 value meal (i.e., cheeseburger, fries, medium drink) and a Number 2 value meal (i.e., double cheeseburger, fries, medium drink), we had reached the front of the line. Before I could say anything, the lady behind the counter said, "For-here-to-go?" I stared absolutely blankly at her. What on earth did that mean? Was she speaking in English? When I did not respond immediately, Gary stepped up and replied, "Here." With obvious relief, the woman turned to him and directed all subsequent questions, including my order, to him. We carried our trays to a small table to which Gary led us. Later, he showed me how to "bus" our table.

In that environment, I undoubtedly was the one with more disabilities, not only in my own perception but also in others'. Over the years, I have related this story to my students on numerous occasions as a springboard for discussion on the social construction of disability. It serves to remind me of the fragility of one's own perception of competence and helps the students to become aware of the arbitrariness with which individuals determine, in each culture, who is "normal."

THE SOCIAL CONSTRUCTION PREMISE

The arguments in this chapter are based on the premise that the parameters for normalcy or deviance are socially constructed. As mentioned in Chapter 1, several theorists and researchers have argued that high-incidence disabilities such as SLD and attention-deficit/hyperactivity disorder (ADHD) are essentially social and/or political categories (e.g., McDermott, Goldman, & Varenne, 2006; Skrtic, 2005; Sleeter, 2010, Stein, 2002). Indeed, this premise provides the basis for the field of disability studies and has been applied to perceived disabilities such as deafness, blindness, mental illness, and physical disabilities (Albrecht, Seelman, & Bury, 2001; Barton, 2007; Davis, 2006). Following the social construction perspective, decisions about what constitutes a disabling condition, who is a person with disabilities (the meaning of disability), who makes these decisions (the models that establish these meanings), and how the disability is to be valued are all culturally specific. Although in some cultures the meaning of disability is established by legal or professional institutions, in other cultures these meanings may emerge more from "folk beliefs" (Groce & Zola, 1993) and from community understanding of people's roles (Edwards, 1997; Helander, 1995). In turn, societal values influence both cultural models and the meanings attached to them.

Research on attitudes toward people with disabilities in different cultures points to differences in the meaning of disability. Findings indicate that the same condition may or may not be perceived as a disability in different societies and that certain conditions may carry more of a stigma than others. For instance, some Yoruba families perceive physical conditions such as goiter, hunchback, and albinism to be punishments for offenses against God and therefore a disgrace; conversely, hydrocephalus is neither a stigma nor a disability (Walker, 1986). Some Asian families consider having a child with a developmental disability a sign of good fortune in the future, others view it as a punishment of past sins, and many consider it an act of God that cannot be changed (Miles, 2002).

Findings also reveal that the value attached to a certain disabling condition differs depending on societal expectations and the established parameters for normalcy. For example, Edgerton (1970) found that among the Manus of New Guinea, the loss of an arm was much more of a disability and much more stigmatizing than the inability to read because being able to handle a canoe was a necessary survival skill.

Conversely, technological availability of prosthetic devices and societal expectations for literacy in the United States combine to create exactly opposite perceptions of the same disabilities.

A key question is whether a diagnosis or label of disability diminishes an individual in the eyes of the law. In Western societies, where the value of individual rights is one of the key underpinnings of disability rights movements, this argument is seen as a civil rights issue. For example, Officer and Groce stated the following:

> Removing barriers is not a matter of goodwill or charity, but of human rights. People with disabilities have the same human rights as everyone else, but these rights have not historically been respected.... People with disabilities have often been denied the right to education and work, to marry and raise a family, to participate in community life, to choose to what extent they will use available health-care services, and indeed the right to life itself. (2009, p. 1796)

Education policy represents another aspect of legal provisions. In the United States, every authorization of IDEA of 1990 (PL 101-476) has required that students be evaluated to determine their eligibility for special education services, a process that results in labeling some students by disability category. As a result, in 2004, 9.2% of all children between the ages of 6 and 21 were identified as having special education needs and received some services (U.S. Department of Education, 2009). Demographic data (Donovan & Cross, 2002; U.S. Department of Education, 2009) continue to show that students earning these labels are disproportionately poor, culturally and linguistically diverse, and male. Evidently, many factors contribute to a student being labeled as having a disability. The two sections of this chapter examine the implications of the cultural specificity of the models and meanings of disability for families whose points of view may differ from the official, mainstream view. The first section consists of two parts. First, it identifies some of the values that underlie special education law and policy in the United States, specifically IDEA of 1990, the IDEA Amendments of 1997 (PL 105-17), and the Individuals with Disabilities Education Improvement Act of 2004 (PL 108-446). Next, it discusses the implications of embedded values for families from contrasting traditions. The second section also has two parts. First, it identifies certain assumptions about the meaning of disability embedded in this process of assessment, particularly as they relate to the issue of disproportionate numbers of certain groups being labeled as having a disability. Next, the section shows how these meanings may contrast with the beliefs of minority families.

CULTURAL UNDERPINNINGS OF SPECIAL EDUCATION LAW

It is well established that education and social policies reflect the core values of prevailing cultural contexts (Levin, 2008; Marshall, Mitchell, & Wirt, 1989; Welles-Nyström, 1996). Indeed, as Marshall and colleagues noted, "We can learn a great deal about a culture by understanding [its] values...and by understanding the ways in which values are built into policy" (1989, p. 6). For instance, in a study of Swedish family policy, Welles-Nyström (1996) identified the ideology of equality as the underpinning for Swedish child health care policies. That is, the rights of women to participate in the labor force and of men to participate in the home and in child care are ensured through legislation for both maternity and paternity leave. In addition, children's rights are ensured through numerous legislative measures including the socialized health care sector for all children, regardless of race or socioeconomic status.

That social policy is a response to the cultural context becomes clear when professionals examine policy changes in the United States over time. For instance, during the latter half of the 19th century, the ideal of individualism as a striving for self-reliance and independence was tied to the national civic goal of efficient and rapid economic development (Marshall et al., 1989). Thus, social policy reflected efficiency measures that sought to exclude those who did not conform to this mold. Concerns about new immigrants from southwestern Europe who might not subscribe to American values as well as attempts to classify races led to federal immigration laws that severely limited immigration (Tyack, 1993). Dependent individuals—for instance, people with developmental disabilities—also were perceived to be undesirable, and their reproductive capability was restricted through compulsory sterilization acts and large-scale warehousing in institutions (Rauscher & McClintock, 1997).

It was only in the latter half of the 20th century that the ideal of equity emerged as the preeminent value and has broadened to encompass disenfranchised groups, including women, people of color, people with disabilities, and children. This process allowed these groups the freedom to make their own life choices, which resulted in radical changes in legal provisions related to marriage and family structures (Friedman, 1996; Grossman & Friedman, 2011). Claiming the same rationale of individual civil rights, the disability rights movement wrought an equally profound change in people's quality of life from rejection and segregation to acceptance and inclusion (Ferguson, 1994; Turnbull, Turnbull, Stowe, & Huerta, 2007). The emergence of new ideologies in human services, such as the principle of normalization, which involves making the lives of people with disabilities as normal as is practicable (Wolfensberger, 1972), and the principle of the least restrictive environment (LRE), which provides an array of programmatic options for students with disabilities to maximize their potential (Turnbull et al., 2007), further reinforced this emphasis on equity, choice, and individual rights. Current assumptions about inclusion are all based on these key principles.

We contend that this interaction of social values and cultural context with legal doctrine influences the ideologies that dominate human services and special education programs. For instance, in the 1960s and 1970s, the movement toward deinstitutionalization on the basis of the principle of normalization emerged from the societal emphasis on rights and individualism (Biklen, 1974; Wolfensberger, 1972). Similarly, the self-advocacy and parents' movements used the platform of civil rights and equality to further their causes, and these ideals eventually became the cornerstone principles for the special education policies enshrined in IDEA (Miller & Keys, 1996; Turnbull et al., 2007). Indeed, IDEA is a product of 20th-century American culture. As Marshall and colleagues pointed out, "Laws are ultimately statements about particular values that dominate within a political system. Such values reflect cultures" (1989, p. 138).

Individuals with Disabilities Education Act as a Cultural Statement

IDEA encompasses six principles of law:

1. Zero reject or the right of every child to education
2. Nondiscriminatory assessment or the right to a fair evaluation to determine appropriate educational placement

3. Individualized and appropriate education to ensure that the education is meaningful

4. LRE to ensure that children with disabilities can associate with their peers who are typically developing to the maximum extent appropriate to their needs

5. Due process to ensure the child's right to challenge any aspect of education

6. Parent participation in the education decision-making process

An analysis of these six principles reveals several core underlying values. Although we acknowledge that other values may be represented in these principles, for the purpose of our analysis, we focus on three core values: individualism, equity, and choice. For instance, the value of individualism underlies the principles of due process and individualized, appropriate education, whereas the principles of parent participation and the LRE are grounded in the right to freedom of choice. Similarly, the value of equity is embedded in the principles of zero reject, nondiscriminatory assessment, and parent participation. We also discuss the implications of these value-embedded principles for families of children with disabilities who may not subscribe to the same values and must negotiate what some have referred to as the "special education maze" (Cutler, 1993; Hayden, Takemoto, Anderson, & Chitwood, 2008).

Individualism in Individuals with Disabilities Education Act   The principle of individualized and appropriate education is operationalized in the policy that all children have the right to an education that is appropriate to each individual's level of skills. Based on the assumption that the individual, not society, comes first, the focus for all education service programming is on the individual. For instance, "person-centered planning" (Turnbull, Turnbull, Erwin, Soodak & Shogren, 2011) places the individual with disabilities at the center of a universe that consists of pertinent domains, such as home, school, and community. Although in an individualized family service plan (IFSP) the unit of analysis might shift a little to accommodate the family, the focus is still on the infant or the toddler with disabilities as professionals identify supports and services that families may need to meet the child's needs.

Furthermore, because the purpose of education is to provide students with the skills that they would need to acquire a job and become independent, productive adults, the underlying assumption in this principle is that a meaningful education for children with disabilities maximizes their potential toward the ultimate goal of independence: open, competitive employment (Powers, Singer, & Sowers, 1996). Such a high value is placed on individuals' becoming self-reliant and responsible for making their own life choices that these outcomes are a major part of most IEPs. Thus, the concept of individualism is embedded in the notions of maximization of potential, competitive open employment, and self-reliance and autonomy.

In the principle of procedural due process, individualism provides the underpinning for the idea that all citizens have rights that are protected under the law; indeed, parents of children with disabilities have the right to be told their rights specific to their child's education. A major aspect of self-advocacy curriculum consists of informing people with disabilities of their rights so that they can demand their entitlements and protest if denied them. Implicit in this argument is the individualistic belief that people are responsible for ensuring their own protection. In other words, although the statutes entitle individuals to protection under the law, ensuring that protection is up to the person, as the following action guide for parents illustrates:

> If you buy a toaster that doesn't work as it's supposed to, you take action.... You don't wring your hands and wait for the company to find you. It's the same with IDEA.... The full implementation of the law depends on parents. (Cutler, 1993, p. 3)

An important aspect of this notion of personal responsibility and self-determination is the right to protest, possibly the most individualistic feature of the principle of due process. Litigation is a process of dispute resolution that involves formal legal mechanisms; the process can be initiated by ordinary citizens and is not imposed from the top down (Turnbull et. al, 2007). Friedman (1996) argued that the tendency to sue is a structural and cultural feature of American society that emerges from modern individualism. As he stated, "It would be hard to imagine much litigation among people who truly believe that it is wrong to make a fuss, or who value harmony and compromise above most other values" (Friedman, 1996, p. 58). What is most significant is that the right to protest or litigate assumes that individuals would be able to express the level of assertiveness needed for claiming their rights and be aware of the appropriate avenues for redress, as the following example of an African American mother illustrates. On discovering that her daughter with disabilities was to be placed in a program that was inappropriate to her needs, this mother did the following:

> I called the local television stations and told them that I'd been trying to communicate with the [school] district and they wouldn't [respond], and somebody sent a camera team out to the district office and I had a little picket sign that said the school district would not talk to parents, only media. And I walked up and down with that sign for awhile and no one from the school district came out. So finally I just went into the office of one of the school district's personnel and talked to them. And after having tried to resolve that problem for maybe a week or so, it was resolved that afternoon.

Friedman suggested that the increase in litigation is in part due to the increase in the scope of the law to a point that almost all areas of life are "potentially justiciable" (1990, p. 16). By mandating an education for all children with disabilities, for instance, the legal system opened the door for parents to protest the violation of this right. The paradox is that although the mandate for parent participation requires school personnel to involve parents in the decision-making process and establish collaborative partnerships, the principle of due process pits parents and professionals against each other and creates adversarial conditions.

Choice in Individuals with Disabilities Education Act

Implicit in the right to freedom of choice are the individualistic beliefs that each person may—indeed, has the right to—aspire to the valued goal of upward social mobility (although the reality of achievement is not guaranteed) and that no individual should be placed at a disadvantage as a result of "immutable characteristics," or those aspects of self that are not within a person's choice, such as disability or gender (Friedman, 1996). In other words, all citizens have the right to the pursuit of happiness and can choose how they wish to attain this goal. Society then distinguishes those who appear to be capable and choose not to be (e.g., in the commonly held perception that the poor are lazy and poor of their own making) and those who are not capable because of an immutable characteristic that limits their capacity.

Certain legal provisions guarantee freedom of choice to ensure that individuals are not placed at a disadvantage because they cannot choose their personal characteristics. Although these compensatory provisions—top-down measures—could be interpreted as welfare or charity, they are defined as entitlements, or rights, that support an independent way of life (Friedman, 1990). In other words, the opportunities to make choices are "rights, not favors" (Cutler, 1993, p. 9) precisely because they enable autonomy and choice making. This distinction of "rights, not favors" is crucial because it contributes to the culture of individual ownership that enhances the sense of personal outrage and, as noted previously, raises the likelihood of conflict resolution through confrontation rather than mediation or "simply swallowing one's anger" (Friedman, 1996, p. 58).

In IDEA, choice is embedded in the principles of LRE and parent participation. The principle of LRE, through its programmatic model of a continuum of services (Turnbull et al., 2007), is most closely identified with the value of choice. In its original intention, this model of services ran along a continuum of environments from most segregated and with the highest intensity of services to least segregated and with the lowest intensity of services (Taylor, 2001) to provide the most individualized educational, vocational, and residential environments for students and adults with disabilities (Bruininks & Lakin, 1985). Similarly, the principle of parent participation, in giving parents the right, among others, to choose from this range of programmatic options, exemplifies the "socialized expectation of participatory democracy" (Marshall et al., 1989, p. 70) that citizens have some choice in decisions about services that they use (Ravitch, 2010). Furthermore, challenging the emphasis on professional decision making, the principle that parents should participate in school policy and programming is another assertion of the choice value.

We acknowledge that, in reality, however, most parents do not have much choice in terms of services. Policy analysts suggest that this is because there is an inherent tension between equity and choice; equity increases as choice decreases (Garn, 2000; Marshall et al., 1989; Ravitch, 2010). The tension exists in terms of how resources are allocated. The greater the effort made to distribute resources and services equitably, the less choice for the recipients of these services. When given more choice for interpretation, school systems often will decide that providing individualized, choice-based services for all is not feasible and that distributing equitably without personal choice is better than offering choices to some and leaving few or no resources for many. The irony of the "choice" paradox was well illustrated by Ravitch, who pointed out that, after the Brown decision of the Supreme Court, the principle of "freedom of choice" was used by many states as a "dodge invented to permit White students to escape to all-White public schools or to all-White segregation academies" (2010, p. 114).

Equity in Individuals with Disabilities Education Act
The value of equity is embedded in the principles of zero reject, nondiscriminatory assessment, and parent participation. Behind the principle of zero reject is a long history that overlays the value of equity. As the role of a child came to be perceived increasingly as that of student, schooling for all children was mandated to avoid inequities and was made available through universal primary education (Turnbull et al., 2007). Next, arguments

against racial segregation in schools were made on the grounds of inequity—that separate schools provided inferior education to certain groups of students on the basis of an immutable characteristic, their race, and placed them at a disadvantage for making equal life choices (Ravitch, 2010). These precedents provided the framework for mandating an education for students with disabilities; excluding students with disabilities from public schools was a discriminatory act because the basis for exclusion was their disability, another immutable characteristic. In addition, the equal protection and equal access doctrines provided the context for the zero-reject policy. Now, students with disabilities cannot be denied an education; furthermore, the education that they receive must enable them as adults to have access to the same life choices as people without disabilities.

Equity also is the underpinning of the principle of nondiscriminatory evaluation. For instance, the mandate for fair assessment and labeling is based on the recognition that classifying students as having a disability when they do not, or classifying them incorrectly, may deny them equal opportunities to an education. Furthermore, the disproportionate representation of culturally and linguistically diverse students in special education has become an increasingly explicit concern of the law (IDEA 2004) and has been one of the main contributors to the agenda of reforming the placement process through the use of the RTI model, as described in Chapter 1.

Finally, the ideal of participatory democracy is embedded in the principle of parent participation, which entitles parents to share as equal partners with professionals in the decision-making process of their child's education. Based on the understanding that parents act on behalf of their minor child, this principle ensures parents' rights to exercise their child's rights to an education. As noted previously, however, when placed in conjunction with the principle of due process, this requirement creates adversarial conditions between parents and professionals. Furthermore, school districts all too often prefer to abide by the letter, not the spirit, of the law so that parent participation is dictated by compliance (Harry, Allen, & McLaughlin, 1995; Harry & Klingner, 2006). Because policy determines special education practice, it is crucial that professionals become aware of these cultural underpinnings, particularly when dealing with families who may not uphold these values and may have differing concepts of self, immutable characteristics, and status.

Contrasting Cultural Traditions

One of the aims of contemporary mainstream American society is to foster individual growth and maximize choices that are open to all individuals equally. This ideal is embodied in the principles of special education law in an effort to ensure that students with disabilities, like all others, have equal opportunities for education in order to maximize life choices and to develop independence and self-reliance and that parents too may participate in a democratic decision-making process toward ensuring this outcome. These constructs assume that both the underlying values and the outcomes are highly regarded universally. This section discusses the implications for families who, in fact, subscribe neither to these values nor to the social outcomes.

Alternative Concepts of Self   Various aspects of the value of individualism, such as the notion that the individual (not society) comes first, freedom of choice, and rights consciousness (including the right to protest and the right to maximize one's potential), are embedded in the principles of individualized and appropriate education and procedural due process. These concepts of individualism, however, may be antithetical to the beliefs of many families with children with disabilities, which may lead to some dissonance when planning an individualized and appropriate education. For example, in introducing issues related to ethnicity and family therapy, McGoldrick, Giordano, and Garcia-Preto (2005) contrasted the dominant Anglo-American nuclear definition of family with the more collectivist orientations of many ethnic groups. Wong, in comparing the values of participatory democracy and individual rights with traditional Chinese values of propriety and individual duties, noted the following conflict:

> The Chinese conception of the individual, in contrast to the Kantian tradition, is not one of an abstract entity. Here, roles and statuses determine one's dignity; differences in abilities are believed to be relevant in evaluating one's worth; one's behaviors are very much constrained by social identity and the related obligations it imposes. As such, it is not difficult to understand why the Western conceptions of "rights" and "equality" are so foreign to the Chinese. (1989, p. 97)

This may be the case for any cultures that hold similar values, such as Jamaican, where Bean and Thorburn (1995) described families as being both unfamiliar and uncomfortable with the prevailing "culture of rights" on which American special education policy and practice are based. Studies indicate that families that have recently emigrated from countries where schooling was not the norm for children are most likely to be unaware of their child's right to education, particularly in cases in which the child has a disability, or of their right to protest if their child's rights are violated (Dentler & Hafner, 1997; Valdés, 1996). Furthermore, even after having been made aware of their rights, they may be unable to assume the level of assertiveness needed for claiming them. For instance, the organizer of a support group of Vietnamese families of children with disabilities described a problem that he faced in helping the families gain access to services: "People are afraid of asking for favors.... I try to show them, to explain to them that they have the right to ask for the services and they are not asking for a favor."

Other scholars have noted that the individualism that is embedded in family–school policies places the onus on parents for initiating involvement in their child's education (Hadaway & Marek-Schroer, 1992; Lareau & Shumar, 1996), an expectation that can be unfair to parents who are "hampered by modesty, language differences, mistrust, and defensive attitudes or who may not have the necessary background and knowledge about assessment procedures and special programs in the schools" (Hadaway & Marek-Schroer, 1992, p. 76). Certainly, traditional habits of deference to professionals have long been identified in research on diverse families (Lynch & Hanson, 2011), and studies of Chinese (Lai & Ishiyama, 2004) and Korean mothers (Cho, Singer, & Brenner, 2003) have continued to make this point. In some families, parents might perceive that their children have little authority to make their own decisions; should there be a discrepancy between what the parents want for their children and what the children want for themselves, the parents' expectations prevail. In such situations, parents are unlikely to believe that their children have rights and even less likely to recognize any violations of these rights. This perspective might lead to conflict when professionals who come from a more individualistic belief system want to overrule the parents' wishes in favor of the child's desires. Such situations are particularly acute when the child involved is a young adult and the parents' conception of the age of majority does not match policy and legislation (Mallory, 1995). For instance, in *Wisconsin v. Yoder* (1972), although the Mennonite parents decided that their high school graduate son had had enough schooling and forbade him to pursue further education, a court of law ruled that the young adult, having attained majority, had the right to continue his education if he so chose and that his rights to education were being violated.

Differing Perceptions of Immutable Characteristics   Choice is such a highly regarded American value that equity-based legislation seeks to ensure that individuals will not be denied opportunities on the basis of a trait—an "immutable characteristic"—that could reduce their chances for making choices toward the pursuit of happiness. Other groups, however, may not regard individual choice as highly and may proscribe personal choices on many aspects (Fong, 2004). For instance, some societies do not allow individuals a choice in the matter of religion (Ross-Sheriff & Husain, 2004). In addition, some families restrict their adolescent children in the choices that they make about making friends, choosing an occupation, and selecting a life partner (Ross-Sheriff & Chaudhari, 2004). By the same token, a trait, such as gender, that in one culture may be perceived as an immutable characteristic justifying equity-based legislation may in another culture be interpreted as justifying specific acts of discrimination. For instance, among some Indian, Muslim, and Chinese families, the belief that a woman need not work outside the home or have a career often precluded girls from receiving an education or pursuing any academic goals more ambitious than an elementary education (Fong, 2004).

Parents for whom choice is not a highly regarded value may not expect to be presented with an array of special education service options (Harry et al., 1999; Smith & Ryan, 1987). Should a school district choose not to inform parents about the various programs and services that are available, the families may not even be aware that their right to freedom of choice is being violated. Indeed, the onus is on parents to identify the types of available options and become informed about the appropriateness of these various programs for their child with disabilities. This presumes a high level of awareness and resourcefulness in parents that may be unfair (Lareau & Shumar, 1996). For instance, in Harry's (1998) study of culturally diverse families, the parents readily agreed to have their children with disabilities participate in inclusive programs when informed of these options by the researchers. Although the children were fully included in their family environments, none of the families had questioned the school system's decision to place their child in segregated environments, primarily because they had not known that they had a choice. Similarly, when a Dominican family received a letter from the school district informing them that their son, Rafael, who had Down syndrome, would be moved to a different school, they were unhappy with the decision but told the researcher, "We weren't going to put any pressure…to fight for him to stay there, because they are the ones who know…. If kids have to be moved to another school, one can't be opposed" (Harry, 1998, p. 195).

Principle of Value Inequality   In the United States, the ideal of equality is so much a part of society's collective conscience that it is easy to be unaware of this underlying value in professional policy. This emphasis on equality, however, may be antithetical to many families who may believe instead in the fundamental tenet of the value inequality of human beings, by reason of birth, caste, skin pigmentation, economic and social status (Miles, 2002). For instance, Wong (1989) noted that among some Chinese families, people are assumed to have different capacities and status owing to different backgrounds (e.g., education) and characteristics (e.g., age); it is therefore accepted that some people should dominate others because of their status. Similarly, because social roles and duties are ascribed among many Indian (Ross-Sheriff & Chaudhari, 2004) and Korean (Sohng & Song, 2004) families, the status of various family members is predetermined in terms of a hierarchical order: Elders have high status, men have higher status than women, and children assert their authority according to birth order. Indeed, Schweder and colleagues noted that to many Hindu families, "the justice of received differences and inequalities,…[the] asymmetrical interdependencies in nature (for example, parent–child), and the vulnerabilities and differential rationalities of social actors [are] universal truths" (1990, p. 160).

To prevent the abuse of power in hierarchical structures, there is the expectation that those in more privileged positions will recognize their obligations toward the less privileged, a sort of *noblesse oblige*, also known as *li*, or rules of propriety, in China (Wong, 1989) or *dharma* in India (Kalyanpur, 1996). By the same standard, professionals, by virtue of their higher status, have a similar duty toward protecting and ensuring their clients' well-being. This understanding conflicts dramatically with the idea of individual responsibility which places the onus for advocacy on parents.

Thus, the belief in value inequality has tremendous implications for parents whose children are in the special education system, particularly with regard to the policy expectation for parent participation. The perception that a professional is a person of high standing and a figure of authority makes it difficult for parents to participate as equal partners in education decision making (Harry, 1992a, 1992b; Smith & Ryan, 1987). Many parents do not participate because they have had a history of bad experiences with schooling and do not perceive that the power dynamics between them and the professionals has changed; this is particularly true of many low-income (Lareau & Shumar, 1996) and African American (Boyd & Correa, 2005; Harry, Allen, & McLaughlin, 1995; Harry, Hart, & Klingner, 2005) families. Other parents may attend IEP meetings, but their silence at these occasions may be due to deference to authority and compliance or even disagreement (Harry, 1992b; Harry, Allen, & McLaughlin, 1995).

Some families also may become uncomfortable with the professional expectation that their child with disabilities be "normalized" (Wolfensberger, 1972)—that is, given the opportunities to lead a normal rhythm of life with outcome and quality of life consonant with that of the child's peers. This effort to level the playing field for children with disabilities is based on an ideal of equality for all children, including all siblings in a family. As indicated by Harry's (1998) study of culturally diverse families, however, although parents might aspire to give their child with disabilities the best life possible, even referring to it as a normal life, they may not mean a life that is the same as for the other siblings, arguing that perforce the outcomes for the child with disabilities will be different, just as the outcomes for the oldest or the male child will be different from that of the younger or the female children.

CULTURAL UNDERPINNINGS OF SPECIAL EDUCATION EPISTEMOLOGY

The previous section analyzed the cultural underpinnings of special education law to illustrate how the cultural specificity of these values can become a source of conflict for families who may have diverse, even opposing, points of view and value systems. As we have stated before, our intention is not to imply that the law is inappropriate—indeed, quite the opposite, for a law that upholds and protects the most highly cherished values of the majority of the people is perfectly suited to its purpose. We are not alone in noting the cultural core of special education law. Other researchers (e.g., Silverstein, 2000; Turnbull & Stowe, 2001) have offered detailed analyses of how key principles of the law are expressed in special education. For example, Silverstein identified four central concepts—equality of opportunity, full participation and/or empowerment for individuals and families, independent living, and economic self-sufficiency. Turnbull and Stowe's analysis expanded this core to nine principles, classified into three main groups—constitutional, ethical, and administrative principles. Our purpose in this book is to indicate that, for some, albeit a minority, the very values on which the law is built may not be consonant with their worldview, thus contributing to the possibility of parent–professional dissonance.

This section examines the cultural specificity of the meaning of disability embedded in special education professional knowledge. In low-context cultures such as the United States (Hall, 1981), where "social relationships and contexts are more impersonal and task specific, and individuals are not related to each other in varied contexts" (Scheer & Groce, 1988, p. 31), a single immutable characteristic such as disability may be used to classify and denote the individual's social identity. As Ingstad and Whyte (2007) observed, despite global progress through international agreements on disability rights policies, people with disabilities are affected locally by the meanings and relationships that obtain where they live. Institutions that define and treat disability are a part of the local social and civic consciousness that influences members' attitudes and values (Hall, 1981). These institutions' greater legitimacy and authority are due to the positivistic belief that the knowledge that they provide is tantamount to the truth because it is assumed to be scientific and, therefore, objective (Hall, 1981; Skrtic, 1995b).

Special education professional knowledge owes its epistemological origins to the similarly positivist fields of medicine, psychiatry, and psychology—in particular, experimental psychology, which provides the basis for education's psychometric approach to assessment and evaluation (Skrtic, 1995b). The roots of these fields are, in turn, embedded in Western rationalist thought.

The Clinical Perspective

The paradigm that has dominated professional knowledge in special education is the clinical perspective, or the medical model (Mercer, 1973; Sleeter, 2010). This perspective of deviance contains two contrasting theories of normalcy: the pathological model from medicine and the statistical model from psychology. The pathological model defines abnormality according to the presence of observable biological symptoms, whereas the absence of these symptoms connotes good health. The medical model implies that abnormality is an unhealthy state that requires alleviation or "fixing." The statistical model, which is based on the concept of the normal curve (Dudley-Marling & Gurn, 2010), defines abnormality according to the extent to which an individual varies from the average of a population on a particular attribute. The statistical model implies an inherent evaluative neutrality in that it is society that defines whether deviance from the average on a certain attribute is good or bad.

Whereas instances of moderate to severe developmental disabilities that have distinct etiologies and characteristics come under the rubric of the pathological model, conditions that are considered mild and that do not have specific biological characteristics come under the rubric of the statistical model, as in a low score on an IQ test. Because a low IQ score is stigmatizing socially, however, ID is regarded as a pathological condition, an objective attribute of the individual (Mercer, 1973; Skrtic, 1995b). Moreover, there is both explicit and implicit bias inherent in the testing process. An analysis of an IQ testing procedure with an African American second grader (Ball & Harry, 2010) demonstrated how bias was present not only in the nature of the questions themselves but also in the process, which included negative interpersonal interactions between the tester and the child as well as an unnatural absence of reciprocity. At one point in the testing, the child had been identifying similarities between objects based on their function (e.g., what do milk and water have in common, you drink them). At one point, however, the child switched to the kind of answer the psychologist wanted, identifying the similarity between an apple and a banana as "food." The tester spontaneously slipped out of her neutral role, exclaiming, "A very good answer!" The child quickly inferred the reason why her answer had been praised and immediately shifted the next sequence of answers to the desired specification of properties, not function (e.g., elbow and knee, body parts; cat and mouse, animals).

The dominance of this clinical perspective in the field of special education has led to two consequences of concern. First, its legal and professional procedures combine to construct an identity of a child with disabilities that often is marked as much by unrelated characteristics as by cognitive or physical bodily functioning. This is indicated by the fact, noted previously, that some groups such as poor, culturally and linguistically diverse, and male students tend to be identified and placed in special education programs more than others. Second, the clinical perspective overlooks the fact that the meaning of disability is not universal and that some families' perceptions about what is a disability and who has disabilities may differ from that of the clinical perspective.

Deconstructing the clinical perspective of disability yields four implicit assumptions:

1. Disability is a physical phenomenon.
2. Disability is an individual phenomenon.
3. Disability is a chronic illness.
4. Disability requires remediation or "fixing."

This section examines each of these assumptions, the first two with particular regard to the issue of overrepresentation of linguistically and culturally diverse students. This is followed by an analysis of the social systems perspective that offers contrasting meanings of disability.

Disability Is a Physical Phenomenon   The Western rationalist belief system and, therefore, the field of medicine dichotomize the spirit and the body, imputing physical causes to all disabling conditions (Fadiman, 1997), including those that affect the mind such as mental illness, which is attributed to neurochemical imbalances in the brain. Accordingly, a disability is assumed to have a biological etiology and an identifiable set of symptoms that constitute that disability; in turn, any individual who exhibits a minimum number of symptoms that are characteristic of a particular syndrome is diagnosed as having that specific disability.

Given the logic that all disabling conditions must have a physical or biological cause, professionals in the special education system determine certain student characteristics to be symptomatic of a specific category of disability. The legal definition of the category reifies this determination. Next, professionals identify which students exhibit these characteristics through both informal means such as classroom observations and formal means such as standardized assessment tests. Furthermore, because current policy requires that a student be deemed either to have or not to have a disability for educational purposes, established eligibility criteria are used to ascertain the presence of a disability.

This process is based on two taken-for-granted beliefs. First, it assumes that the problem is intrinsic to the child and downplays or ignores contextual explanations such as environment, culture, or what Hruby and Hynd (2006) referred to as the complex "dynamics of change over time in organic entities due to…transactive relationships" (p. 555) between brain structure and function. This decontextualized explanation is evident in the official definition of *learning disability*, which, despite changes in the legal provisions for service delivery, continues to exclude environmental, cultural, and economic effects as possible causes (IDEA 2004). Second, it assumes that identification of the disability occurs through a scientific and objective process because professionals are involved. These assumptions have significant implications for students from culturally, linguistically, and socioeconomically diverse backgrounds.

One problem is that approximately 91% of the children who are classified as having disabilities in school environments are accounted for by just 5 of the 13 categories. These categories often are referred to as the "judgment" categories—SLD, speech and language impairments, ID, other health impaired (OHI), and EBD—because no biological bases can be clearly identified. One of the most ambiguous categories, SLD, accounted for 46.4% of all classified students, whereas OHI accounted for 8.4%, this being a category that very often is used for children diagnosed with ADHD (U.S. Department of Education, 2009).

Second, many students are placed in special education programs by a process that in reality involves a high level of professional subjectivity. For instance, it has long been shown that, despite vast variations in teacher tolerance for student behavior, teacher referral is the leading reason that students are screened for service eligibility (Algozzine, 1977; Hadaway & Marek-Schroer, 1992; Mehan, Hartwick, & Miehls, 1986). The idiosyncratic nature of the labeling process is powerfully illustrated in a study by Mehan and colleagues, which found that although teachers would allow behavior (e.g., hitting a classmate) from some students, they would not permit this inappropriate social behavior from other students whom they had already targeted and identified for intervention. These trends continue to appear in research on referral, as in a study of the perspectives of 66 urban teachers (Skiba et al., 2006) that indicated great cultural variability in tolerance levels for different behaviors. This is reminiscent of long-standing arguments that differing interpretations of behavioral and cultural styles result in inappropriate classification (Delpit, 1995; Harry, 1994; Harry & Anderson, 1994; Kalyanpur, 1995). For instance, Delpit (1995) noted that, often, African American students, coming from home environments where they are more familiar with imperatives such as "Put the scissors in the box," are misperceived as being defiant when they do not comply immediately with their Anglo-American teachers' less directive instruction, "The scissors go in the box."

The arbitrariness of classification processes is also indicated by changes that have occurred in eligibility criteria over time. For instance, in 1969, by reducing the IQ cutoff point for mild mental retardation from 85 to 70, the official definition and therefore the meaning of *mental retardation* was changed overnight. Moreover, wide variations among states in classification policies, including differences in terminology, key dimensions, and classification criteria, are another indication:

> It is highly unlikely that there are over nine times as many students with mental retardation in Alabama as in New Jersey; that there are over three times as many students with SLD in Massachusetts as in Georgia; or that there are 40 times as many students with SED (severe emotional disturbance) in Connecticut as in Mississippi.... These variations are more likely to be related to unique state-by-state practices regarding how children and youth are identified as disabled than to real differences in student populations. (McDonnell, McLaughlin, & Morison, 1997, p. 76)

If professionals can recognize that a disability, particularly among the high-incidence categories that lack clearly defined etiologies, is in reality a set of criteria that are established by professionals and that are subject to change and are very vulnerable to individual interpretation, then they become aware of the possibility that many students may be wrongly labeled and placed in special education programs. Further, the challenge of distinguishing between second-language learning and disability continues to result in disproportionate identification of English language learners (Connor & Boskin, 2001; Klingner, Artiles, Mendez-Barletta, 2006; Sullivan, 2011). Harry and Klingner's (2006) ethnographic study of the placement process for black and Hispanic students in 12 urban elementary schools clearly delineated a process marked by irregularities and arbitrary decision making.

Disability Is an Individual Phenomenon   A second implication of the medicalized view is the extent to which ownership of learning or developmental disabilities is seen as belonging to the individual or to the group. A medicalized attribution of disability locates the problem within the individual rather than within the family unless there is clear evidence of genetic etiology. Monks and Frankenberg suggested that this focus emerges from the notion of personhood in Western industrialized societies wherein "the location of individuality in consciousness has been associated with an emphasis on rationality, responsibility, and the continuity of a self that exists independently of both the sociocultural environment and bodily changes" (1995, p. 107).

This point of view has two paradoxical assumptions. On the one hand, in mainstream American culture, a medicalized explanation of disability generally is seen as mitigating stigma because the condition is viewed as an accident of nature, an event beyond our control for which nobody can be blamed (with the exception of conditions with a clear behavioral etiology, such as fetal alcohol syndrome). The increasing reliance on this kind of belief is evident in the medicalizing of substance abuse or, in the field of education, hyperactivity (Conrad, 1976; Stein, 2002). Even when a condition is thought to be genetically determined, the notion of blame is not part of the diagnosis.

On the other hand, a medicalized explanation attributes a child's failure in school to a difference within the child in a context in which, as Artiles (1998) argued, difference is linked to abnormality or stigma and, by the same token, sameness is synonymous with equality. Referring to this phenomenon as the "dilemma of difference," Artiles noted that, difference being a comparative term, mainstream American culture represents the norm against which comparisons are made; as a result, minority people traditionally have been defined for what they are not—for example, non-Caucasian—and "deficit thinking has permeated dominant conceptions of minority people" (p. 4). When all students are compared with the norm of the majority Caucasian culture, students who might have different cognitive and verbal skills that represent "concepts formed through exposure, experience, and their unique backgrounds" (Roseberry-McKibbin, 1995, p. 14) are perceived to have a deficit (Artiles, 1998; Roseberry-McKibbin, 1995).

Much has been written on the fundamental flaws in standardized tests and diagnostic tools used for measuring IQ, particularly for students who are considered to have mild to moderate disabilities (Skrtic, 1995a). Yet, standardized tests continue to be the primary—and sometimes the only—means by which students' school performance is measured to ascertain the presence of a so-called "deficit" (McDonnell et al., 1997). For instance, in an analysis of the tools used to assess students' readiness for kindergarten, Cooney (1995) noted that the instruments used tended to invalidate the indigenous drawing and storytelling skills of culturally and linguistically diverse students because these skills were not consonant with the schools' expectations for understanding of print concepts and sequential narration. She pointed out that, as a result, "children and their families are blamed for having deficient skills upon school entry" (Cooney, 1995, p. 164). Similarly, many students are classified as having speech and language impairments because of low proficiency in English or because their differences in language patterns or dialects are perceived as deficient (Roseberry-McKibbin, 1995; Wolfram, 2007).

The problem with IQ and other standardized tests is that they overlook the fact that children are competent in multiple domains, such as kinesthetic and interpersonal skills, and not just in the academic domains that IQ tests measure (Sternberg, 1996; Serpell, 1994). The tests also overlook the fact that the process of learning is mediated by the environment whereby children exhibit the acquisition of these skills in culturally specific ways (Bérubé, 1996; Serpell, 1997; Trawick-Smith, 1997). A study by Serpell (1994) on the cultural construction of intelligence illustrates dramatically the need to develop alternative means of assessing students' innate skills. Serpell noticed that Zambian students who grew up in an environment in which children's books and crayons were scarce could create quite sophisticated skeletal three-dimensional model cars from scraps of wire, which demonstrated their ability to reproduce patterns, but did less well in a drawing version of the same task. Conversely, English students had no difficulty with copying a two-dimensional picture with pencil and paper but did not perform as well as the Zambian students on the wire-modeling version. What is interesting is that both groups, who were equally familiar with clay, did equally well on the clay-modeling version of the task.

Disability Is a Chronic Illness   Related to the aforementioned beliefs is the assumption that disability is a chronic phenomenon, since the Western rationalist dichotomy between spirit and body explains all etiologies of disability in terms of physical or biological dysfunction (Zola, 1986). Furthermore, the Judeo-Christian belief that an individual has only one bodily life on this Earth leads to the interpretation that a chronic condition is permanent rather than temporary. In contrast, for people who believe in reincarnation, for instance, a lifelong condition would be perceived as temporary (Ayala Moreira, 2011; Danseco, 1997b; Vanleit, Channa, & Prum, 2007). Western time is both linear—it runs on and out—and abstract:

> The artifactual time of decontextualized, abstract hours, minutes, and seconds...where time is controlled and where it is used as a medium for the translation of labor power into a monetary value...is not a human universal. It belongs firmly to the history of Western economic life and paid employment. (Adam, 1995, p. 28)

Although life is predicated on natural (e.g., circadian) time all over the world, this clock time that Adam described forms an integral part of contemporary Western societies' time consciousness. As a finite, measurable resource, it conveys a message of time running out for the human body and death as the final end (Hall, 1983). The concept of time as linear and arbitrarily divided has implications for transition and personal futures planning in special education.

Because it is assumed that a single lifetime is all the clock time that individuals have to maximize their potential, most mainstream families will consider and pursue courses of treatment and interventions to ameliorate the effects of the disability. Indeed, special education and rehabilitation policy is based on this belief. In other words, families are more likely to seek help if they think that this lifetime is all the time that they have. An example of this is the notion of transition planning, a legal requirement, which contributes to the popularity of practical tools for personal futures planning.

Disability Requires Remediation The related fields of special education and rehabilitation are based on the premise that disability is a problem that needs to be and can be fixed or remediated. Furthermore, because it is assumed that the disability is intrinsic to the child, interventions are geared exclusively toward remedying this condition within the child, ignoring the impact of environment (Bogdan & Knoll, 1995; Brantlinger, 2006). Two cornerstone tenets of special education—normalization and behavior modification—emerge from these assumptions. The understanding is that individuals with disabilities can be "normalized" when provided with the repertoire of environments and activities to which typical peers without disabilities would have access and when taught the skills for successful participation through a process of behavior modification. In other words, given the opportunities for the same outcomes of life as their peers without disabilities, individuals with disabilities will have socially valued roles (Wolfensberger, 1972).

The value of equity underlies all policy and practice that are aimed at remediating or compensating for an individual's disability. It is also the underpinning for ideologies such as mainstreaming or inclusion, which are based on the understanding that the life with the best quality is one that most closely resembles the pattern of lives of peers without disabilities. The intent is to mitigate the inequality that is inherent in this immutable characteristic by mandating and providing accommodations for students with disabilities (Turnbull et al., 2007).

Contrasting Traditions in Defining Disability

The pivotal role played by the law and professionals in constructing disability, which we take for granted in a low-context culture such as the United States, is not a universal phenomenon. In high-context cultures, impairment often is interpreted in cosmic or spiritual terms (Ayala Moreira, 2011; Ingstad & Whyte, 2007). High-context cultures also lack the level of abstraction and belief in the immutability of science that characterize low-context cultures (Hall, 1981). This difference contributes to an alternative perspective of disability: the social systems perspective (Mercer, 1973). In this context, disability has no inherent meaning but is defined by any given community's understanding of people's roles, and the degree to which one is able to fulfill the tasks of membership determines the degree of one's physical ability or disability (Edwards, 1997). For instance, although certain descriptors such as *pêros* (*maimed* in ancient Greece [Edwards, 1997]), "No-Eyes" (*blind* in many American Indian tribes [Locust, 1988]), or *dhegoole* (*without ears* in Somalia [Helander, 1995]) imply a set of conditions, the image intended by the term varies from usage to usage, informed by the context (Edwards, 1997), and is not meant to signify the individual as being a member of a category of people with disabilities (Helander, 1995; Locust, 1988).

Furthermore, the value that is attached to a specific condition varies among families, in terms of whether it is perceived as disabling and/or stigmatizing. For instance, Joe noted that although many Navajo families would disagree that the professional diagnosis of Down syndrome implicitly connotes a disabling condition because, in their perspective, "the child functions well at home and exhibits no physical evidence of disability…[has] all the body parts and in their appropriate places… walks, eats, and helps others at home" (1997, p. 254), Navajo families who have high academic expectations for their children would be devastated by the diagnosis. Among many Hmong families, epilepsy is neither a disability nor stigmatizing but an illness of "some distinction…and a sign that the person has been chosen to be the host of a healing spirit" (Fadiman, 1997, p. 21), a position of high social status (Fadiman, 1997).

In this section, we examine four assumptions of the social systems perspective that contrast with those of the medical model:

1. Disability is a spiritual phenomenon.

2. Disability is a group phenomenon.

3. Disability is a time-limited phenomenon.

4. Disability must be accepted.

In noting that the assumptions of the social systems model contrast with those of the positivistic medical model, we are not implying that the former are irrational but rather that they emerge from a set of values that often are diametrically opposed to those embedded in Western rationalist thought. Indeed, there is always a perfectly rational explanation for a belief (Kleinman, 1980). For example, the various seemingly irrational behaviors of many families in most non-Western societies to ensure good health and longevity, such as imposing taboos on pregnant woman, conducting naming ceremonies for newborns well after birth when their survival is reasonably assured, and avoiding all actions that might appear to savor of complacence about one's good health, are responses to the scientific reality of high maternal and infant mortality rates. By the same token, rituals such as baby showers and planning the nursery, customary in societies in which the pregnancy is assumed to end in the birth of a healthy child who will grow to become an adult, can be seen as unimaginable, almost irrational behaviors in societies in which such an outcome is not guaranteed.

Disability Is a Spiritual Phenomenon

Adherents to the contrasting or alternative perspective do not necessarily rule out the possibility of a physical etiology to a disability; the difference is that they may also ascribe spiritual or sociocultural causes. Some Native American and immigrant Vietnamese families impute to illness a natural cause, such as the environment, weather, or unsuitable food or water; but by far the most common attribution of illness is soul loss or "ghost sickness" (Locust, 1988) or a bad or ill wind that invades the body (Davis, 2000). Studies of Southeast Asian families' interpretations of epilepsy, for instance, found strong spiritual attribution (Ayala Moreira, 2011; Eisenbruch, as cited in Ovesen & Trankell, 2010; Fadiman, 1997). For instance, in her study of a Hmong family whose daughter developed epilepsy, Fadiman (1997) noted that the Hmong term for epilepsy is *quag dab peg*, which literally means "the spirit catches you and you fall down" or soul loss caused by fright (Fadiman, 1997). Along similar lines, Ayala Moreira's study (2011) noted that the Khmer term for epilepsy is *skon mday deum* which literally means "evil spirit of one's previous mother" and refers to "the attempt of the newborn's previous mother in the form of an evil spirit to take back the child that she lost through an unfortunate event" (p. 40). Eisenbruch as cited in Ovesen & Trankell (2010) makes the significant point that, although these terms are used by traditional healers and modern doctors alike for similar conditions, the *cultural meaning* of the term is far different from its meaning in western or modern medicine. As a result, health workers in hospitals and traditional healers in communities will treat the same condition very differently.

Similarly, the Mexican American families in Mardiros's (1989) study attributed their child's disability both to biomedical causes such as pollution or chronic health problems during pregnancy and to sociocultural beliefs such as marital difficulties and divine punishment for parental transgressions. Research suggests that deeply religious families (Rogers-Dulan & Blacher, 1995) and families who engage in traditional healing practices (Davis, 2000; Locust, 1988) are more likely to attribute sociocultural beliefs as a cause of disability than are others.

The "evil eye," curses, and other metaphors of spiritual malevolence also are seen as common causes for sickness and disability among many African (Helander, 1995), Hmong (Fadiman, 1997), Jewish Oriental (Stahl, 1991), Native American (Locust, 1988), and Latin American (Groce & Zola, 1993) families. Roman Catholic beliefs about guilt and retribution also account for these views, as evidenced in the study of Latina mothers by Skinner, Correa, Skinner, and Bailey (2001). These spiritual concepts have a distinct social component and are believed to have been triggered by some neglected duty or obligation of the victim. In a case in which the victim is a child, the cause may be envy from those less fortunate (Devlieger, 1995; Helander, 1995). As a result, many deem it a bad omen to express admiration for anything good, such as a large and healthy family (Fadiman, 1997). This belief in the concept of the evil eye has an impact on the families' responses to illness and disability, including beliefs about causes and treatments sought. For example, some Maasai families distinguish between congenital anomalies, which are viewed as being caused by a divine curse—an act of God—and acquired disabilities, which are caused by sorcery—a human act—in response to a social transgression; whereas nothing can be done about the former, the latter condition might be ameliorated through the services of a shaman and/or by righting the wrong (Talle, 1995).

Another spiritual explanation for a disability is that it is direct evidence of a transgression in a previous life of either the parents or the child, a belief strongly held among many Southeast Asian and Indian families who believe in reincarnation (Danseco, 1997b; Groce & Zola, 1993). Among many Songye (Devlieger, 1995) and Hmong

("Hmong Family," 1991) families, a child who is born with certain characteristics some-times will be considered to be an ancestor who has come back into the family; that is, the child is said to be born with "the spirit of the ancestor" (Devlieger, 1995). For example, in the case of a child who is born with a clubfoot, the Songye interpretation is that the ancestor was not well buried—a coffin was too small and caused the feet to be pressed (Devlieger, 1995). The Hmong interpretation is that the ancestor had been wounded in the foot in a battle ("Hmong Family," 1991) and, in this case, the condition is seen as a divine blessing. Indeed, despite the often negative spiritual at-tributions, many families interpret their child's disability as a gift from God, as shown in studies of Mexican American (Smart & Smart, 1991), African American (Rogers-Dulan & Blacher, 1995), and Tswana (Ingstad, 1995) families. Thus, families may have several nonphysical explanations for the causes of disability; this phenomenon has implications for families' help-seeking behavior.

Disability Is a Group Phenomenon   A tacit understanding in all of the nonphysical explanations for the causes of a disability is that the child is not solely responsible for its occurrence but that the entire family is implicated. For instance, many Native American tribes believe that although a spirit may choose to inhabit the body of a person with a disability for some purpose that the spirit and the Supreme Creator have determined, "the causes of a body's being handicapped may lie with the parents (as in the case of fetal alcohol syndrome), and consequently the blame for (prenatal) mutilation of a body falls on the parents" (Locust, 1988, p. 326). Similarly, many Maasai families believe that although the supernatural punishment for an an-cestor's sins—for example, dereliction of duty to one's parents—comes in the form of the child with a disability, the child him- or herself cannot be blamed for it (Talle, 1995). What is interesting is that although many of the Tswana parents of children with disabilities whom Ingstad (1995) interviewed claimed that their child was a gift from God, or *mpho ya modimo*, even in some cases naming the child Modimo, or God, other families in the community referred to the child as *mopakwane*, a condition be-lieved to be caused by breaking taboos against sexual intercourse during pregnancy; however, this decidedly negative label stigmatized the parents, not the child. Again, among many Songye families, disability is made a relational problem between human beings and the occurrence of disability in the family the starting point for an inquiry into the relations of the family; the assumption is that "the problem of disability is not a problem of the individual but rather a problem of the family" (Devlieger, 1995, pp. 100–101).

There are positive and negative implications for this perspective of group re-sponsibility. On one hand, the stigma that is attached to a condition affects the entire family. On the other hand, the stigma is mitigated by a holistic view that interprets disability and illness in terms of family rather than individual traits (Harry & Kaly-anpur, 1994). For example, in Harry's (1992a, 1992d) study, the Puerto Rican Ameri-can parents tended to describe individual difficulties in terms of a normal range of diversity within the family pattern, allowing for a less stigmatizing interpretation of a child's slowness in reading or a quick temper as being "just like his aunt" or "just like her father." Similarly, many Asian families often interpret their child's school-based difficulties as "laziness," oppositional behavior, or indications that they may not have trained their children adequately (Lau, 2010). Another positive aspect of group responsibility is the collectivistic support that becomes available to the family. For example, Locust noted the following:

(American) Indians believe that an individual's spiritual illness can affect the group (family and friends), and thus group efforts are required to return all members of the group to wellness. As a result, students who are not ill may be absent from school in order to assist a sick relative in returning to wellness. Although this group effort is of vital importance to tribal, clan, and family members, it often becomes a point of antagonism between group membership and school officials, resulting in discriminating actions by school authorities. (1988, p. 319)

Disability Is a Time-Limited Phenomenon   Beliefs about the causes of disability can affect a family's perspective on whether a condition is chronic. Among many non-Western cultures, time is cyclical and, therefore, infinite (Fadiman, 1997; "Hmong Family," 1991; Locust, 1988; Meyers, 1992). The past, then, is not necessarily that period of time that occurs between an individual's birth and the present moment, as might be understood in most Western cultures, but also the preceding period, which includes previous lives (Fadiman, 1997). Similarly, the future need not be the period between the present and the moment of death but can include the period following the death of the corporeal body, wherein the spirit will go on to inhabit yet another body (Locust, 1988). Those who see a spiritual explanation for the disability, such as soul loss, view the child's condition as temporary, with the hope that either the soul will be recalled (Fadiman, 1997) or the child will outgrow the problem (Smith & Ryan, 1987). Danseco noted that among families who believe in reincarnation, "disability is perceived as a temporary condition when viewed along several possible lives" (1997b, p. 44); the disability itself is seen as the result of an event in a previous life. In some cases, this perception also contributes to a sense of fatalism, of acceptance of the disability, as is discussed later.

The notion of cyclical, infinite time has implications for transition and personal futures planning. First, the future is intangible and death is merely a transition into the realm of possibilities for new and unknown lives, making futures planning an exercise in futility. Second, to plan for the future is to assume a certain life expectancy that may be inappropriate, especially for an individual with a disability (Whyte & Ingstad, 1995), or may appear as though one were unappreciative of the present (Locust, 1988). Thus, many families might not have a place for transition planning in their repertoire of needs if they believe that the disability is a temporary condition and that the present is more significant than the future.

Disability Must Be Accepted   A family's perceptions of the cause of disability have a great impact on 1) whether they will seek help and 2) the types of interventions that they will seek (Danseco, 1997b). Reasons for accepting the disability are many. For instance, a study of familial attitudes in Africa (Serpell, Mariga, & Harvey, 1993) found that families who attributed a condition to witchcraft, an act of God, or natural causes were likely to seek help; whereas those who linked the condition to family ancestors tended to accept it without seeking external help. Similarly, among many Maasai families, a child with a disability is a fact of life that must be accepted, and statements such as "We met him just like that" (Talle, 1995, p. 62; referring to a child who was born with a disability) convey the message that the child's impairment is an act of God and is beyond human comprehension and ability to cure. Again, the belief among many Hmong families that the body must be whole to reincarnate as a whole being compels them to reject invasive medical procedures such as surgery, prostheses, dental fillings, and autopsies (Fadiman, 1997). The belief among many

Hubeer families that individual deviance is given "cosmological sanction and religious legitimation by the astrological system" (Helander, 1995, p. 75) facilitates a fatalistic acceptance of a disability.

It is important to note, however, that most families do seek intervention, and the type of service often depends on what is perceived to be the cause of the disability. For instance, in their study of African families, Serpell and colleagues (1993) noted that families who attributed a condition to an act of God were likely to seek help from a modern medical facility, whereas those who believed that witchcraft was involved were as likely to visit traditional practitioners as a medical facility. The Hmong family in Fadiman's (1997) study treated their epileptic daughter with the anticonvulsants prescribed by American doctors and a soul-calling ceremony, performed by a shaman, to retrieve the soul. Among Songye families who believe that disability is a response to disharmony in the relationships among family members, the father of the child with the disability may ask his wife to redistribute her bridewealth among the members of the family to restore harmony (Devlieger, 1995). Helander (1995) noted that many Hubeer families initially might seek different medicines or healing techniques, both traditional and modern; but the few, if any, results and the cumulative costs of health care combine to fuel feelings of despair and resignation, at which point the terms *naafo* or *boos* (meaning *hopeless*) are used to describe the person to imply that nothing more can be done.

Whether families choose to do nothing or to seek help, their actions are grounded in an acceptance of the disability. Indeed, among many groups, there is little awareness of the potential for rehabilitating, finding roles, or developing adapted lifestyles for adults with disabilities (Helander, 1995), and the notion that a child with disabilities can be helped by early intervention or stimulation may not be part of common knowledge (DeGangi, Wietlisbach, & Royeen, 1994) or, in the case of many developing countries, even the standard knowledge base of medical and educational professionals (Groce & Zola, 1993).

One factor that accounts for this level of acceptance is the belief in fate, or "karma" (Vanleit, Channa & Prum, 2007), which is enhanced when the cause for the disability is perceived to be divine retribution for one's sins. This fatalism has been instrumental in some Christian Scientist families' choosing not to seek medical treatment even for a child with a life-threatening illness (Fadiman, 1997). Another factor is the belief in value inequality, referred to previously, which, in assuming that every individual has his or her own niche within a social hierarchy with its ascribed roles and status, runs counter to the concept of maximization of potential. Attempting to change this status quo by seeking treatment or interventions would be tantamount to destroying the existing social equilibrium and harmony, an act that would affect the entire community ("Hmong Family," 1991).

CONCLUSION

This chapter identified the cultural underpinnings of special education policy and professional knowledge. Because the values that underlie policy are congruent with those held by the mainstream culture, most families benefit from the provisions of policy and legal mandate. The conflict arises when families do not subscribe to these same values and yet are required to use services within this framework. Furthermore, professional epistemology is based predominantly on the clinical perspective of the medical model. The assumptions of the medical model—that disability is physical, is chronic, is individually owned, and can be fixed—have serious implications for students from linguistically and culturally diverse backgrounds as well as for families who may believe that disability has spiritual causes, is temporary, is group owned, and must be accepted. The process of cultural reciprocity is essential in developing collaborative relationships with families who may hold any of the alternative world views described in this chapter.

REVIEW QUESTIONS

1. Examine your own beliefs on the issue of the accuracy of a psychological assessment. Using your personal identity web, examine the source of your definition of intelligence and how it affects the value that you place on formal psychological assessment. How would you explain the professional view of this psychological assessment to a family?

2. Many parents are aware of their responsibility to be involved in their child's education but are unaware of two taken-for-granted beliefs that are embedded in special education law: 1) that parents are expected to be partners in their child's education and that, ideally, their knowledge about their child is perceived to be as important as the knowledge of the professionals and 2) that if parents do not agree with professionals' recommendations, then the onus is on them to advocate on behalf of their child for an appropriate education, even if it results in an adversarial relationship. It is often the case, however, that parents defer to professionals, even when they do not like a decision, because they believe that the professionals know best. At the same time, many professionals operate within the traditional model of positivism, which values professional knowledge more than parental knowledge—contradicting the partnership expectation of the legal mandate. Think of a family you have worked with or heard about who seems to fit the profile just described. Imagine that you are an advocate for this family. Using your personal identity web, identify those aspects of your own value system that might affect your view of this family's participation. Then, work through the steps of the process of cultural reciprocity to assist this family in becoming a more effective advocate. Specify some actual events on which you would work with family members.

3. Many parents have found that learning the language of the system is an essential part of their effective advocacy and that they must use not only educated language but also the jargon of the field. What are some of the cultural underpinnings of this belief? We believe that much of special education language is based on a belief that the more "objective" the language, the more accurate and professional it is.

   - How do you respond to parents' language? Does the educated quality of their speech affect you? Does their ability to use special education language or jargon affect you? Use your personal identity web to examine the sources of your attitudes, both socially and professionally, toward language.

   - Think of your own professional training and identify some words and phrases that are commonly used in the profession, then translate them into the language that you think would be used by parents. In addition, identify some terms or phrases that may seem acceptable to professionals but might be offensive to parents.

Chapter **4**

The Role of Professional Expertise and Language in the Treatment of Disability

Beth's Story

My introduction to the language of special education in the United States came during a very sensitive period of my life. My 4-month-old daughter, Melanie, had been diagnosed as having incurred brain damage in utero and/or at birth, and I was in the earliest phases of accepting and adjusting to the shock of this event. One of my best friends was coming from Canada to visit, and I sent her the following cable: "Longing to see you. Bring books on brain-injured children and cheese." The displacement of "cheese" in the sentence was intentional; I hoped to amuse my friend, who knew my great love of cheese, while also letting her know of my anxiety over my daughter's condition. My friend understood both my need for new information and for the reassurance that life would still go on as normal. She brought both books and cheese.

I embarked on several months of intensive reading of the current theories and instructional approaches regarding disabilities in young children. I have no idea how much of what I read I absorbed, engrossed as I was in the day-to-day realities of caring for an infant with severe feeding difficulties. What I recall most from that reading was how struck I was by the strangeness of the language. On the level of semantics, there were phrases that were new to me despite my advanced education in the English language—for example, *multiply handicapped,* which I kept reading as though it were the verb *to multiply* because I had never heard this used as an adjective. To me, the word *label,* which I had never heard used to refer to a classification or a designation of a person, was something that you put on a jar.

On a practical level, the language of the texts that I was reading seemed too technical for a field that I expected to be very personal and humanistic. The phrase *service delivery system* was one that seemed particularly strange. Pausing to think about my discomfort with this phrase, I found that it brought to mind an image of a delivery van doing its rounds. The connotations that went along with this image included a predetermined schedule, neat packages to be dropped off at designated addresses, fixed fees for these services, and uniformed drivers carrying out the simple, clearly specified task of delivering a package on time. I found the image disturbing: Would the delivery van not stop for a while at my home? What if I needed someone to talk to? What if I opened the package and discovered that it wasn't quite what I needed or that I didn't know how to use it? What if I wasn't home when the van came?

The verbs of the service delivery system were equally disconcerting. They seemed to me appropriate to physical or nonhuman phenomena rather than to the supremely vulnerable children and families with whom the field of special education would have to deal—for example, the word *service* as a verb for providing services related to disability. Until that time, I had heard the verb *service* used only in reference to servicing vehicles or machines. Similarly, the word *measure* connoted for me physical phenomena, which, when related to humans, could refer only to features such as height, weight, blood components, and so forth. Yet I read of researchers who were measuring parents' attitudes and emotions as well as babies' attachment to their mothers. Furthermore, did *intervene* mean that professionals would move in and take over? Until that time, I had expected that verb to be applied mainly to the resolution of disputes by a third party.

Now, more than 30 years later, I am occasionally startled to hear myself using some of these terms. Others are still strange to me, but even when I disagree with the appropriateness of much of the language commonly used within the field, I do understand the reasons for its use. For example, I now see that the use of technological vocabulary and concepts is driven by the field's concern to prove its place in the scientific paradigm from which it claims authority. I understand that credibility resides in the ability to appear objective and that objectivity is taken to mean the documentation of phenomena in ways that make them seem measurable. I believe that the field has sought to apply the goals and methods of the physical sciences to a set of phenomena that are, very often, unmeasurable, such as intelligence, social adaptation, or interpersonal attachment.

We, the authors of this book, are not unique in disagreeing profoundly with much of this way of framing disability. As stated in earlier chapters, many other scholars have noted its social and political implications and have proposed a social constructionist perspective that acknowledges the role of human decision making and judgment in the creation of the construct of disability. Yet the categorical language of the special education system continues to predominate in professional circles, and, more important, it continues to be the primary vehicle for communication with the families of children who are designated as having disabilities. Our personal experience and our research have convinced us that whether this language is used deliberately to exclude people who do not share membership in the field or is used unconsciously on the assumption that it is universally comprehensible; it too often functions as a source of alienation and disempowerment for families of children with disabilities.

Language, however, is only one manifestation of the persona of the professional. At the heart of that persona is a simple requirement: To be professional, one must retain an impression of objectivity and factuality. That is not to say that one must be cold or inhuman but that one's reasoning and judgment must be based on evidence that can be demonstrated objectively. In matters of disability, however, the problem is that the evidence is all too often of a subjective, unmeasurable, and socially constructed nature.

This chapter addresses the way in which professional preparation uses the positivist paradigm to develop beliefs, practices, and language that reinforce the impression of objectivity. We discuss these issues in the light of the experiences of parents who come as outsiders into the maze of special education services.

THE CHARGE FOR EXPERT DIAGNOSIS AND TREATMENT

A teacher's role is to teach. This simple truism contains several assumptions (Danseco, 1997a; Harry, Allen, & McLaughlin, 1996; Valdés, 1996). First, parents consider themselves responsible for the social and moral development of their children, whereas teachers are expected to be responsible for children's cognitive and academic growth. Second, although these areas of development may overlap somewhat, the teaching occurs in exclusive domains; that is, academic instruction takes place in school, whereas socialization and moral behavior are taught at home. Third, teachers have the expertise to teach, which comes from many years of specialized training; parents lack this expertise because they have not undergone training.

Although this tacit knowledge has been identified primarily within the realm of general education, it is equally relevant to special education—more so, in fact, because professionals in special education are assumed to have the expertise not only to instruct through remediation and other appropriate mechanisms but also to identify who should be the beneficiaries of these specialized services. In addition, professionals in special education are charged by law to undertake this responsibility based on their professional knowledge (Turnbull et al., 2007). Consequently, in the special education arena, this charge establishes a clear hierarchy of knowledge in which professionals' expertise ranks higher than parents'. As in any hierarchy, this creates a certain imbalance of power (Fine, 1993): Professionals have it, parents do not. As Fine (1993) noted, professionals can choose to give parents power by involving them in the education decision-making process, but even this delegation of authority tends to be initiated and controlled by professionals.

The legal mandate for parent participation attempts to restore this power differential caused by the hierarchies of knowledge and, by extension, of status by requiring parental input and parent–professional partnerships in the decision-making process. As this chapter illustrates, however, the issue of power continues to affect families and professionals in the implementation of the mandate.

Expert Knowledge as Categorical and Objective Knowledge

The traditional paradigm of professionalism, what Schön (1983) called *technical rationalism,* has contributed to the implicit assumption that professionals have the expertise to evaluate, classify, and provide appropriate special education services to students who exhibit a specified number of characteristics of a particular disability, an assumption that is further reified under IDEA of 1990 and the IDEA Amendments of 1997 (Skrtic, 1995a). Rooted in positivism, technical rationalism also assumes that the scientific method can be used systematically to accumulate objective knowledge about reality (Skrtic, 1995a).

Objectivity is highly valued in the low-context culture of Western professionalism (Hall, 1981), the assumption being that professionals are likely to diagnose and remediate more effectively when they are not emotionally involved with their clients

(Swick, 1997) and when the process is informed by a scientifically based and, therefore, objective body of knowledge that yields universal solutions. Indeed, the concept of objectivity itself is essentially Western. As Pedersen noted, "Western culture emphasizes objectivity and the scientific method of discovering the truth as more valid and reliable than subjective and spiritual access to knowledge" (1981, p. 324). Objectivity implies a level of decontextualization in that a specific body of knowledge is stripped of its context so that, conversely, it has the same meaning across all contexts. This categorical knowledge, as a universal truth, does not permit the possibility for alternative points of view.

Furthermore, professionals expect and are expected to have a great deal of autonomy in their jobs and to make decisions on the basis of their own professional competence. As Schön (1983) noted, the mechanistic world of the technical rationalist presents professionals with the challenge of maintaining professional distance or objectivity while asking the right questions toward identifying the problem and then providing the answers themselves. Heshusius (1994) has argued for a move away from either subjectivity or objectivity toward an interpretation of competence as emerging from participation in human transactions.

The Language of Objectivity

Beliefs about the objectivity and universality of professional knowledge are reflected in the language that professionals are taught to use. We recognize several positive aspects of this process, including the drive to make language more accountable by systematizing it and the desire to develop language that is respectful of people with disabilities and their families. We believe that as professionals, however, we should develop a critical perspective that will allow us to see the paradoxes in the best of our efforts. We address three aspects of concern in this process.

First, the categorical nature of the labeling and diagnostic process leads to a reifying tendency that is widely known (Bogdan & Knoll, 1995) and has been described in earlier chapters. Once a label has been assigned, it is all too easy to attribute all of a child's difficulties to this presumed fact. This was the process at work when, for example, a professional in Harry's (1992c) study of Puerto Rican parents exclaimed impatiently to a parent who wondered whether instructional practices might account for her child's difficulty in reading, "Well, you see, it's because her disability is in learning to read. That's her disability."

Second, the desire to be seen as a source of objective knowledge often leads professionals to hide behind their jargon. This is particularly disturbing in light of the fact that much professional knowledge is ambiguous and impressionistic. The tendency to use jargon as a disguise often is encouraged by the professional's own knowledge that his or her perspective may not be shared by the parent with whom he or she is communicating. These conflicts can result in situations such as the one in Box 4.1, which was reported in Harry, Allen, and McLaughlin's (1995) study of the experiences of a group of African American parents of preschoolers.

Third, the jargon itself is created by means of strategies that have the effect of excluding or at least confusing outsiders to the field. Some of the most common strategies are what we refer to as the value-neutral or euphemizing process, the abstracting process, and the medicalizing process.

BOX 4.1   Parent Conference
Hiding Behind the Jargon

At an annual review conference, a parent asked the meaning of the term *Level IV*, which, in that state, meant a particular level of service, such as the number of hours, types of services, and so forth. However, the district also used *04* as a code for intellectual disability. The parent was told the meaning of Level IV, but, noticing the notation *04* on the child's file, the parent went on to say, "Oh, so that's 04." The mistake in interpretation was allowed to pass without correction or clarification by the professional. Because the parent had not asked in which category the child had been classified for special education services, the term *intellectual disability* had not been introduced. (This was a strategy noted in annual reviews for children in the 3–6 years age range, in which professionals were hesitant to affix a label on such a young child, yet the classification had to be given for services to be received.) The professionals in this case seemed relieved to be able to let the moment pass. The avoidance of a label in the early childhood years has since become official in many states, where the regulations allow only a designation of *developmental delay* (DD) until the age of 6. The institutionalization of this approach has become entrenched in the light-hearted professional expression—"The DD drops off at 6!"

In this case, professionals practicing cultural reciprocity would have reflected on their own feelings about the label of intellectual disability and examined whether their discomfort with this concept or language was resulting in their "hiding behind the jargon." Having come to terms with their own feelings, the professionals should then have taken the time to ensure that the parent understood that one code referred to the intensity of services the child would receive whereas the other code referred to the disability label. Asking the parent to share his or her own view of this label that was assigned to the child, the professional would need to be clear in explaining the official meaning to the parent and also be willing to engage in a conversation about the parent's view of the appropriateness of this label for this child.

Source: Harry, Allen, and McLaughlin (1995).

The Value-Neutral or Euphemizing Process   As noted at the beginning of this book, one way to offer an impression of objectivity is to replace words that evoke emotional responses, or subjective judgments, with technical or supposedly value-neutral language. This strategy is not peculiar to special education. We spoke, for example in Chapter 1, of the difference between using the word *airplane* as opposed to *equipment*. Ready examples of this process also can be found in books on family life education, where the traditional vernacular words for sexual organs or activities are replaced by medical language. What, for example, might be the difference in effect between the word *womb* as compared with *uterus*? For anyone raised on the Bible, it is likely that *womb* brings to mind "the fruit of thy womb, Jesus," or any other of the widely known biblical stories that refer to the birth process. Thus, the word is likely to have a much more emotional connotation than would the technical word *uterus*. What might be the difference in effect between using a term such as *self-stimulating sexual behavior* as compared with *masturbation*?

The same process can be seen at work in special education as the field struggles to replace derogatory language with language that is either value neutral or, at best, respectful. Most obvious in this regard are the changes in the terms used to refer to different disabilities. For example, old terms for particular conditions of ID are now not only obsolete but also offensive, such as *mongol, cretin,* and *moron*. These originally were used as technical terms that specified supposedly precise levels or syndromes of mental impairment. Society's abhorrence and consequent rejection of individuals with these conditions, however, resulted in the terms themselves having taken on the unpleasant connotations associated with the people to whom they referred. Replacing these terms with the supposedly neutral term *mental retardation* was an attempt to soften the diagnosis, as the word *retardation* should imply a delay only in mental development. Within a couple of decades, however, the new term had come to reflect the continuing stigma attached to people with the condition, and derogatory terms such as *retard* soon came to serve the same purpose as the old terms *mongol* or *moron*. In 2010, the U.S. government amended its laws to replace all references to the term *mentally retarded* with ID. Schalock, Luckasson, and Shogren (2007) explained several reasons for the change in terminology, including that ID indicates that the construct belongs within the construct of disability, is based in a social-ecological framework that allows for a better focus on functional behaviors and contextual factors, and is less offensive to individuals with the disability.

An interesting by-product of the labeling process is its potential for backlash by the people to whom the labels refer. Usually, terms that describe marginalized individuals or groups are assigned to them by the mainstream and not by the people themselves. As the society becomes aware of its prejudice against such people, it struggles to soften its perspective by using language that it hopes is more technical or less value laden. Often, however, the recipients of the terminology come to a point at which they begin to resent and ultimately reject being described as "other" and seek their own redefinitions. Often, their solution is to return to the traditional, stigmatizing language in an effort to reclaim and redefine the marginalized identity. The black power movement is a prime example of this, whereby the previously stigmatizing term *black* became the rallying cry of the reclamation of identity. Although many have since come to prefer the term *African American*—another step toward reclaiming a long-devalued history—many black youth have taken the ultimate step: using the term *nigger* as their way of throwing in the face of society its own prejudice while restating a pride in all that had previously been reviled by whites (Logan, 2001). The term *Indian* has undergone the same process, in place of the mainstream's *Native American* (Red Horse, 1980). In the field of disability, the same has been true of the Deaf community, for whom the term *deaf* is used to emphasize deafness as something of which to be proud (Livingston, 1997).

Another way of neutralizing language is to borrow words from technical activities, thereby emphasizing the mechanistic and more systematic aspects of a process. For example, the word *service*, when used as a noun, loses all of its traditional connotations of something offered through serving, which is further underscored by the use of the same word as a verb, which traditionally referred to the maintenance or repair of a machine. Thus, we hear early interventionists speaking of "servicing" a family. By contrast, the word *serve*, which is the source of all of these terms, seldom is used, and then only by someone who wants to emphasize that professional efforts ought to focus on humanistic or altruistic practice.

Another technical term is the word *system*, which, as was commented on in the opening anecdote to this chapter, when paired with *service*, connotes a level of mechanistic practice that really is neither desirable nor feasible. Even the term *family system*, although intended to emphasize the interconnectedness of family members and functions, also has the effect of understating the very human unpredictability that so often confounds professionals' best attempts at prediction and planning.

This is the main point about the borrowing of technical terms: Its purpose is to make activities sound more systematic and more objective, whereas, in reality, they continue to be marked by human ambiguity and often are driven more by intuition than by reason. But human judgment is just that—judgment—and the discrepancy between the ideal of objectivity and the reality of subjectivity results in the undermining of professionals' confidence in their ability to make true professional judgments.

The Abstracting Process   Another strategy is to use language that effectively abstracts the essential properties of a range of materials or activities so as to be able to refer to general categories without specifying individual items. This process results in some words that are tremendous favorites of teachers, such as *manipulatives*—a sensible word that can include a wide array of toys, learning materials, and miscellaneous items but that carries no meaning for most parents. Another version of this is the use of words that refer to processes or services that are universally recognized by professionals but that may be unknown to the uninitiated. The most common of these tend to be acronyms, such as *IEP, OT, PT, SLP,* and so forth. Although the goal of this process is to establish a universal, shared meaning that all professionals inducted into the culture of special education can recognize, local variations in terminology can defeat this effort: In Florida, for example, the term *staffing* refers to the process of meeting and making decisions about a child's placement. Thus, "staffings" are routinely held for the purpose of children's being "staffed in" or "staffed out" of special education services. Of course, it seems ironic that the term reflects a focus on the professionals in the process rather than on the child.

The Medicalizing Process   The attempt to make language seem objective is perhaps most evident in the use of jargon that originates in the fields of medicine and physical sciences. For example, whereas, in the past, teachers might comfortably have used terms such as *hearing/listening* or *looking/seeing*, words such as *auditory, visual,* or *perceptual* now are among those in common professional usage, and student teachers quickly learn how to use them. It may be that professionals may prefer using these terms because of their greater precision in identifying a specific physiological process rather than a social activity, but they are preferred also because using these words avoids referring to the person who is doing the action. For example, we can see the difference between saying, "He doesn't hear very well," as compared with, "He has difficulties in auditory reception." By minimizing the actor's role, the sense of objectivity and factuality is increased because interpretations of whether the person was listening, whether the language spoken was appropriate, and so forth would have been ruled out. Thus, it would be assumed that any observer would come to the same conclusion. The use of such jargon can become so entrenched that professionals do not even know how to translate it into everyday English. This was evident in an IEP conference reported by Harry and colleages (1995), during which a therapist stated that the child she had evaluated had an "auditory processing deficit"; when asked to say that another way, she replied that the child "has trouble processing information auditorially!"

Expert knowledge and the language used to convey this knowledge, then, is marked by its objectivity and universality. By the same logic, the experts are those who have acquired this knowledge—that is, the professionals.

The Training of Experts

How do professionals acquire objective and universally applicable knowledge? To ensure that professionals have the competence to diagnose and remediate, they are socialized through a process of training or professional education that is directed toward helping participants acquire these special competencies. The understanding is that members of a profession form a community with similar education, training, and practices as well as commonalities in culture, tradition, language, and qualifications, which are in large part a consequence of their professional education (Skrtic, 1995b). As Skrtic (1995b) pointed out, however, this process of induction has two major flaws. First, it assumes that the body of knowledge that is imparted to students in training is objective because its scientific base renders it value neutral and of universal applicability. Second, it does not permit opportunities for inductees to question the objectivity of the knowledge that they receive and identify the values that, in reality, undergird it. Indeed, Jacob noted the following:

> Many of the values and concepts promoted in schools and teacher preparation programs are so deeply embedded culturally that they operate without our conscious awareness. Facing and accepting the reality that specific assumptions or values are not universally true can be very threatening. (1995, p. 453)

For instance, many professionals may question why the parents who belong to the same social class as themselves are also the parents with whom they are "most comfortable" and who are the "easiest to work with," whereas the parents who belong to a different social class are the ones whom they find more "difficult to work with" (Dinnebeil & Rule, 1994). Those professionals who do ponder the point might recognize the discrepancies between the assumption of universal applicability embedded in their professional training and the reality of social class differences. For example, some early intervention professionals who assume that their knowledge is universal might focus on educating families about the child's development and on sharing observations and concerns about the child; the family, conversely, might have very different concepts of child development and of the need for early intervention (DeGangi, Wietlisbach, & Royeen, 1994; Miles & Miles, 1993).

Indeed, professionals are trained to believe that professional knowledge, because it is objective, is akin to the "truth" and that, in the hierarchy of knowledge, it carries greater authority over parents' everyday knowledge of their child because the latter is subjective and personal.

Ensuring Accountability

Recognizing the potential detrimental effect of cultural bias in the process of diagnosis, the law calls for assessment to be provided by highly trained specialists whose expert use of validated tools ensures the objectivity of the process (Turnbull et al., 2007). Were the process of evaluation to lead to a status-enhancing outcome, it is extremely likely that few families would complain about the event. But the facts are that placement in special education is stigmatizing, that often the labels stay with students throughout their academic lifetime or even beyond, that the instruction that students receive in special education keeps them excluded from general education, and, probably most troubling of all, that students from culturally and linguistically diverse (CLD) backgrounds and of low-income status tend to end up in special education more than any other group of students (Donovan & Cross, 2002; Harry & Klingner, 2006).

The policy to involve parents in this process, then, is an effort toward restitution and professional accountability (Turnbull et al., 2007). The intention is twofold. First is the hope that involving parents will elicit alternative perspectives on students' abilities and performance, thus reducing the chances of professional misdiagnosis. Second is to ensure that students who do need remediation will receive, through the advocacy efforts of their parents, an education that is neither inferior in quality nor inappropriate.

It is significant that the onus for informing parents and ensuring their participation is on professionals, although parents also may choose to initiate and sustain their advocacy efforts. As a result, professionals are caught in a web of traditional notions of objective knowledge with themselves as experts and a contradictory mandate to invite the input of parents whose knowledge of their child is presumed to be unscientific because it is subjective.

THE CONFLICT OF EGALITARIANISM AND EXPERTISM

As Fine asserted, the issue is about "(ap)parent power" (1993, p. 682). The mandate for parent participation directly contravenes the traditional notion of the professional as expert and attempts to overturn the balance of power in favor of parents by its recommendation that parental input about a child be taken into account in the decision-making process. Professionals, trained to believe that their knowledge gives them authority to make decisions about a student's education, must now grapple with the seemingly radical idea that parents can be experts too.

From the point of view of parents, the conflict is even more bewildering. Many people from nonmainstream cultures tend to view experts as the source of unquestionable knowledge and therefore expect professional expertise to be delivered in a categorical manner (Cho et al., 2003; Correa, 1989; Harry et al., 1999; Lai & Ishiyama, 2004). They do not expect to be collaborators or decision makers in the process (Cloud, 1993; Rhodes, 1996) and may neither offer their input, even when solicited, nor disagree with professionals' recommendations (Kalyanpur & Rao, 1991). What results, as this section describes, is considerable miscommunication as professionals attempt to convey professional knowledge to parents while, in turn, parents struggle to acquire professional knowledge.

Egalitarianism and American Professionals

On the basis of the common law doctrine that parents have both a duty to support their children and rights that they can exercise on behalf of their children, IDEA gives parents the right to exercise their child's right to have an education (Turnbull et al., 2007). IDEA's regulations require state and local education agencies to establish procedures for the participation and consultation with people who are concerned with the education of children with disabilities, including the students themselves and their parents or guardians. Parents must be informed and their consent must be obtained for pre-placement evaluation, initial placement of their child in a special education program, and reevaluations. What is most significant is that it is the responsibility of the local education agency to inform parents of the procedural safeguards and their rights pertaining to their child's education. Parents have access to students' and system records as well as the right to confidentiality of students' records. School districts must notify parents when personally identifiable information is on record, and parents have the right to inspect these records and challenge the contents.

Implicit in these requirements are three taken-for-granted beliefs. First is that parents have the right to know; that is, they are equally entitled to have access to the same knowledge about their child as professionals have. Second is that parents will advocate for their child by exercising these rights and by demanding redress should these rights be violated. Third is that all parents are equally knowledgeable and have a "shared understanding" (Harry, 1992c) about the first two beliefs.

As several scholars (e.g., Bowers, 1984; Brantlinger, 2003; Coots, 1998; Harry et al., 1995, 1996; Lareau & Shumar, 1996; Serpell, 1997) have noted, however, a significant and/or culturally diverse families often do not have this shared understanding about the system and may not have the means to learn. Apple and Beane (1995) referred to the acquisition of the tools for success in the mainstream as "cultural capital," or, as Bowers put it, the "knowledge of relevant issues and conceptual frameworks of a culture that enable individuals to successfully negotiate themselves within it" (1984, p. 2). Members of the culture acquire this knowledge "from infancy to adulthood, continuously and effortlessly" (Bowers, 1984, p. 33), without being consciously aware of it, as part of their socialization into the culture. For outsiders to the culture, however, this knowledge has to be learned as a conscious process at the point and time of contact—and, indeed, many may never acquire it. Bowers noted, for example, that an individual who has no knowledge of the tacit assumptions that are embedded in political ideas, such as the Bill of Rights,

> Is not likely to possess a set of taken-for-granted beliefs pertaining to the importance of maintaining civil liberties…. The lack of knowledge and exposure to the collective traditions that enable an individual to share in the collective memory will not lead to the individual being influenced by the authority of this area of the culture. (1984, p. 6)

With professionals socialized into the culture of special education, which, in turn, is based on the values of the dominant mainstream culture, it is hardly surprising then that many professionals find mainstream (i.e., Anglo-American, middle-income) families "easier to work with" (Dinnebeil & Rule, 1994). Where there is this "intimate culture" (Serpell, 1997, p. 589) of tacit understanding about family values, professionals do not expect to or need to explain their practice.

Given the tradition of technical rationalism, most professionals do not expect to explain their practice to families who do not participate in this shared understanding either. On the contrary, historically, parents have been expected to attempt an understanding, however rudimentary, of the professionals' culture (Correa, 1989). As Mlawer (1993) asked, how fair is this advocacy expectation? For instance, a comparative study of the advocacy efforts of parents of high and low incomes with children in special education (Coots, 1998) found that mothers with high-income ratings were able to "customize" their child's schooling if it did not meet the child's needs, for instance, by engaging a phonics tutor to teach a child whom the school had deemed unable to read phonetically. Conversely, mothers with low-income ratings did not take action to find additional services to meet these needs but kept pushing the school to meet the needs; as a result, their child continued to receive inadequate services and the parents were labeled "difficult" or "noncompliant." In a similar study (Fine, 1993) of parents of children in general education, the low-income mothers did not have access to the elaborate networks of support and information that prevailed among the high-income mothers. Common avenues of access to the school authorities—for instance, by becoming a volunteer in the classroom or a member of the PTA—were, in effect, not available to the low-income mothers because most of them worked outside the home.

Professional compliance without meaningful communication negatively affects all families, including those who have access to the intimate culture of the professionals, those who have access to the information and resources that allows them to customize their child's education to meet his or her needs, and those who are aware of their rights and of the avenues for participation and for redress. We assert that the pattern of discourse needs to be changed. Compliance is adequate, although barely so, for middle-income families: If they receive written notice, then they can read and understand its content and then act on it. Most professionals are trained to believe that this pattern of discourse, because it is objective and universalistic, is good professional behavior and that parents are receiving quality service (Fadiman, 1997).

Consider, then, the implications of this pattern of discourse for families who lack this cultural capital. For instance, many Hispanic migrant families do not attend parent meetings because they have limited communication skills or believe that they will not make a difference if they complain (Leon, 1996; Rhodes, 1996); some even fear that if they complain, then the teachers and the system will retaliate by suspending their children (Leon, 1996). Similarly, in Harry's study, professionals could not understand why the Puerto Rican American parents would agree to everything at the meetings and then "would go away and say they did not like the decisions that were made" (1992c, p. 480); the parents, on their part, found it difficult to disagree openly or challenge the professionals because of a deep-rooted deference toward teachers.

In a study attempting to promote parental involvement in their middle-school child's education and prevent school dropout, Garlington (1991) noticed that many of the inner-city African American parents were not aware that they could call a meeting with their child's teacher if they had a concern. Those who were aware of this avenue hesitated to do so and often put off calling a meeting, however serious the concern might be, because of their history of poor communication with teachers. As a result, concerns that might have been dealt with at early stages often were not addressed until they became serious enough to merit the school's attention. Over a decade later, Harry and Klingner (2006) reported similar deference to school authorities among families of minority status, sometimes in extreme circumstances. For example, an African American mother of a second grader referred for behavioral difficulties was distressed when the school administration decided to restrict her son to only 3 hours of school attendance per day. Yet, the mother tolerated the situation for 5 months before she finally summoned up the courage to insist that the school lift this decision and go ahead with a behavioral evaluation of her son.

In such ways, the advocacy expectation makes assumptions about parents' knowledge of taken-for-granted beliefs about American culture and the special education culture in particular. Parents who lack this shared understanding are at a disadvantage despite the legal mandate for parental participation and often need professional support, guidance, or explicit advocacy. Turnbull and colleagues (2011), calling for professionals to "keep [their] conscience primed" and regard themselves as advocates, cited the analogy of everyone thinking the job should be done by someone else and ending up with a situation in which "Everybody blamed Somebody when Nobody did what Anybody could have done!" (p. 152).

The Professional as a Parent

Historically, information about parents' perspectives on the experiences of having a child with a disability was presented by researchers and professionals who were not themselves parents of children with disabilities (for a comprehensive review of parents' roles, see Turnbull et al., 2011). Much of their analysis resulted in a theory of pathology and a deficit model of families. For instance, having a child with a disability was assumed to be a burden with few positive outcomes for the family.

The induction of parents into the ranks of professionals contributed considerably to a change in these traditional perspectives. Research on parents, conducted by professionals who are themselves parents of children with disabilities (e.g., Behr & Murphy, 1993; Ferguson, Ferguson, & Jones, 1988; Harry, 1992a; Turnbull et al., 2007) as well as first-person accounts by parents (e.g., Beck, 2000; Bérubé, 1996; Harland, 2002; Harry, 2010; LaSalle, 2003; Mont, 2002; Park, C.C., 1982, 2001) have helped to shape new theories of resilience and strengths-based models of families and affected some of the perceptions about professional knowledge and objectivity.

In response to this growing realization that every person brings to a situation a different point of view as well as an increasing demand for relevance over rigor, professional education began to acknowledge both the impact of individuals' cultural and ethical values on their ability to make professional decisions and the significance of diverse points of view in the development of professional knowledge. This recognition that professionals may have experienced circumstances similar to their clients', indeed, may have "walked in their clients' shoes," was a big step away from the objective stance of professionalism.

For many parents, the decision to become a professional is motivated by the need to gain knowledge about the system (Traustadottir, 1995) and often does result in familiarity with professional knowledge such as the terminology of the field, availability of service options, and current professional practices. Although this does not necessarily change the status differential and many professional parents continue to experience a "feeling of dread" about approaching conferences with professionals (M.J. Blue-Banning, personal communication, April 14, 1998), becoming a professional is an option that is available primarily to middle-income families (Carpenter, 1997).

Although many families may be denied the opportunity to become professionals for economic reasons, other parents' opportunity to become professionals may be tied to the issue of equity because becoming a professional means putting oneself on a par with professionals. For middle-income parents, who in other spheres of life may already enjoy professional status, this may not be as much of a leap as it might be for low-income parents. For culturally diverse parents who believe professionals to be authority figures, any effort to place oneself on an equal footing with a professional would smack of extreme conceit and disrespect.

Finally, the experience of being a parent of a child with a disability does not necessarily signify that an individual may relate to all families who have a child with a disability. Indeed, the process of socialization into the profession (Skrtic, 1995a) and individual cultural and ethical values (Dinnebeil & Rule, 1994) can become barriers to collaboration even for those who have had the parental experience firsthand.

Scientific Knowledge versus Everyday Knowledge

Besides ensuring parents' right to have access to professional knowledge, IDEA also seeks to include parents' knowledge about their child to reduce the field's excessive emphasis on professional knowledge with regard to diagnosis and remediation. Despite these legal efforts to balance the power differential, professional expertise in assessment continues to carry greater clout because it is based on a sequence of evaluation tools that are assumed to be scientifically based and therefore objective, whereas parents' everyday knowledge about their child's difficulties traditionally has tended to be dismissed as subjective and anecdotal (Turnbull et al., 2007). It is no wonder, then, that parent–professional collaboration is so inordinately difficult to accomplish. The ideal of parent participation is based on the macrocultural value of equity and participatory democracy, whereas the ideal of professional as expert is based on the "bureaucratic ranking system" (Hall, 1981, p. 21) of the microculture of special education. For instance, when Bérubé (1996) "politely" gave the audiologist three valid reasons for why the results of a hearing test for his son might be inaccurate—Jamie would have responded more often to the familiar voices of his parents than to the unfamiliar audiologist's, he would have responded to being called "Jamie" rather than "James," and he turned more often to see the animal move when the audiologist spoke than in response to the sound of her voice—the professionals reacted in the following manner:

> They were understanding. After all, Pt. [patient] was so young, it was difficult to read his responses, and we'd know better in 3 months or so. They were also quite sure that he had a pretty serious hearing loss and that I wouldn't help anything by pretending it wasn't there. They said so very politely, too. (Bérubé, 1996, p. 131)

The professionals' response to Bérubé's objection to the results of the test is representative of the dominant positivistic paradigm and the belief that a validated evaluation instrument has universal applicability because it is objective. Similarly, the suggestion that Bérubé was "in denial" is also fairly typical of the dominant pathology model that imputes deficits in families and individuals with disabilities (Bogdan & Knoll, 1995); as a result, his everyday knowledge about his child's actual skills and hearing ability is dismissed because it is subjective.

Deficit Views of Culturally and Linguistically Diverse Families   Professional bias in favor of scientific knowledge can be compounded into deep prejudice when deficit views of historically marginalized minorities are involved. The impact of this deficit model is heightened in that the child's culture itself is seen as somehow being at fault, as this comment by a low-income, African American mother about her young son's evaluation reveals:

> She is judging *me*. I met this lady once, *one time,* and she judged me…. She kept saying his environment is making him act like that. [But] I am his environment. So what is she trying to say? That I am not a good mother or something? (Kalyanpur & Rao, 1991, p. 527)

What, asked Correa, is the message being conveyed when a professional tells a young Hispanic mother that she must "be a good mother and talk to her child" (1992, p. 6)? Similarly, Markey (1997), an African American mother, wondered whether the psychologist who was examining her son with autism recognized the deeper cultural implications of questions such as "What do fathers do?" and, "Do you like policemen?" Again, in Kalyanpur's study, the professional identified a language delay in the bilingual Native American children because she had observed that they did not engage in much verbal interaction with their mothers, and she concluded that "their culture was hurting them" (1998, p. 322). Finally, Valdés's study powerfully illustrates how the cultural deficit model creates a discrepancy between Mexican American immigrant families' and the mainstream teachers' understanding of parent involvement in their child's education:

> When American teachers expected that Mexican working-class mothers would "help" their children with their schoolwork, they were making assumptions about abilities that the mothers did not have. Moreover, they were also making assumptions about the universality of what, in American schools, counts as knowledge.... The parents were not aware that for many teachers, knowing the alphabet was an indicator of children's abilities and of parents' "involvement" in their education. By not making certain that their children arrived in school with the "right" knowledge, they were, in fact, condemning their children to placement in the lowest reading groups. (1996, pp. 166–167)

What often is overlooked is that parents with very little education can be very insightful concerning their child's difficulties. For instance, Harry's (1992a, 1992d) study of the views of low-income Puerto Rican American parents demonstrated that despite limited education, the parents' theories paralleled three arguments that are current among scholars in the field: 1) Labeling is detrimental to children, 2) special education curriculum frequently is repetitive and infantile, and 3) their children's difficulties were attributable to the difficulties involved in acquiring a second language rather than from any intrinsic learning deficits.

Operating within a system that is hierarchical, parents from culturally diverse or low socioeconomic backgrounds are doubly disadvantaged by the "cultural clash" of beliefs (Boyd & Correa, 2005) because of their societal status and restricted economic choices (Harry, 1992c; Lareau & Shumar, 1996). As Harry noted,

> Parents who do not believe that they can challenge school authorities are likely to withdraw from participation. Out of a traditional respect for authority, however, they may continue to defer to professionals yet fail to cooperate with professional recommendations or even to respond to invitations to participate. (1992c, p. 475)

A study by Lea (2006) showed plainly the lack of trust and mutual disdain between teenage African American mothers of children with disabilities and their service providers. One young mother said that she had not told her child's case worker about private speech therapy the mother had arranged for the child because the professional saw her as "just another young Black girl who had a baby and not married....I know she look down on me but I just play the game....They don't know me. They don't know nothing about me." (p. 271)

Joe made a similar point regarding Native American families who, "aware that mainstream society has the power to determine what resources will be made available to those with disabilities and by whom" (1997, p. 253), will quietly refuse services or withdraw from interaction with the agencies when faced with a conflict. Studies indicate that this practice of agreeing and "then going away and saying they do not like the decisions that were made" (Harry, 1992c, p. 480) frustrates many professionals and often leads to misunderstanding (Bernheimer & Keogh, 1995; De-Gangi et al., 1994; Harry et al., 1995) and, in some instances, to parents' being labeled *noncompliant*—a term, asserted Fadiman, that implies "moral hegemony" (1997, p. 260) and coercion rather than mediation.

Box 4.2 shows the extreme gap in communication that can occur when professionals find it impossible to collaborate with parents whose explanations of disability

BOX 4.2 The Spirit Catches You and You Fall Down

In her study of a Hmong child with epilepsy and her American doctors, Fadiman (1997) found that the family, immigrants to the United States, held traditional beliefs about their daughter Lia's epilepsy, attributing it to spiritual causes; indeed, the word for epilepsy in Hmong literally means "the spirit catches you and you fall down." The doctors that the family came into contact with, however, knew and understood only the physical explanation for the condition. They assumed that, like most middle-income Anglo-American families, this family, too, would believe that epilepsy is caused by—and only by—neurochemical imbalances in the brain; that they would also believe in the healing effects of drugs and invasive surgical procedures; and, finally, that they would be fully conversant and literate in English and therefore understand complicated instructions about medications and side effects. Their efforts to treat Lia with modern medicine through a very complex regimen of drugs failed to take into account two significant factors: 1) the family's spiritual beliefs required a mixture of treatments involving both modern medicine and traditional healing through a spiritual ritual performed by a shaman; and 2) the parents' inability to speak, read, or write English prevented them from telling the doctors this. As a result, when the parents stopped administering the drugs, they were viewed as being noncompliant rather than, perhaps, as getting a second opinion or pursuing alternative treatments. On the physicians' recommendation, the child was removed from her family and placed in foster care. As Fadiman points out, the professionals were caring and genuinely concerned for Lia's well-being, but their oversight of the need to consult the parents for other possible explanations for her condition resulted in a major collision of the two cultures.

　　Had the professionals applied the process of cultural reciprocity, they would have learned about the family's alternative explanation for their daughter's condition and their tradition of seeking a spiritual healer for its treatment. They would have used this as a springboard to acknowledge the parents' caring efforts to heal Lia and presented their modern medicine as another possibility rather than assuming that by stopping the treatment after a seizure ended, Lia's parents were uncaring and "noncompliant." The parents would have been more willing to learn about alternative forms of treatment if they had felt respected for trying as best they could.

are totally outside of the scientific paradigm. Despite the legal requirement for eliciting parental input in the education decision-making process, the greater weight that is given to professional expertise in the hierarchy of knowledge skews the balance of power against parents. As a result, parents are expected to know and understand what professionals know, such as the meaning of a diagnosis or a placement. They also are expected to know how to gain access to this knowledge—for instance, by exercising their right to be informed. However, many parents may be denied access to professional knowledge because of a lack of cultural capital and a lack of awareness of this advocacy expectation. Furthermore, families whose cultural beliefs offer opposing points of view are more likely to be perceived as deviant or defiant than different, whereas families from low socioeconomic backgrounds who have limited resources are unfairly situated in a structure that is weighted heavily in favor of professional access to resources.

EQUITY VERSUS HIERARCHY IN THE STRUCTURING OF PARENT–PROFESSIONAL COMMUNICATION

The tension between the requirement for equitable participation and the prevailing hierarchical structure that emerges from the positivist paradigm is also felt in the status that parents are accorded in the decision-making process and the patterns of communication between parents and professionals in formal conferences.

The Mandate of the Law Regarding Parental Participation

In the interests of participatory democracy—that is, the political opportunity of those affected by a public agency's decisions to participate in making those decisions—IDEA provides for shared decision making between parents and professionals (Marshall et al., 1989; Turnbull et al., 2007). This vision of parents as collaborators was reaffirmed in the reauthorization of and amendments to IDEA in 2004 (Turnbull et al., 2011).

The primary forum for such parent–professional partnerships is the IEP meeting, the formal conference during which an IEP is developed from both parental and professional input. As Turnbull et al. (2007) noted, the law requires local education agencies to take specified steps to facilitate parental attendance, such as using various communication methods to ensure that they have been notified, documenting all such efforts, scheduling meetings at mutually convenient times, and providing information in the native language when feasible and interpreters if necessary. Only when efforts to have parents attend have been unsuccessful can the meeting be held without them. Schools must give parents a copy of the IEP if they ask for it. Thus, the law provides opportunities to facilitate parent participation and shared decision making. Again, however, in reality, the implementation of the mandate falls far short of the vision of collaboration and participatory democracy.

Implementation of the Mandate

As discussed in Chapter 2, the legal fiat that requires professionals to collaborate with parents emerges from the ideal of participatory democracy and equity, both central values in the dominant mainstream culture. This is also reflected in the climate of school reform that has contributed to the movement for a restructuring of parent involvement in general education (Fine, 1993).

Ware (1994) pointed out, however, that these reforms have not affected the prevailing model of professionalism that values professional autonomy and hierarchical authority, both barriers that remain significant impediments to collaboration. She asserted that the expectation of autonomy leads more to professional compartmentalization than to interdisciplinary interdependence and shared responsibility with parents. Similarly, centralized power structures traditionally have denied parents' roles outside of their participation in children's homework and parent–teacher conferences and in school events such as open house and fundraisers, where the agenda and limits of participation are clearly delineated by the professionals (Fine, 1993; Ware, 1994). In the special education system, these barriers are exacerbated by the medical model, which reifies the notion of professional as expert (Harry, 1992c; Skrtic, 1995a; Ware, 1994).

Ware's (1994) argument is underscored by the accounts of parents' unhappy experiences with the special education system. In a study by Coots, one mother noted, "Sometimes it appears that [the school personnel] want you so frustrated that you just say 'fine'" (1998, p. 513). Furthermore, the societal status of low-income, culturally diverse parents often determines the way parents are treated. For instance, Garlington (1991) noted that as the African American director of an inner-city community outreach project, she was ushered in to administrators' offices upon arrival while the low-income African American parents with whom she worked were kept waiting in the hallways. Similarly, a low-income mother in Coots's study reported that her child's teacher was always "too busy to talk with her" (1998, p. 513). Harry, Hart and Klingner (2005) reported the gross disrespect shown by professionals toward a low-income mother who, despite consistent and thoughtful participation in all of her son's conferences, was made fun of literally behind her back in a child study team conference.

The low-context, bureaucratic, and hierarchical structure of schools also has an impact on school personnel's efforts to comply with legal requirements to inform parents fully in writing or another suitable manner of communication, in their native language, of any school-initiated special education decisions. Often, compliance becomes an end in itself rather than a means for facilitating communication and shared decision making with parents. For instance, although the responsibility for giving notice to parents lies with the school district, the burden rests on parents to make sure that they have understood the notice (Turnbull et al., 2007); in other words, if the information was clearly stated, according to the law, then the school has complied, even if the parent does not understand it.

Accustomed as people are to the bureaucratic, legalistic phrase *notice given in writing*, it is easy to overlook the cultural assumptions that are embedded in it. First, there is the assumption of literacy. In a country where a majority of the population is literate, indeed where illiteracy is stigmatized, ubiquitous reliance on the written word for communication is a natural outcome, to the point that even informal, everyday situations such as learning how to open a milk carton or filling up the gasoline tank in one's car require a certain level of reading skill. The reason, and this leads to the second assumption, is that, as Hall (1981) noted, in low-context cultures, most transactions are mechanistic and decontextualized—acquiring the milk or gasoline, for instance, can be accomplished with a minimum of personal interaction because it maximizes efficiency. As a result, information is communicated in similarly mechanistic and impersonal ways. Indeed, using low-context, written formats to communicate information about an issue as personal as the educational well-being of children would not be considered inappropriate.

This "highly rational, efficient, 'quick-fix' approach" (McGowan, 1988, p. 62) to communication can be disconcerting to people who are accustomed to a slower, more personal, yet more generalized approach. The dominant value behind the latter approach is the kind of personalism that has been identified as central to high-context cultures. Personalism brings to communication a holistic, relational perspective (Falicov, 1996) that increases considerably the significance of contextual details such as the status of both listener and speaker and assumes a high level of tacit understanding. Because the focus is more person-centered than task-centered, the rules of communication often require a more indirect style that would include, for instance, discussion of seemingly tangential issues before coming to the topic at hand (Kalyanpur & Rao, 1991) and the use of allusions, parables, or proverbs to convey an opinion

(Falicov, 2005). As McKenzie-Pollock (2005) explained, "To an American observer, the Cambodian style of communication often appears elliptical and indirect, [sometimes causing] confusion and miscommunication as Cambodians experience confrontation or direct questioning as very rude and threatening" (p. 293). McKenzie-Pollock also gave the following example of using personalism within the indirect cultural style of Cambodians:

> I once asked a Cambodian teacher for advice about the most effective way to intervene in a case where teachers were referring a child who had talked about domestic violence. She said she would handle this situation by visiting the couple with a gift of food. She would sit with them and chat about family life and values without mentioning the reports of violence. Therefore, the couple would not be shamed by having the problem named, but they would get the message that there was a problem with their or his behavior. (1996, p. 308)

In contrast, the low-context culture of the special education bureaucratic machinery provides parents with written information on the assumptions that 1) they are literate, 2) a written document is the most appropriate means of communication, and 3) they will understand the contents of such a decontextualized message. Indeed, a study of parents' preferences and priorities for receiving information about challenging behaviors (Turnbull & Ruef, 1996) found that the well-educated, Caucasian mothers chose printed material over other formats such as audiocassette, videocassette, or parent matching. However, a disproportionate number of people with low levels of literacy are members of minority groups and/or of low socioeconomic status (Weiss & Coyne, 1997), many of whom are likely to have children who are at risk for academic failure and are, therefore, likely to receive written notices to this effect. Furthermore, typical handouts used to inform individuals about their rights are written at the tenth-grade level or higher, whereas most of the recipients of these documents might be, at best, at third- or fourth-grade reading levels (Weiss & Coyne, 1997). The National Assessment of Adult Literacy survey (U.S. Department of Education, Institute for Education Sciences, 2003) reported that 29% of a national sample of adults scored at the basic level and 14% scored below basic—basic being defined as "able to read and understand information in short, commonplace prose texts" (p. 16). The report specified that adults who had not graduated from high school and those who had not spoken English prior to…were overrepresented in the below basic group. These numbers clearly have increased relevance for many immigrants and minorities of low educational level. For instance, the modern Hmong script was developed in the mid-1950s (Fadiman, 1997). As a result, illiteracy is common among many Hmong families:

> To the Hmong, the numerous consent forms, individualized education plans or individualized family service plans, and permission forms that parents must sign when their child is in an early intervention program are alien and overwhelming. Illiteracy in Hmong or English or both further complicates the process of written documentation required by local, state, and federal mandates, even though English forms may be translated to the Hmong language. (Meyers, 1992, p. 741)

Various sources have suggested that many culturally diverse and low-income families are more comfortable with alternative formats to written communication (Rao & Kalyanpur, 2002; Weiss & Coyne, 1997). These formats include direct communication by telephone or in person through an interpreter and nonwritten materials, such as picture books, slide or tape presentations, audiotapes, videotapes, and mod-

politeness, frustration, disagreement, or anger, and, similarly, would consider making direct eye contact with a speaker extremely impolite, in complete contrast to the dominant Euro-American belief (Brooker, 2003; Davis, 2000; Ovesen & Trankell, 2010; Rao & Kalyanpur, 2002).

There are also logistical factors that work against effective parental participation. Despite legal regulations to the contrary, school districts might schedule IEP meetings according to their—not the parents'—convenience (Harry & Klingner, 2006). If parents cannot attend because of a conflict of time, transportation, or child care problems and are not aware of their right to participate, then they may not dispute the scheduling, choosing instead not to attend. This decision often is misperceived as an indicator that they do not care. With regard to the role played by parents in such conferences, their low status often is reinforced by the fact that they are the only outsiders or nonprofessionals among the participants, particularly when they are unaware that regulations allow them to bring a lawyer or a parent advocate to the meeting. Sometimes parents may not be introduced to the other participants, all of whom, as professional colleagues, may know each other. Whereas professionals are addressed by titles or last names, parents may be addressed by first name only (Harry, 1992b, 1992d; Marion, 1979).

These behaviors convey to parents the message that they have little or no status as members of the IEP committee. Often, parents are ushered into a room where all of the other participants are already present and seated, leaving the parent no choice in seating, thus amplifying the sense of being an outsider. Equally often, parents and other temporary members of the committee are required to leave the room while the actual decision about placement is being made (Mehan, Hartwick, & Miehls, 1986). As Mehan and colleagues asserted, this action is an unequivocal declaration of who holds power, and it denies parents influence in an area in which most might be expected to hold an opinion. These attitudes are reinforced further when parents perform the ultimate "subjective" act: cry! Harry and colleagues (1995) reported a meeting at which a mother who burst into tears was ushered sympathetically out of the meeting until she regained her composure. This excluded her from relevant matters that were discussed in her absence.

Because parents are cast in the role of temporary members, their participation is defined by the professionals. If parents lack the cultural capital that would enable them to negotiate a change in this pattern of discourse, then the formal meeting becomes yet another forum for compliance with the law rather than communication in the full meaning of the term, and the absence of meaning in parent participation is startling. This is powerfully illustrated by Harry's (1992a, 1992b) description of a case in which Dora, a Puerto Rican American mother, was not even aware that a meeting that she attended was an IEP meeting. Although the event met none of the criteria for an IEP meeting in that it was initiated by the parent, not the teacher; it took place well beyond the 30-day time limit for such meetings; and no one from the evaluation team was present, it was conducted and recorded as an IEP meeting. At the end of the meeting, the parent was handed an IEP document simply as documentation of the meeting; its nature and importance were not mentioned. As Harry noted, Dora signed the IEP

> Not knowing that an IEP was required or that there were specific procedures for its implementation…quite unaware of its meaning and importance in the system, and certainly unaware that the conduct of the meeting was out of compliance with state requirements. (Harry, 1992b, p. 485)

From Dora's point of view, the event was simply one in which she "went to the school and talked to the teacher."

Structural Factors: The Order of Speakers and the Types of Reporting

A significant barrier to equitable collaboration among IEP committee members is the hierarchical structure of schools. The effect of this structure was first studied by Mehan and colleagues (1986) and Mehan (1993) and subsequently by several authors including Bennett (1988), Harry and Klingner, (2006) and Knotek (2003). The hierarchy of status in special education conferences does not seem to have changed much over more than 2 decades. This hierarchy is evident in the order in which the participants present their information about the child and the manner in which this information is presented. For instance, in his study, Mehan (1993) noted clearly defined parameters in keeping with the hierarchical professional structure of the school: The school psychologist presented first, followed by the child's special education teacher, the nurse, and finally the child's mother. Furthermore, the psychologist's information was presented in the form of a "single uninterrupted report" that was read aloud, "augmented by officially sanctioned props" that included the case file, test results, and prepared notes. Although the psychologist's report contained fairly technical language such as "poor mediate recall" and "high auditory association" as well as abbreviations such as "ITPA" for the name of a test, there were no explanations for the terms used and no questions were asked. The general education teacher's and mother's information was elicited by other members of the committee in the form of a question-and-answer session. Both spoke from memory and had no notes; and, although they used no technical terms, they were asked to clarify what they meant.

Similarly, in Bennett's (1988) study of the interactions between Hispanic parents of deaf children and special education professionals, a parent was prevented from discussing the possibility that the classroom environment was affecting her child's behavior because this knowledge did not conform to the professionals' analysis of the child's behavior. Thus, despite the parent's best advocacy efforts, she was effectively silenced.

Knotek's (2003) study of parent conferences demonstrated the detrimental influence that hierarchical assumptions can have on decisions made about children. This study painted a distressing portrait of the intense social class bias expressed in all aspects of placement and review meetings. First, the attitude toward the families was marked by disdain of families known to have low economic and educational status or problematic marital issues. Second, the priority given to the opinions of high status professionals was evident in the order of reporting (as in Mehan et al., 1986) and in the fact that these members' interpretations, offered early in a meeting, would become a dominant motif in explanations of a child's skills and needs. For example, the use of the metaphor of the "lightbulb" (cognitive ability) working intermittently in a child's brain overshadowed an explanation offered later by a classroom aide that the child's variable performance might reflect inconsistent routines at home, such as bedtime. Such attitudes strongly influenced the educational decisions made about children's disability designations and educational placements. Very similar processes were reported by Harry and Klingner (2006) of negative attitudes toward poor African American families having a detrimental influence on the decisions made by school teams. This entire 3-year ethnographic study of the placement process was marked by the common phrase on the part of school personnel—"the parents are the problem!"

CONCLUSION

The authority that technical rationalism, the dominant paradigm of professional education, bestows on professional knowledge about the diagnosis and remediation of a student in special education tends to undermine parents' knowledge about their child. Furthermore, this hierarchy of knowledge and status directly contradicts the legal requirement for parent–professional collaboration in the education decision-making process, placing both parents and professionals in a precarious and unpleasant situation. To have their views considered, parents are expected to advocate vigorously—an expectation that is particularly unfair to parents who may lack an awareness of both this responsibility and the avenues for participation, such as the IEP meeting. Parents who do attend the IEP meeting then are confronted by the rigid, positivism-based hierarchical structure that belies the legal mandate. Differences in interpersonal communication style serve only to increase further the barriers to collaboration between parents and professionals.

The approach of cultural reciprocity places significant responsibility on professionals to initiate ongoing dialogue with family members toward the goal of mutual understanding and respect. There is a crucial place for professional expertise in developing effective educational programs for children. There is an equally crucial place for parental expertise. For these to come together, professionals must first understand the cultural basis of their knowledge so as to understand the cultural basis of parents' knowledge. This mutual understanding provides the ground for collaborative decision making.

REVIEW QUESTIONS

1. We, the authors, believe that values such as equity and individualism underlie the philosophy of inclusion. However, although these values are cornerstones of American culture, the idea of the equal importance of each individual is not universally held. In fact, there are societies in which the concept of inequity is accepted; that is, it is accepted that differential value will be placed on individuals according to factors such as social status, biological limitations, age, gender, or other factors. Describe your own concept of equity and explain how it influences your view of inclusion. Using your personal identity web, examine the source of this view.

2. The differences in defining disability indicate that the parameters of what is considered normal differ according to cultural expectations. What is your own definition of disability? In your opinion, how severe do an individual's disabilities need to be in order to be considered a person with disabilities? How does your view compare with the official definitions used by the special education system? What implications might differing definitions have for your communication and interaction with families from diverse cultural backgrounds?

3. This chapter described several contrasting traditions with regard to beliefs about disability. Where would you place yourself on these various aspects? Does acculturation play a role in where you placed yourself?

Chapter **5**

Professionals' Perspectives on Parenting Styles

Maya's Story

At a dinner party at my home, I noticed my American friend's eyes grow rounder and rounder as she watched my Indian friend sit her almost 4-year-old daughter on her lap and proceed to feed her swiftly and efficiently. Later, she shook her head in amazement: "My kids learned to eat by themselves by the time they were 2! We Americans like our kids to be independent as early as possible." Then, she continued, "Speaking of kids, we need to be getting home soon. We have an early day ahead of us tomorrow. My husband is the baseball coach for our son's team, and I promised our daughter I'd watch her soccer game." Listening to her, I tried and failed to recall a single instance when, growing up in India, my parents played with me beyond toddlerhood. As soon as I reached an age when I understood the rules of a game and could be expected to share with my peers, I played with other children. There were no parents on the sidelines cheering, keeping score, or coaching. What a high level of independence was expected of us children, I thought. It struck me that parents in all cultures seek to make children independent but that the milestones toward that goal may differ.

I remembered this incident when, some months later, I was introduced to a Native American mother, living on the reservation, who agreed to let me interview her about her adult daughter with developmental disabilities. She told me with pride that all of her adult children, many with children of their own, lived in proximity of each other on the reservation, and she beamed as she described the sundry shop that she and her husband had been able to set up in an annex of the house for their daughter with disabilities after her graduation. This way, their daughter, who was unlikely to get married or to have children of her own, could enjoy financial independence while enjoying the comforts of home. Yet another culturally defined understanding of independence, I thought.

Then I met the middle-income, Anglo-American professional who had organized a parent support group on the same reservation. She described enthusiastically how she had come up with the idea and was excited that the first meeting had been fairly well attended and considered a success by all. Agreeing that it might be interesting for me to attend the next meeting and meet the mothers, she wondered in what capacity I could be introduced to them. Then she remembered that the mothers brought their children with them and that she was looking for someone who could supervise the children while the mothers attended the meeting. "Could you look after the children during the meeting?" she asked. "Do you have parenting skills?"

I realized that, like many of us professionals, she was assuming a universality of meaning to the term *parenting skills,* believing that milestones toward independence are the same and that bringing up children occurs in the same way across all cultures. Here we were, trying to use her knowledge of parenting in the Anglo-American culture to assess my skills as an Indian mother and decide whether I could look after Native American children. Implicit and equally disconcerting was the unquestioning acceptance that the term conveyed an objective truth and the belief that we were demonstrating true professionalism.

When did parenting cease to become something that only parents and families did? When did it become acceptable, indeed, appropriate, for professionals to ask parents whether they had parenting skills? Perhaps the timing of this blurring between what schools or professionals should do and what parents should do is less significant than the fact of its existence. The blurring is more so for the field of disabilities, in which professionals target as education goals traditional parenting tasks, such as self-help and leisure skills, as much as traditional academic tasks, such as reading and writing. Indeed, professionals are legally mandated to ensure that parents are involved in the child-rearing process of getting their child to learn to eat, dress, and make friends. For instance, Part C of the IDEA 2004 specifically suggests that the goal of family education and training about exemplary models and practices to the families of children in early intervention is to enhance the capabilities of parents (U.S. Department of Education, 2007). In this climate, it is perfectly appropriate for professionals to question a parent's parenting skills and to assume that the professionals are the experts on parenting.

By the same token, with the increasing overlap between child rearing and educational tasks, the responsibility for involving parents in the development of their child with disabilities has fallen on professionals. Under the law, professionals are required to inform parents of any changes in their children's educational placement, of steps for an evaluation or assessment, of their rights to due process, and so forth. Chapter 4 described the implications for CLD families if these procedures that determine the legal parameters for enlisting parent involvement are too narrowly interpreted, with the reality falling far short of the ideal of parent–professional collaboration (Harry, 2008).

This chapter focuses on another outcome of professional responsibility for parent participation: the enlisting of parents as helpers in achieving their child's education and child rearing goals. Because the next step after identifying appropriate education goals is to implement them, it is commonplace—indeed, natural—for professionals to expect parents to participate in reinforcing learning and helping toward generalizability of skills across various contexts. What needs reinforcing and how it should be reinforced is prescribed by professionals and forms the basic premise of parent education programs and IEP goals. However, as we explain in this chapter, many professionals, in the belief that they must teach parents parenting skills, often overlook the cultural specificity of their own professional knowledge about child rearing and development and conclude that different parenting practices are wrong or at least inappropriate. This has serious implications for the partnered process of identifying and implementing appropriate education goals for the child or young adult with disabilities.

This chapter is divided into three sections. The first section examines two assumptions about parenting skills that are embedded in professional practice—universality and deficit. The second section describes how differing social orientations, with specific reference to family values, structure, and interactions, inform "parental ethnotheories" (Harkness & Super, 1996) or parents' belief systems on child rearing. The third section examines the cultural contexts that have informed or instantiated (Harkness & Super, 1996) parental ethnotheories on parenting practices, with specific reference to discipline.

ASSUMPTIONS ABOUT PARENTING SKILLS

Most professional practice manifests two inherent assumptions about parenting skills. The first is that, because child development and developmental psychology are scientifically based, the theories are objective and therefore universally applicable. Indeed, behaviors considered normative by the mainstream have become the standards of behavior for all other groups. The second assumption is that any variation from these norms is a deviation or wrong practice that needs correcting.

Assumption of Universal Applicability

As infants and toddlers become students and eventually young adults, they and their families encounter myriad situations in which they are presented with a value system, rules, behaviors, and expectations that may not coincide with their own. In some situations, the conflict may seem obvious, such as an IEP goal to teach an Asian child with a disability to eat with a fork and a knife when the child uses chopsticks at home. Other instances, however, may be less overt, as in the case of the Native American parents of a young woman with developmental disabilities who found that the highly recommended self-advocacy course in which their daughter was enrolled at the local community college was making her "rebellious;" the professionals had recommended the course in the hope that she would become "assertive" (Kalyanpur, 1998). Similarly, M. Smith-Lewis (personal communication, February 1992) pointed to the incongruence in introducing American Sign Language, the signs and symbols for which emerge as much from English etymology as from the cultural context—for example, the sign WOMAN is a reference to bonnet strings—as an alternative means of communication for nonverbal children whose native language is not English.

Genetic determinism, or the belief that ability or disability is inherent in an individual, precludes the possible impact of external influences such as environment (Scherzer, 2009; Valsiner, 2008). This belief is embedded in traditional and dominant behaviorist and developmental paradigms such as Piagetian theory. As a result, the developmental milestones of children in Western industrialized countries have come to be considered the norm for all children regardless of their economic and cultural milieu. One example of this is the use of assessment instruments such as the WISC-5 (Wechsler, 2004) and the Vineland Adaptive Behavior Scales (Sparrow, Cicchetti, & Balla, 2005) on populations that are not included in the standardized sample.

Assumption of Right versus Wrong Practice

With the rules, behaviors, and values of the dominant culture becoming established as the norm within professional domains, the values and behaviors of other cultures, not being the norm, began to be perceived as deviant and the cultures themselves deficient; parents who adhered to the so-called "deviant" sets of rules were "a tangle of pathology" and their children "culturally deprived" (U.S. Department of Labor, 1965, p. 51).

Thus, not only are professionals not trained to be aware of the cultural underpinnings of their practice (McCall & Skrtic, 2009), but they also are, in fact, trained to remediate what is perceived to be wrong practice. For instance, an occupational therapist who might develop for an Asian child an eating goal that requires the use of knife, spoon, and fork does so on the basis of two embedded assumptions: 1) The ability to eat independently involves these and only these implements, and 2) eating with chopsticks is not a socially appropriate skill. Instances abound of African American children whose language is demeaned in school because it is not Standard American English (Delpit & Dowdy, 2002; Filmer, 2003; Heath, 1983; Piestrup, 1973), in some cases to the point that preschoolers who were articulate and master storytellers at home were placed at risk for academic failure in school.

This deficit model has permeated all of the helping professions. In health, social work, and mental health services, it contributes to the medical model that identifies innate deficits in children. In special education services, it contributes to the overrepresentation of culturally and linguistically diverse students in special education (see Chapter 3). In child welfare services, as shown in the following sections, the deficit model provides the rationale for parent education programs and for legal safeguards against abuse and neglect by families whose parenting does not conform to the professional definition of appropriate practices.

Negative Effects of Assumptions of Universality and Deficiency on Parent–Professional Interaction

These dual assumptions of universality and deficiency tend to affect parent–professional interactions adversely. Caught between the ideal of excellence and the reality of failing students, policy makers were faced with the choice of either forgoing excellence and a standard curriculum or targeting the students who are likely to fail in school or in life and providing them with a separate curriculum (Frattura & Topinka, 2006). The decision to go the latter route resulted in compensatory programs and parent education models. The intention was that the deficiencies of the children and of their parents, who lacked the ability to teach their children the skills necessary for academic success, could be overcome through these compensatory and at-risk programs. Children who were identified as being most at risk for academic failure were those whose home conditions included "poverty, low educational attainments of parents, single-parent families, and non–English-speaking families" (Levin, 1990, p. 284). The National Commission on Children asserted the following:

More and more families, overburdened and debilitated by the conditions of their lives, struggle to survive in settings where poverty, unmarried child bearing, absent fathers, unemployment, alienation, and violence are common. Under these circumstances, it is difficult for parents to teach children the value of marriage, steady work, and a healthful lifestyle. Children have few opportunities to acquire the skills, attitudes, and habits that lead to success in school, productive employment, and strong, stable families. (1991, p. xxv)

Thus, parent education programs set about the task of teaching appropriate parenting skills to "culturally disadvantaged" parents, whether poor, less educated, or linguistically diverse. Appropriate parenting skills were those that would show parents and thereby children that "character, self-discipline, determination, and constructive service are the real substance of life" (National Commission on Children, 1991, p. xxv) and disciplinary practices that avoided the use of physical punitive measures (Lau, 2010).

Although professionals acknowledge the reality of economic and environmental disadvantages that can threaten family security and stability (Ceballo & McLoyd, 2002), they are concerned here with the pernicious effects that can result from stereotypical assumptions based on cultural assumptions. For example, a Korean mother of a child with disabilities described the cultural miscommunication that arose between her and a professional, Amy, on Amy's first visit to the mother's home. Amy initiated some activities, and the child responded well, while the mother sat back and observed. When told later that Amy's interpretation of the situation was that the professionals would need "to make her interact more with her child," the mother commented as follows:

First of all, I was not sure what the purpose of the visit was. Also, in my culture, we do not show off our affection in front of strangers. However, if I had known that she wanted to see if I could interact with my child all right, I would have done it. We are very shy people and were taught not to show our emotions. Also, I was being humble and nice to Amy. I thought I could always interact with my child when professionals are not there and I would just let Amy interact with Sung-Hee for the purpose of letting Sung-Hee be exposed to diverse individuals. Amy visited my home only once. She probably had some information about my family, but I never had an informal or formal conversation with her. Was it appropriate for her to judge that my behavior indicated an inappropriate, inactive mother?

CULTURE AND PARENTAL ETHNOTHEORIES

For many years, behaviorist and developmental paradigms dominated, spotlighting the child as an isolated unit of analysis. Later, the work of Bronfenbrenner and Vygotsky developed more dynamic, interactive models of parent–child interactions that used a broader lens to incorporate an understanding of culture into explanations of parenting (see Feeney, Christensen, & Moravcik, 2005). Cross-cultural research on parenting indicated that, far from being universal, parenting styles tend to differ not only from culture to culture but also within cultural groups from family to family. In their seminal research, Harkness and Super (1996) contended that "parental ethnotheories," or parent belief systems about child rearing and development, are affected by culture and personal history in ways that are unique to each family, even as the cultural context is shared by members of a culture at particular periods in time and beliefs are appropriated directly from the culture. For instance, the idea that children learn by exploring their environments is both an unspoken and overt message of our times, conveyed tacitly through the availability of childproof devices and directly through the Montessori and the more recent constructivist methods of teaching. However, how each individual transacts an understanding of this shared knowledge based on his or her own personal history creates a parental ethnotheory that is unique. Therefore, although parents from the same broad culture are more likely to share similar ethnotheories than parents who belong to opposite traditions—for example, Asian versus western European—there still would be individual variations depending on whether the western European parents were, say, Italian or English. Box 5.1 illustrates the application of the process of cultural reciprocity to enable professionals to understand families' parental ethnotheories.

     BOX 5.1   Annie
The Good Mother

When Annie, an African American mother of two toddlers, was reported to child protection services by her social worker, Caroline, for spanking her children, she became bitter and angry about being accused of abuse and about the betrayal of her trust in Caroline. On her part, Caroline saw no need to change her mind about Annie's parenting skills. The relationship between the two women deteriorated. If, instead, Caroline had applied the process of cultural reciprocity, how might this scenario have played out?

Caroline asks herself why she expects Annie to bring up her children without spanking them. She realizes that in her professional training, she was taught that when parental behavior places a child in danger or serious harm, she is required to issue a report; in addition, her training taught her that verbal disciplining is good and physical disciplinary practices such as spanking a child are wrong. A middle-income Anglo-American herself, she agrees with this position, leading to her conclusion that Annie is a bad parent.

Investigating how Annie's view differs, Caroline learns that although Annie does spank, she makes a distinction between beating and spanking and is fully aware that beating is an abusive form of punishment. Annie believes that spanking is a sign of good parenting and that a spanking when the occasion demands will help her children to grow up responsibly. She clarifies that she uses spanking only on occasion and then, too, as a last resort, after nonphysical and verbal discipline have not worked.

Caroline and Annie exchange stories: Caroline talks about how she was trained to ask questions when she saw a bruise on a child and how she was disciplined as a child herself. Annie talks about her hopes for her children and describes what it is like to be living on the brink as a low-income single parent with no guarantees of a less precarious life for her children.

Are the two points of view so completely incompatible that it is impossible to find a middle ground and work out a solution acceptable to Caroline without compromising Annie's beliefs? By now, Annie and Caroline have built a deeper understanding of each other, each recognizing why the other believes what she does. Caroline recognizes that parenting styles differ and that these differences do not constitute deficits: They certainly do not mean that a person is a good or a bad parent. She recognizes that Annie, in fact, is a good parent and that her values and expectations for her children are similar to those of any parent. Thus empowered, she introduces ideas that Annie could add to her repertoire of skills, empowering Annie in turn.

For instance, in a study of Dutch, suburban American, and Tanzanian mothers' ethnotheories, Harkness and Super (1996) noted that the Dutch and American mothers had similar explanations for their 2-year-old child's tantrums—that is, a demonstration of independence—which the authors attributed to the similar traditions of Western individualism that the two groups shared. However, differences between European and American ethnotheories became apparent when the Dutch mothers further associated the behavior with a situational cause, such as a disruption in the child's sleep or daytime routine, whereas the American mothers associated the behavior with an aspect of their child's strong-willed personality. Conversely, through a more collectivist orientation, the Tanzanian mothers accepted the behavior as one of the innate characteristics of a child at that age, or *kasinyin* (roughly translated as "that is what a child's work is"), rather than as an expression of independence. Similarly, Lau (2010) found that parenting styles and disciplinary practices among Chinese American immigrants differed according to levels of acculturation.

These perspectives challenge the implicit assumption of universal applicability for almost all aspects of child development and related fields, including those that might otherwise be assumed to be innately or developmentally determined (Valsiner, 2008). More significantly, they indicate that members of the same culture have distinctive ethnotheories. If professionals can recognize that myriad variables including ethnicity or race interact to create an infinite combination of commonalities and divergences in families both from the same and across cultural groups, then the unit of analysis becomes, appropriately, the individual family. And if professionals can understand that cultural values and beliefs inform family structure and interactions, which, in turn, affect parenting practices, then they might be less likely to label as "wrong" certain child-rearing practices that emerge from a family's reality (Harry, 1997). The following sections analyze and illustrate the impact of family values, structures, interactions, and community identity on parental ethnotheories.

Impact of Family Values, Structures, Interactions, and Community Identity on Parental Ethnotheories

A considerable body of literature has sought to recognize non-Western cultural variations in family values, structures, and interactions (e.g., Lynch & Hanson, 2011; McGoldrick, Giordano, & Garcia-Preto, 2005). Although this information provides a crucial starting point at which professionals can recognize the possibility of alternative worldviews, there are some caveats in applying this "us versus them" approach to understanding individual families' values and belief systems. First, it further exacerbates a sense of distance between professionals and parents. Second, it tends to reinforce stereotypes about cultures by presenting groups as seemingly homogeneous, when the process of understanding the social orientation and cultural values of families cannot be reduced to a formula that places them in a finite quadrant. The next section presents an analysis of these alternative realities, with specific reference to hierarchical versus egalitarian family values, extended versus nuclear family structures, enmeshed versus disengaged family interactions, and group versus individual status in community identity and their implications for service delivery.

Family Values: Equality versus Hierarchy   Families who subscribe to the notion of equality and individualism tend to have egalitarian family structures (Lau,

2010). For instance, as the democratic tradition in Western cultures changed to in-clude women, people of color, and children as having equal rights, previously patri-archal family structures also changed so that in many middle-income families, spouses now share authority and household responsibility equally (Wheelock, Oughton, & Baines, 2003). In response, the field of early childhood special education has begun to acknowledge fathers' roles in caring for a child with a disability and to recognize the need to involve fathers equally with mothers in daily activities (Parette, Meadan, & Doubet, 2010). Similarly, families who emphasize equity among siblings, whereby the same rules apply to the child with disabilities as to the other children, might pre-fer that the other children not take on responsibilities that are perceived as more pa-rental, such as caring for their sibling with disabilities (East, Weisner, & Reyes, 2006). Studies indicate that this is less of an issue with some large Anglo-American families (Gibbs, 1993) and Hispanic families (Harry, Rueda, & Kalyanpur, 1998) "where the achievement expectations and caregiving responsibilities can be spread out among siblings" (Gibbs, 1993, p. 347). Conversely, there are families who believe in a more collectivist rather than individualistic approach, whereby family priorities and con-cerns take precedence over the individual and the need for interdependence and cooperation is of paramount significance (Brooker, 2003; East et al., 2006; Lau, 2010; McHatton & Correa, 2005). Such families tend to establish a social organization that is hierarchical with ascribed roles and status for its members, stressing duties rather than rights.

How might a family with these differing social orientations respond to a child with a disability, and what are the implications of such a response for professional practice? Some Native American and Southeast Asian parents of a child with disabili-ties may be required to inform or consult the grandparents or other concerned com-munity elders and may have to acquiesce to their decision (Manuelito, 2005; Tajima & Harachi, 2010; Wilder, Jackson, & Smith, 2001). Although professionals may want decisions to be made quickly, they need to respect this process and allow time for it to occur. For example, noting that child-centered intervention services and individual-focused substance abuse programs evoke low levels of participation among Native Americans, Dorris (1989) suggested that professionals adopt a more communal ap-proach by appealing to a community to become responsible for the welfare of their addicted members and the good health of their children with fetal alcohol syndrome.

Family Structures: Extended versus Nuclear   Based on traditional norms of family structure (e.g., nuclear families) and individual roles (e.g., father is sole breadwinner, mother is primary caregiver), some professionals might structure home-based service provision around the mother–child dyad. This unit of analysis, how-ever, may have little meaning in families in which 1) no one is designated as the primary caregiver (Hodges, Burwell, & Ortega, 2003); 2) the mother–child dyad is no more important than the father–child dyad, the older sibling–child dyad, the co-wife–child dyad or the grandmother–child dyad (East et al., 2006; Gona, Hartley, & Newton, 2006; Parette et al., 2010); or 3) the social context of development rarely in-cludes any form of dyadic formation as there typically is more than one person inter-acting with the child at any given moment (Brooker, 2003; Kalyanpur, 1996; Rao, 1996). If the mother is unable to fulfill the responsibilities placed on her by profes-sionals who assume that she is the sole caregiver, then it might be easy to conclude that she does not care or is not involved with her child. Therefore, professionals who recognize and incorporate the alternative caregivers into service planning would be more in keeping with the family's realities (Harry, 2008).

The traditional definition of a nuclear family—two parents and their children constituting a single household—has undergone a change to accommodate the many variations in family constellations, such as single-parent, blended, adoptive or foster, and gay or lesbian families (Turnbull et al., 2007). Theories on family systems have incorporated these demographic shifts toward developing more responsive professional practices. In all of these various configurations, however, the spousal relationship still assumes primacy, an implicit assumption that may not apply to all families. For example, in "kin-corporate" families (Turner, 2003), the brother–sister relationship serves as the fundamental structuring principle between the genders. Here, family systems may be either matriarchal or patriarchal; same-gender siblings and their respective spouses form a large, extended family. In such families, spousal rights are secondary to sibling rights. This traditional pattern has been noted among African and Native American families (Taylor, Chatters, Hardison, & Riley, 2001; Wilder et al., 2001). Similarly, in Maya's extended Indian family, child-rearing decisions about a child with Down syndrome were made by the mother and her sisters—not by the mother and her husband. Furthermore, when the child grew up, she became the responsibility of her eldest brother, a responsibility acknowledged and unquestioningly accepted by his wife because, in this situation, the rights of the sister superseded those of the wife.

Another variable of family structure is size. In some cases, families may extend beyond the immediate nuclear group to include blood relatives such as grandparents, aunts, and uncles as well as what McAdoo (2002) referred to as "fictive kin," such as godparents, community elders, and neighbors. Extended family members may or may not reside in the same household, a situational fluidity that may be misread as a sign of instability to those familiar only with the nuclear family experience. For instance, among many African Americans, the extended family consists of a multigenerational, interdependent kinship system that includes neighbors and church members who are treated with the same deference and respect and enjoy similar ties and obligations to the family accorded to blood relatives (McAdoo, 2002). Similarly, *padrinos,* or godparents, and *compadres,* or confidants, are examples of the adoption of non-kin among many Latino families (Hodges et al., 2003).

Studies of Native American families provide compelling evidence of the benefits of including grandparents and elders as appropriate in the therapeutic or education decision-making process (Sutton & Broken Nose, 2005). Similarly, in Rao's (1996) study of Bengali families of children with disabilities in India, the families appealed successfully to the neighborhood children's "spirit of community and family" when inviting them to participate in play groups that included the child with a disability and when trying to stop them from teasing the child.

Overlap and fluidity of roles also may occur. In families in which roles and responsibilities depend on age as well as gender and an emphasis is placed on developing a sense of collective responsibility in children, older siblings often are caregivers for the younger children (East et al., 2006; Harry et al., 1998; Hines & Boyd-Franklin, 2005; Hodges et al., 2003; Tobin, Hsueh, & Karasawa, 2009; Valsiner, 2008). In many migrant and black families, this may be primarily for economic reasons: The parents are freed to perform subsistence tasks (Hines & Boyd-Franklin, 2005). Among some Japanese families, the goal is more social: Duty to others is inculcated from an early age (Tobin et al., 2009). Indeed, in some Asian and African extended family systems, the responsibility of caring for and disciplining children often is shared among several parental figures—natural parents, father's other wives, aunts and uncles, grandparents, and older siblings (McAdoo, 2002; Tobin et al., 2009); often, children spend as much time with alternate caregivers as with their biological mother (Brooker, 2003; Hodges et al., 2003; Tajima & Harachi, 2010).

For families of children with disabilities, this flexibility in caregivers has implications both for informal respite and child care options and for the levels of acceptance for the member with the disability. For instance, in Harry and colleagues' (1998) study, a Dominican family assumed that their son with moderate intellectual disability would accompany his siblings and participate in their recreational activities. Through this responsibility, the siblings and their friends became an additional resource for playmates in an environment that was completely accepting of the boy's disabling condition. Harry (1998) also noted that some families expect significant sibling responsibility, including child care for the sibling with disabilities, and also expect and prepare siblings for a greater role in adult responsibility for the child with the disability.

Family Interactions: Enmeshment versus Disengagement

Patterns of interaction between family members and with those outside the family differ from family to family; boundaries may be open or closed and establish the level of family cohesion or family members' close emotional bonding with each other as well as the level of independence they feel within the family system. Turnbull and colleagues (2011) noted that cohesion exists across a continuum with high disengagement on one end and high enmeshment on the other and point out that the assumption that most effective functioning occurs toward the center is culturally based. Indeed, the blurring of roles and boundaries that occurs among highly enmeshed families often is interpreted as being negative and indicative of chaotic family interactions rather than as a strength. For instance, as Hines and Boyd-Franklin (2005) pointed out, the perception that many African American families consist of "female-headed households" actually is an adaptive response to role reversal among husbands and wives who are faced with low employment for males. Similarly, the practice of informal adoption or "child keeping" in times of economic necessity among extended family members in the African American community means that children and other relatives may have lived with different families at different times. Emotional bonds in these cases may have little connection with physical proximity or bloodline.

Studies on the issue of privacy and space in interpersonal communication styles also reveal differences across cultures (Brooker, 2003; Hall, 1983). For instance, a Guyanan father was highly distressed when his preschool son with autism, who would fall to the ground to indicate that he did not want to be touched, was taught to push his classmates away instead. Although the professionals believed that they were teaching the boy a survival skill toward assertiveness, the father saw the learned behavior as extremely rude and very socially inappropriate.

Strongly enmeshed families who prefer to resolve problems within the boundaries of the family or, at the most, the extended family may view the professional as an outsider. Such families might resent the professional's insistence on being included in the problem solving. For instance, in Rao's (1996) study, the Bengali mothers believed that when family problems were discussed with an outsider, the cohesion of the family was threatened. When professionals operate from the deficit model, this interaction may be misperceived. In Kalyanpur's (1998) Native American study, the mothers on the reservation interpreted their phrase "We look after our own" as an indication of the close and caring nature of their culture, whereas the professionals translated it in terms of a closed, even hostile, community. By the same token, professionals who respond to families from a strengths-based perspective are less likely to be viewed as outsiders (McAdoo, 2002; Sutton & Broken Nose, 2005).

Research indicates that the intercommunicative structure and group-dynamic expectations of the support group, a popular and common mainstream strategy for uniting individuals with a common issue and addressing parents' emotional and educational needs, often is antithetical to patterns of interactions in some families. For instance, in their study of a Latino parent support group, Shapiro and Simonsen (1994) found that the tradition of *confianza*, or trust, initially made many Latino parents of children with Down syndrome reluctant to share their experiences in the "instant intimacy" environment of the support group. Similarly, in a study of Latino families, Lieberman (1990) noted that the mothers sought opportunities to be alone with the group coordinator rather than attend the group meetings, preferring the privacy and closeness of the individual sessions to discuss freely the same personal and child-rearing issues scheduled for discussion at the group sessions. Using an example of service provision within a Native American community, Box 5.2 illustrates how applying the process of cultural reciprocity can help to reduce the adverse impact of the differences in interactional styles.

Community Identity: Group Status versus Individual Status   Some families perceive status to be a shared commodity whereby social transgressions by an individual have shameful consequences for the entire family or community. In these circumstances, idiosyncratic or individualistic behavior rarely is tolerated, and, instead, a high value is placed on conformity. Thus, the stigma of deviance or disability affects not only the individual and his or her immediate family but also the group associated with this family. As Harry's (1992a, 1992d) study of Puerto Rican families demonstrated, the professional labeling of an individual child as "retarded" was devastating to the families because it implied that the entire community was at fault. Similarly, Ballenger (1999, cited in Scarlett, 2005) noted that disciplinary practices among the Haitian families whose preschool children she taught made the children accountable to the entire community: They were told that if they behaved badly, then they would make their parents, aunts, and uncles "sad."

Furthermore, as mentioned earlier, individual status is relational and dependent on one's position in society. In many Native American and Asian families, for instance, elders and young children are accorded high status (Rao & Kalyanpur, 2002; Sutton & Broken Nose, 2005). Certain families may have higher status within a community than others (Kalyanpur, 1998; Kalyanpur & Gowramma, 2007). Under the hierarchical structure, status may also be gender specific or according to birth order, such as the firstborn son's having higher status than his younger brothers and both older and younger sisters. By contrast, in the mainstream culture, in which the ideal of equality generates social mobility, individuals acquire status through their own identity or occupation, such as a profession or a successful business (Wheelock et al., 2003). Because parameters of status are an aspect of "invisible culture" that becomes apparent with sustained contact (Philips, 1983), professionals who in initial interactions impose inappropriate understandings of status when working with parents may show disrespect when none was intended. For instance, the mainstream service providers in Kalyanpur's (1998) study of a Native American parent support group

BOX 5.2   Nancy
Their Culture Is Not Helping Them

When Nancy, a child psychologist, was hired to provide developmental screening and diagnostic evaluation services to Native American preschool children, she applied her expertise and prior knowledge about the community to identify what she termed a "language delay" in the children, even though they spoke their native language and some also spoke English. According to her, the language delay was a cultural deficit justifying the need for intervention:

> *It's because of the culture. The children aren't encouraged to talk very much. So their receptive language is very good, but not their expressive. But it's difficult to tell the parents. I mean, how do you tell them that their culture isn't helping their children?*

If Nancy had applied the process of cultural reciprocity, how might this scenario have played out?

Nancy recognizes that her emphasis on verbal skills is a yardstick for language development of the mainstream culture. She also implicitly assumes that becoming mainstreamed is a desired, even a necessary, outcome.

Listening to the mothers, Nancy discovers that, in their culture, learning occurs by observing. One mother describes how she "learned as she watched" her child in physical therapy. Nancy observes that parent–child interactions are physical, warm, and frequent but nonverbal. At the parent support group meetings that she organizes, the children run to their mothers, who hold them silently, almost absentmindedly, while continuing to speak to the other adults. At the end of the meetings, the children do not regale their mothers with stories of what they did but allow themselves to be bundled into their coats without protest while the mothers speak over their heads to each other. Nancy realizes that just because the Native American mothers do not talk directly to their children does not mean that the children do not acquire language and that the notion of difference as deficit is wrong. She recalls that, until the 1940s, the Protestant ethic that children should be seen and not heard prevailed in many mainstream families.

Nancy asks if the mothers intend to send their children to the mainstream school outside the reservation and tells them the mainstream expectations for academic achievement. She discusses with them the possibility of creating a preschool program or other group opportunities in which both she and the children (with the mothers on hand) learn the other's sociolinguistic style and the children develop socialization and language skills considered important within the mainstream culture using the Native American style of interaction with which they are familiar.

accorded a high status to the Native American professionals and a lesser status to the participants, although the latter group included members of the two highly respected families on the reservation, thus quite unwittingly alienating themselves from the Native American mothers.

In studies on community and social networks, researchers have identified socioeconomic status (SES) as a major variable in the types of supports that individuals developed (see Kalyanpur, Harry, & Skrtic, 2004 for a review). These studies found that members of middle SES tended to develop networks and friendships based on such commonalities as occupation and/or profession or recreational interests, whereas working-class families sought kin- and neighborhood-based communities and friendships. Other factors also may contribute to a sense of community. Although in some cases African Americans tend to divide along socioeconomic lines, the common experience of racism and being black also can facilitate a sense of a larger community across all classes as well as among voluntary immigrants from Africa and the Caribbean (Foster, 2004; Ogbu & Simons, 1998). Similarly, as Harry pointed out, although the racial, national, and socioeconomic heterogeneity of Latinos makes generalizations about this group difficult, the Spanish language, despite many prevailing dialects, is a single common bond that "seems to stand as an important symbol of their cultural heritage and solidarity" (1992a, p. 25). Among Asians, communities are more tightly drawn along country of origin; families tend to migrate and settle in pockets that are already occupied by their fellow compatriots, historically for economic reasons, as in the case of Chinese railroad and laundry workers in San Francisco (Pfaelzer, 2007) or the Indian Sikh farmers in California (Gibson, 1987) and, more recently, through government intervention, as in the case of the Hmong (Fadiman, 1997). Certain commonalities such as history, ethnicity, and religion can help create a common context among groups, whereas geographic isolation on reservations, as occurs with many Native American communities, in ghettos such as Harlem and Chinatown, or in certain neighborhoods such as within inner cities can enhance group identity (McAdoo, 2002; McGoldrick et al., 2005).

The impact of these variables as contributory factors to group identity often is overlooked. For instance, for many parents whose first language is not English, whose child with a disability may have difficulty acquiring language, the decision to forgo teaching the child the native tongue in favor of English, the language preferred in the mainstream, may be akin to the loss of connection with one's cultural heritage. As an Indian mother noted, the "major, immediate impact" in switching from Hindi to English to communicate with their daughter with a hearing impairment was accepting that they "would raise a child not rooted in Indian values" (Das, 1995, p. 6). Similarly, in Harry's (1992c, 1992d) study, the geographical differences in the boundaries of the Puerto Rican community and those of the school district had the parents alarmed that their children were being sent to schools "so far away" from the Hispanic neighborhood in which they lived.

Thus far, the impact of family values, structures, interactions, and community identity on parental ethnotheories on child rearing and the implications for professional practice have been examined. The next section looks at discipline, in which professional expectation for parent involvement is highest and, if intersected by differing ethnotheories, also the most conflicted.

PARENTING AND DISCIPLINARY PRACTICES

Professionals examine the process by which the inculcation of values, or the process of socialization, occurs. More specifically, they analyze the shared cultural context that affects parents' decisions about the process—that is, why parents choose certain parenting and disciplinary practices over others to socialize their child, a process that Harkness and Super (1996) refer to as "instantiation." Some of the ideological and societal changes that have taken place in the United States and that have contributed

to a shift in beliefs from an authoritarian to a democratic mode of parenting are identified and how this change in focus affects families who may not have adopted this
canon is described.

Authoritarian versus Democratic Parenting Practices

Adults are responsible for facilitating children's acquisition of appropriate behaviors
through a process of socialization. This process can involve explicitly teaching children the rules for behavior—in other words, disciplining them. The specific disciplinary practices in which parents engage emerge from their general beliefs about child
rearing, which, in turn, are influenced by the information that they read on the subject, by people from whom they seek advice, and by their own experiences both as a
child and as a parent (Raghavan et al., 2010). What follows is an analysis of the religious, sociological, and epistemological traditions that have affected the ethnotheories about discipline that parents over the years may have acquired (for an extended
review, see Holden, 2002).

Religious Influences The religious tradition that has influenced disciplinary practices in the United States most significantly is the Judeo-Christian ethic that
originated in the Hebrew, Greek, and Roman traditions. In these traditions, parenting
styles primarily were authoritarian. All three civilizations agreed about the necessity for discipline and control both at home and in school. Children were seen as
unformed and moldable with tendencies toward disorder if left unguided but also
valued as the future of the family and society. Initially, parents were responsible for
bringing up their children to be moral citizens; children, in turn, were expected to
show unquestioning obedience. Later, the role of parents as educators was taken over
by professional teachers. Corporal punishment was clearly emphasized; children received spankings, beatings, and whippings in the course of their education. Although
Puritan conceptions of the child varied in that children were seen as entering the
world imbued with original sin and needing both instruction and strict discipline
from their parents to ensure their moral salvation, disciplinary practices stayed much
the same: To shame a recalcitrant child, parents could admonish, beat, whip, or spank.
These aspects of Judeo-Christian traditions of disciplining were incorporated into
American philosophies of childhood. As recently as the 1950s, the dominant parenting style in the United States was authoritarian, with physical disciplining widely
accepted. Indeed, given this historical context, the recent mainstream rejection of this
disciplinary practice is remarkable.

Sociological Influences In the early 1900s, Western rationalist thought encouraged parents to appeal to the rational side of children in their discipline. Philoso-
phers such as Locke and Rousseau believed that punishment would merely teach
children to avoid externally caused pain rather than to develop rational self-control.
The concept of self-discipline or taking moral responsibility for one's own behavior
and of raising children to work to their full capacity became guiding themes of the
Protestant work ethic as well as enduring American ideals. At the same time, the new
ideals of independence, individualism, and self-sufficiency engendered by free mar-
ket economics led to an erosion of authoritarian and patriarchal structures (Friedman,
1996). These ideals were seen first in the emancipation of slaves, then the women's

suffrage movement in the 1920s, the civil rights movement (on whose coattails the disability rights movement was built) in the 1950s, and finally the culmination of the children's rights perspective in the 1970s. The last movement, spearheaded by the International Labor Organization in an effort to repeal child labor practices, encapsulated a paradigmatic role shift for all children from member of the labor force to student endowed with rights. In particular, the basic rights to protection and development sought to keep children safe from abuse and ensure them access to education.

Epistemological Influences   Since the mid-1940s, ideas about child rearing have changed dramatically as professional beliefs about disciplinary practices were influenced by the newly developing fields of child and behavioral psychology. Under the guise of scientific objectivity, the rational authoritarianism of medical experts began to replace parental authority; the view of "mother knows best" changed to "experts know best"; and the ethnotheories of many parents, mostly Caucasian middle income, were instantiated in these new directions.

Two tenets in child psychology have contributed most to theories about discipline (Holden, 2002). One is the importance of continuity in children's development, in which the assumption is that a child learns best if all of his or her caregivers are consistent about how and when to discipline. Another is the importance of reinforcement, in which the assumption is that children can be taught to increase desirable behaviors through positive consequences (i.e., rewarding) and reduce undesirable behaviors through negative consequences (i.e., punitive). Punishment included the contingent use of aversive verbal, physical, or psychological techniques such as scolding, spanking, isolation, or withdrawal of privileges.

Although these basic tenets of behavioral psychology remain essentially unchanged, modifications have allowed that thoughts and emotions have an impact on the child's reactions. For instance, child psychologists noted that if a child did not think of a particular action or object as desirable, then the object would not be effective as a reward to reinforce certain behaviors. A child who gets noticed only for inappropriate behavior may actually perceive the punishment as a reward. In other words, the intentions of a reward or a punishment may be defined by the disciplinary agent, but its effects are determined by the child.

This new understanding, along with the idea of the child having rights, contributed to the relatively recent mainstream movement away from the use of corporal punishment as an appropriate disciplinary practice to using verbal, redirective approaches, and even as recently as the late 1990s, to using positive behavioral supports (Sugai & Horner, 2002). A process of instantiation then occurred within this cultural context: As professional beliefs about disciplinary practices changed, so, too, did the beliefs of those middle-income, mainstream parents who were most likely to seek professional advice and to be influenced by reading information on the subject. The next section illustrates the impact of this process on parents who do not subscribe to the practices that fall within these parameters.

Cultural Parameters of Child Abuse versus Acceptable Discipline

The shift from corporal punishment to redirective discipline or positive behavioral supports has been adopted so universally among most professionals and many Anglo-

American middle-income parents as the current canon or recommended practice that legal safeguards against what are perceived to be inappropriate practices have been established (McCarthy & Soodak, 2007; Sugai & Horner, 2002)). Indeed, in their zeal to proselytize parents to the cause of positive discipline, many professionals forget how recent the conversion of their own field has been and are apt to perceive parents whose parenting styles fall outside these norms of acceptable discipline as inadequate, even abusive, and in need of parent education programs. An analysis of two issues—spanking and healing practices—surrounding this controversy follows.

Spanking   Perhaps on no other topic has the difference in perspectives on acceptable forms of discipline generated more controversy than the issue of spanking. For instance, Janko's (1994) study reported that although many middle-income, Anglo-American families engaged in democratic, dialogic disciplining styles, many Anglo-American families of low socioeconomic status did not, constituting the majority of parents who were reported to child protection services for being "abusive." However, Kalyanpur and Rao's study (1991) found that low-income African American mothers took great pains to distinguish between "beating up" and "spanking," the former being perceived as an abusive form of punishment. Similarly, both the foreign- and native-born Mexican American mothers in a study by Buriel, Mercado, Rodriguez, and Chavez (1991) used spankings, although less often than scolding or deprivation of privileges. The spankings were always accompanied by an explanation. The mothers were reticent about recommending agency intervention in cases in which the child's welfare was not threatened, which the authors attributed to the cultural value of "familism," or the belief that the family is primarily responsible for the welfare of its members, and issues such as how children are reared are internal matters. It is significant that although all of these families amply demonstrated their ability to be responsible parents and used spanking as one kind of disciplining practice, usually as a last resort, the very fact that they did made them potential targets for being reported to child welfare services as being abusive.

More recent studies on mothers' disciplinary practices and attitudes toward child maltreatment have continued to question the commonly held assumption that low-income and/or immigrant families are more likely to maltreat their children and also indicate that parents from such backgrounds are keenly aware of the difference between corporal punishment and physical abuse (Burchinal, Skinner, & Reznick, 2010; Fontes, 2002; Lau, 2010; M.S. Park, 2001). In particular, the studies suggest that level of acculturation plays a significant role with immigrant families, providing further evidence of the importance of responding to each family as an individual unit rather than on the basis of stereotypic assumptions relating to their cultural or linguistic background. For instance, Burchinal and colleagues (2010) found that a small section of mothers in their study disciplined their infants, as young as 6–9 months of age, by "popping," in which the mother gives a quick slap with her hand to the child on the legs or bottom. This group included more European American than African American mothers, the latter being more likely to be poor, single, and less educated. Similarly, investigating the use of physical discipline in Chinese American immigrant families, Lau (2010) found that although all of the families believed in firm parental control, parents were less likely to use physical discipline than commonly assumed because they valued restraint over the expression of emotional impulses. Equally significant, Lau also found that families with high levels of conflict relating to acculturation (e.g., feelings of marginalization, perceived discrimination, struggles with language barriers) were more likely to use physical discipline and concluded that "adaptive culture" or the ability of a family to acculturate is a stronger predictor for the use of physical discipline than cultural values per se.

Healing and Medical Practices   A common healing or medical practice in one family might be considered unacceptable or even abusive in another. Some cultures perform circumcision on male infants; other cultures would consider the practice abusive. In some Pacific Islander families, crying infants are quieted by gentle rubbing of their genitals (Cross, 1995), a practice that would constitute sexual abuse in the United States.

Forjuoh (1995) noted that traditional healing practices among some Ashanti families of Ghana might entail intentionally inflicting burns by flame or contact with a hot object to cure childhood convulsions and seizure disorders. However, the bruises that result from these practices are indicators of abuse by mainstream American standards (McLeod & Polowy, 2000). Similarly, as Davis (2000) noted, the practice of *cao gi* or *ko k'chawl*, whereby a warmed coin is rubbed briskly over an ailing child's body until redness occurs, is a common, almost routine, folk remedy among many Southeast Asian families. Although "a highly regarded cultural practice with deep meaning attached to family, tradition and beliefs" (Davis, 2000, p. 92), the immigrant Vietnamese families in her study found that their physicians in the United States viewed it in a negative way. Many of the recent immigrants reported that they had been warned by older immigrants that this treatment was often misinterpreted as child abuse; in one case, an elderly woman was very upset because she had lost face when her physician yelled at her to stop doing it. Similarly, "Mongolian blue spots," or flat, benign, blue-gray skin markings that appear on many children of color at birth or shortly thereafter often mistakenly are thought to be bruises and signs of abuse (Al-Jasser & Al-Khenaizan, 2008).

Once again, in all of these traditional practices, there is no malice and no intent to harm the child. On the contrary, these most extreme measures are attempts at healing by parents and caregivers who care intensely about the welfare of their child. Indeed, as Galanti (1997, cited in Davis, 2000) asserts, "Americans abuse their children by having thin pieces of metal wrapped around their teeth and tightened until their teeth move out of place. Braces are often applied for primarily aesthetic reasons. Coin rubbing, at least, is an attempt to heal." And yet, once again, the very practice of engaging in an "unacceptable practice" makes parents vulnerable to intervention from child welfare services.

CONCLUSION

We, the authors, are not implying that we advocate a kind of laissez-faire attitude of "anything goes." Professionals do not need to accept situations with which they disagree. The cultural reciprocity approach provides us an avenue for understanding the rationale behind unfamiliar practices and an opportunity to use it as a springboard from which to present families with alternatives, couching them in terms that are meaningful to the families. To attribute neglect or abuse and remove a child from his or her present family conditions would hardly endear any intervening professionals to a family. If, however, after examining one's own assumptions and biases, one seeks the parents' views and explicitly acknowledges their efforts, one can then point out that providing a child with medical care can extend and complement the family's efforts. This collaboration will be more likely to yield a favorable response and will eventually benefit both parent and child.

Over the years, the shift in professional thinking about disciplinary practices in the United States, from an authoritarian style that allowed the use of corporal punishment to a democratic mode that emphasizes verbal redirection and other alternatives to physical disciplining, has contributed to changes in parental ethnotheories about child rearing among many middle-income, Anglo-American families. However, many families' ethnotheories do not conform to this new paradigm. Because the ethnotheories emerge from families' alternative realities, or the social and philosophical factors that have an impact on their lives, families' child-rearing strategies are perfectly adequate for helping their children grow into competent adults within their specific environments. The deficit model of parent–professional interaction, however, overlooks these alternative realities or cultural traditions altogether; as a result, many of these families are labeled "bad" or "abusive." This "cultural arrogance" (Davis, 2000) also assumes that appropriate parenting can be taught through parent education programs. As a result, numerous programs have been developed to teach parents how to parent in the hope that increased parenting abilities will result in decreased incidence of child abuse and neglect (Barth, 2009). Despite the seemingly preventive focus of these models, however, the parents who are adjudicated to undergo this training are not new or prospective parents who might indeed benefit from some helpful tips on parenting but families who, lacking economic resources and social supports, have struggled over a period of time to maintain a fragile equilibrium before collapsing (Katz, 2010). The next chapter examines educational expectations and goal setting, yet another area that can be a potential source of conflict in parent–professional interactions.

REVIEW QUESTIONS

1. Families have "individual" cultural identities, in that the norm of the two-parent, two-child, and a dog family that often is projected on television commercials is now more the exception than the rule. Understanding these differences in family structures and interactions is a step toward understanding the differing values and beliefs of the families with whom you will be working. One way to do this is by developing your family web.

    *   Using the same structure as the personal identity web, draw your family web. Put yourself in the middle, then draw lines to the other members you consider to be your family. To show the differences in structures and interactions, you could keep the lines short if the relationship between you and a person is strong and long if the relationship is distant. You could use wavy lines to indicate people who are related to you by blood, straight lines for those who are related by marriage, and perhaps dotted lines to show those who are connected to you by friendship or because you go to the same church or college. Geographical proximity may also play a part: You may be emotionally close to people who are living far from you or vice versa. In the United States, many people also consider their pets as family. If your friends are closer to you than your blood relatives, you might find that you have more short dotted lines than long wavy ones.

- Now, draw another family web based on your family circumstances 5 or 7 years ago. How different are the two webs? What does it indicate to you about changes over time in family relationships and structures?
- Share your family webs with your classmates. Are their webs similar to or different from yours? Why is that? What does this indicate to you about the concept of a "typical" family?

2. In describing differences in family values, structures, and interactions, the purpose of this book is not to accentuate a sense of "the other" but to reveal other equally viable and rational ways of being and thinking that exist in the United States and across the globe. In a way, the intention is to put you in Lucy's shoes and have you walk through the culture of special education as a foreigner. As you read through the book, were there points at which you were surprised or even shocked by these "other ways"? Use these "shock points" to reflect on which of your own values made you react this way.

3. Differences in interaction styles among families means that, in many families, there is a great deal of coming and going of visitors or extended family members, less predictability regarding planning meetings or other activities, and a more tangential style of conversation. Think about any meetings or home visits that you have paid to families. How would you describe the organizational and interaction styles of those families? With which kind of style were you more comfortable? Use your personal identity web to explore the source of your preferred interaction style and consider how you might or did react to a family with a different style. What kind of limits do you think you would want to set as you offered assistance to the family?

Chapter 6

Goal Setting for Students

Parents' versus Professionals' Expectations

Maya's Story

A few months after I moved to Cambodia, my husband decided to surprise me for our 25th wedding anniversary by planning a weekend trip to the seaside for just the two of us. We felt it was appropriate that our son, then age 16, would stay behind at home, as arrangements could be made to have the housekeeper sleep over. I mentioned this to my colleague, who responded in utter bewilderment, "But why would you leave your son behind? It's your wedding anniversary!"

A week later, on February 14th, I received a barrage of text messages on my phone from several Cambodian friends and colleagues, male and female, wishing me "Happy Valentine's Day to you and yours!" with a string of *x*s and *o*s signifying hugs and kisses. Yes, there are street vendors that day selling red roses and pink greeting cards for young sweethearts, but Valentine's Day in Cambodia dismisses the notion that the day represents only romantic love between sweethearts and claims it, instead, as a day of love for families and friends. There is something quintessentially Asian in this concept that the relationship between a husband and wife belongs as much to the family, including the children and extended family. The family is enmeshed in a togetherness (*cha'ik kneah ruh,* or "share to live,", as they say in Cambodia) that almost completely precludes the concept of privacy or personal space, the need for same-sex siblings to have separate rooms, or the need for parents to ask permission before entering their children's room.

As an Indian, perhaps this is why I was not taken aback when a colleague, a mother of a toddler, asked if she could share a room with me at the guest house during one of our visits to the provinces because she had never slept alone and I was the only other female colleague on this trip. As a child, she would have shared her parents' bed until she was moved into her sisters' room, before moving into a separate bedroom with her husband. Indeed, I realize how much my 25 years in the United States have changed me that I even notice these events as quaint or different as I recall a situation from my own life. As a young teenager in India, I was introduced to an American woman in her early 30s who was to become a relative by marriage. To make conversation, I asked her what she did and where she lived. She told me that she worked in the media and lived in her own apartment 15 minutes away. My horrified response? "You mean you live all alone?!"

It is easier for me now, having returned to my Asian roots, to understand that my prospective American aunt was seen as quaint and different by us Indian women; after all, at 32 years of age, she was unmarried, had no children, and was living alone (even as she relished her own independence in having a job and home of her own). Similarly, my 32-year-old Cambodian colleague might be seen as quaint and different by Americans for never having slept alone in her life (even as she relishes her high social status as a wife and a mother within her culture). I don't believe that we could say that one woman was more independent than the other; indeed, both were equally socially competent and independent within their individual cultures.

When the responsibility of targeting instruction to meet certain education and socialization goals is shared between families on the one hand and professionals on the other, examining the assumptions underlying those very goals is important. What are the markers by which people are deemed to be adults within a society—socially competent and independent? What are the markers by which children and young adults are perceived to be moving toward that eventual goal of adulthood?

Much of special education practice is based on the assumption that children's developmental milestones are biologically determined—a yardstick that ensures scientific objectivity and therefore universal applicability. Thus, most adaptive behavior scales are developed on the understanding that children acquire mastery over specific tasks at particular ages (Scherzer, 2009). Increasingly, however, cross-cultural research points to the cultural specificity of developmental expectations or timetables. Comparisons of mothers' timetables across cultural communities have found variations in acquisition of skills as "biologically predetermined" as infant crawling and toilet training as well as those more socially defined such as verbal communication (Burchinal, Skinner, & Reznick, 2010; Scherzer, 2009; Schum, McAuliffe, Simms, Walter, Lewis, & Pupp, 2001). For instance, Scherzer (2009) studied the reliability of an easy-to-use developmental milestone chart, modified from screening tools used in the west and developed to better enable early identification of and intervention with children with development delays in Cambodia, and found that as many as 31.5% of Cambodian children tested failed to achieve one or more milestones in their appropriate age groups. He concluded that this indicated both the need for more culturally accurate local milestones and the recognition that what constitutes "delay" in one culture may not in another.

Indeed, developmental expectations (e.g., education and socialization goals) emerge from the culture into which children are being socialized to become competent and responsible adults; those deemed most appropriate and significant by the adults in that culture are most likely to be the focus of the socialization process (Harkness, & Super, 2006; Keller et al., 2006). Brooker (2003) describes differences between Bangladeshi and Anglo mothers in the United Kingdom in their expectations of their child's participation in household routines: Whereas the Anglo mothers reported that their children "helped" around the house, in fact, the children tended to role-play adult responsibilities, with the mothers washing the dishes again after the child was done or hiding the knives to protect the child; on the other hand, although the Bangladeshi mothers stated that their children were too young to work, in fact, the children were already assuming adult responsible roles by chopping vegetables, soothing babies, and serving food.

Because of the uniqueness of parental ethnotheories, rationalizations can differ from family to family. Furthermore, although certain tasks such as getting dressed or communicating with others may appear universal, the goals that are embedded in a specific task might differ. For instance, separate studies on Anglo-American, Nepali, and Tanzanian families found that although all three cultures focused on verbal skill acquisition as a desirable goal for their children, the Anglo-American families, valuing individuality and independence, wanted their children to become verbally assertive and to state their own needs; the Nepali families expected their children to develop moral reasoning, reflecting their Hindu orientation that self is constituted from membership in society; and the Tanzanian mothers, bringing a collectivist perspective of society, hoped that their children would learn obedience and responsibility (Edwards, Gandini, & Giovaninni, 1996; Levy, 1996; McGillicuddy-De Lisi, & Subramanian, 1996).

Families develop parenting styles that are appropriate to the family or the environment in which the child is being reared. For instance, an African American grandmother, mindful of the violence that surrounded her grandchildren who were growing up in an inner city, had taught them to "move away" from the scene of the crime:

> If you see a body laying on the street and you see people crying around it, you don't go there and touch that body, try to help. Because just as you do that, the police walk up on you with your hands on it, you did it. When you could have went the other way. You know, not running away from trouble, but avoiding it if you see it coming, you go the other way. You ain't got to go to it. (Danseco, 1997a, p. 96)

This parenting style starkly contrasts with the style of a Jewish American professional mother who taught her children to "become involved in the community and always help if you see someone in trouble" (S. Sonnenschein, personal communication, July 14, 1997). In both cases, the parenting styles matched the requirements of the environment in providing the children with the skills necessary to survive and become competent adults.

CORNERSTONE GOALS IN SPECIAL EDUCATION PRACTICE

To describe all of the variations in maturational milestones that might occur both across and within cultures is beyond the scope of this chapter (for a review, see Rubin and Chung, 2006). For our purposes, we focus on three that have become cornerstone goals in special education practice: independence, individuality, and work.

Independence

Parents in all cultures seek to make their children independent, competent adults in their respective societies. However, the meaning of independence as well as the milestones or transition markers might differ from family to family.

Differences in the Meaning of Independence   The contemporary term for independence is *self-competence,* a multidimensional construct that seeks to develop self-esteem, self-determination, and effective coping in children and adolescents with disabilities by enhancing their perceptions of personal efficacy and worthiness (Test, Fowler, Wood, Brewer, & Eddy, 2005). Perceptions of worthiness and efficacy are acquired through positive attachments to caregivers, friendships, and opportunities for expressions of increasing levels of independence and autonomy; self-esteem is grounded in these perceptions. *Self-determination* is the ability to decide and act on one's own behalf; *coping* refers to individual responses to manage stressful situations (Test, Fowler, Wood, et al., 2005).

Most significant to our argument about differences in the meaning of *independence* is the emphasis in all of these constructs on the individual. Although the definitions do acknowledge relationships with caregivers and friends, the embedded assumption is of an egocentric social orientation whereby the ultimate goal is to make individuals with disabilities totally self-reliant (Renz-Beaulaurier, 2003), thereby minimizing their dependence on other people.

This dedication to self-competence may appear singularly misplaced to families for whom the sociocentric alternative of interdependence is perfectly viable (Brooker, 2003; Lau, 2010). First, in such families, members can be independent and have distinct identities without expecting autonomy. Second, being dependent is not necessarily a devalued position; indeed, members are expected to turn to each other for help and to provide that help. For instance, in a study of parental ethnotheories of American and immigrant Indian mothers in the United States (Raghavan, Harkness & Super, 2010), American mothers wanted their daughters to be active and independent and used words like "independent," "well-rounded," "athletic," "assertive," and "outspoken" to describe them; in contrast, the Indian mothers expected their daughters' lives to center on the family, both natal and marital, and used descriptors like "responsible," "obedient," "respectful," "hospitable," "modest," and "nonargumentative" as desired attributes for being a good daughter, wife, and daughter-in-law. For instance, an Indian mother explained that she wanted her daughter to meet all visitors to the home as a matter of form, as a skill she would need later in her married life, and she believed that American children who did not engage in polite conversation with their friends' parents were being disrespectful to their elders.

Differences in the Milestones Toward Independence   Checklists of developmental milestones as measures of children's growth become inadequate when the milestones themselves differ. For instance, in Cambodia, where many children are not registered at birth, resulting in some ambiguity about their ages, often children are deemed old enough to go to school when they can reach their left ear by taking their right arm over their head (Hun, Berkvens, & Kalyanpur, 2008). Joe (1997) noted that many Navajo mothers are more likely to be able to remember their child's first laugh rather than his or her first words or steps.

Similarly, Mallory (1995) distinguished between developmental transitions (e.g., puberty) and institutional transitions (e.g., graduating from high school) and noted that these two types of transitions often do not occur at the same time in an individual's life. While this has implications for social policy overall, differing perceptions of transitions to adulthood can have especially significant implications for services for young adults.

Independence in Adulthood   Attaining identity as an adult is a crucial aspect of the transition to adulthood. The symbolic construction of an adult identity often is marked by rites of passage that may vary among families. In some families, the transition may be biologically determined through the onset of puberty and signified, for instance, through ceremonies that mark the onset of menstruation in a young girl. In other families, the marker may be chronologically based and be signified in coming-of-age parties and debuts at the age of 16 or 18. Although in some cases this developmental transition may be sufficient to acquire identity as an adult, in others, the institutional transition of marriage may be the more widely acknowledged rite of passage to adulthood.

In other families, achieving adult status may involve another central aspect: the practical setting up of a household (Wheelock, Oughton, & Baines, 2003). The understanding is that when individuals acquire financial independence, they will set up a physically separate establishment; where gender equality is valued, expectations will be similar for both sons and daughters. Indeed, the two dominant themes of transition services, as defined in federal policy, are gainful, competitive employment and emancipation from the family home (Smith & Routel, 2010).

Analyzing the role of social policy in life-cycle transitions, Mallory (1995) asserted that policies have been more responsive to institutional transitions than to developmental transitions. He cited the issue of guardianship, whereby the age of majority is defined in state laws as 18 regardless of whether young adults with disabilities have indeed acquired the levels of maturity and competence needed to make independent decisions, as an example of institutional transition that may not reflect "the complex issues of time, individual and family transitions, and sociocultural context" (Mallory, 1995, p. 218). This discrepancy might affect both mainstream and diverse families. For instance, many parents express concern about being required by mandate to send their 3-year-old child with disabilities to an educational, non–home-based program, in a transition that they perceive to be neither developmentally appropriate nor culturally normative (V. Turbiville, personal communication, November 22, 1997).

Studies on secondary transition among Native American students with disabilities have pointed out that the two themes of transition services, independence and competition, are based on the values of an urban, Anglo culture that may conflict with the values of cooperation, interdependence, and communal responsibility of the Native Americans (Shafer & Rangasamy, 1995; Wilder, Jackson, & Smith, 2001). Wilder and her colleagues (2001) found that many Navajo young adults restricted their choices of vocations to those that were available to them on the reservation because they felt "uneasy" about leaving their homeland. Those who chose to make the transition to the European American–dominant educational and vocational settings outside the reservation experienced it, in the words of one student, as "the difference between a nurturing mother and a demanding father" (p. 122). Similarly, noting that more than 75% of both general and special education Apache students who exited the school system continued to live with their parents and that 25% of both groups indicated that they were not interested in leaving their family home, Shafer and Rangasamy (1995) questioned the validity of the policy-driven focus on the movement from the parental or natural home to other living arrangements.

Indeed, among many families, it is assumed that the son will continue to live in the parents' home, regardless of economic or marital status, and that the daughter will leave after marriage only to move in with her husband's family (Harry & Kalyanpur, 1994; Harry et al., 1998; Turnbull et. al, 2011). In Turnbull and colleagues'

(2011) study, for instance, the Latin American parents viewed the possibility of their unmarried children moving out of their home and establishing homes of their own upon attaining majority as a tragedy and a shame on the family.

Differences in families' orientation toward time also have implications for planning for transition. Whereas some families may prefer not to look too far ahead, others may not have such an option. For instance, the Latin American families in Turnbull and colleagues' (2011) study generally tended not to think about the future but to take life a day at a time, attributing this tendency to the value placed on interdependence. This contrasts with the expectations of some migrant families, whose children are forced into early independence for economic reasons (Green, 2003).

All families aspire to make their children independent, but the markers for and meanings of independence may differ. Some families seek an interdependence whereby dependence is not a devalued position, all members depend on each other for help, and identities are distinct without being autonomous. Differences in the milestones toward independence suggest potential conflict in education goal setting, particularly in the context of social policies that tend to focus more on institutional rather than developmental transitions. Box 6.1 looks at culturally different interpretations of the concept of self-advocacy, suggesting the need for professionals to understand what it means to families prior to making recommendations for services.

Individuality

The ideal of self-competence includes independence not only on a practical level, whereby individuals with disabilities rely minimally on others in performing everyday activities, but also on a philosophical level, whereby people can take control of their lives through the power of choice, a process that is referred to as *self-determination.* The concept of self-determination has its ideological roots in disability rights movements, which have focused on the rights of individuals with disabilities to be integrated and have equality of opportunity (Kalyanpur, 2009). This section examines aspects of self-determination in which there is potential for conflict in education goal setting: the expectation that children are individuals with rights to maximizing their potential and the ideal of personal choice.

The Child as an Individual with Rights to Maximize His or Her Potential   The idea that children have the right to maximize their potential is embedded in the philosophy of self-determination and emerges from the mainstream-value emphasis on individualism. There are two values that are implicit in this premise: 1) that children are individuals and have rights and 2) that children, as individuals with rights, should be given opportunities to maximize their potential. The fact that arguments for changes in services and attitudes toward people with disabilities in the United States have been made on the platform of individual rights and equality is no coincidence: These values are part of the collective conscience (Renz-Beaulaurier, 2003). It also is not a coincidence that these same values are an integral part of educational programming. Asserting that teaching self-determination needs to start as early as possible, scholars have described models for implementing these principles in early intervention programs as well as in early elementary levels (Blasco, Falco, & Munson, 2006; Erwin & Brown, 2003; Palmer & Wehmeyer, 2002). The main objective of self-advocacy courses for adolescents and adults with disabilities is to enable each indi-

BOX 6.1 Cultural Variations in Self-Advocacy

What does the term *self-advocacy* mean? Test and his colleagues (2005) reviewed several self-advocacy intervention studies in the United States to find a universal definition of the constructs of self-advocacy and self-determination. They defined self-determination as "a combination of skills, knowledge and beliefs that enable a person to engage in goal-directed, self-regulated, autonomous behavior" (Test, Fowler, Brewer, & Wood, 2005, p. 101). Its components include choice making, decision making, goal setting and attainment, self-advocacy, self-knowledge, independence, and internal locus of control. Similarly, they identified four components of self-advocacy: knowledge of self, knowledge of rights, communication, and leadership (Test, Fowler, Wood, Brewer, & Eddy, 2005). Knowledge of self and rights are the foundations of self-advocacy, relating to knowing one's own interests, attributes of one's disability, and one's rights as a citizen and an individual with a disability. Whereas communication includes negotiation, persuasion and compromise, and body language and listening skills, leadership involves a person's moving from individual self-advocacy to advocating for others as a group of individuals with common concerns.

One may agree with these definitions. The values embedded in the constructs are those most closely associated with Anglo-European cultures (e.g., personal control over the environment; individualism; self-help; competition; future orientation; goal orientation; a focus on rights that provides a platform for demanding equal status, opportunity, and outcome).

Again, depending on one's cultural identity, one may not agree with these definitions; indeed, scholars have shown that these definitions may not be universal. Smith and Routel (2010), using qualitative research to study how people with disabilities and their families understood self-determination, asserted that the idea most likely means something different to each person and that it is important to remember that self-determination is a right—not a skill that must be taught.

Comparing American and Taiwanese teachers' encouragement of self-determination of students with disabilities, Zhang, Wehmeyer, and Chen (2005) found lower levels of awareness among the latter, suggesting that they may have encouraged different values. The authors concluded that cultural variables may affect understandings of both the concept and the skills involved. Based on their experience with Navajo Native Americans, Wilder and colleagues (2001) asserted that contextual variables that affect self-determination values can include country of origin, school environment, family and individual beliefs, neighborhood, religious beliefs, socioeconomic status, group affiliations, and parent education. Similarly, in Afghanistan, Coleridge noted that the term *empowerment* was rejected in favor of *enablement*, adding that "even this concept was not easily understood in a situation where people may not aspire to individual development at all, imbued with cultural values that are dominated by the need for collective family survival and kin-group solidarity" (2000, p. 18). In India, Kalyanpur (2009) found that the primary goals of advocacy are less individualistic and more societal, with a focus on seeking to change public attitudes to become more accepting and the environment to become more accessible to people with disabilities. Noting that about 92% of adults with disabilities live with their spouse and/or other members of their family and based on his personal experiences with rehabilitation services after his spinal cord injury, Ahluwalia (2004) stressed the need to include the family in designing a program even for adults, because "in Indian society, human bondage among family members is deep and ties are strong. In Indian culture,

> an individual is not as important as the whole family; any major decision taken for an individual in many cases comes from a collective decision" (p. 315). The underlying assumption is one of interdependence, not independence, and the understanding that the quality of life of people with disabilities will be improved not by a self-centered expectation of individual entitlement but rather, as Miles (2002) noted, by a sense of a collective obligation, or "ehsaan," of a community acting rightly.

vidual "to speak for yourself, to make decisions for yourself, to know what your rights are, and to 'stick up' for yourself when your rights are being violated or diminished" (Lehr & Taylor, 1986, p. 3).

Such an approach focuses on the individual and assumes that all individuals, including children, have certain inalienable rights. This might be counter to the approach that a family with a more communal orientation might adopt. Families who define *self* in terms of other people through a web of reciprocal relationships, whereby an individual's identity is connected to his or her social identity, may neither emphasize autonomy or self-determination nor believe that depriving individuals of the opportunity to acquire such a self-concept is a violation of their rights. Such parents may not want to have their adult child with disabilities attend self-advocacy courses (Kalyanpur, 1998). Similarly, Manuelito (2005) noted that "from a Ramah Navajo perspective, self-determination is based on commitment to the community [and] has a communal goal" whereas the Anglo-American notion of self-determination was viewed as "supporting unfair competition and creating selfishness among individuals" (p. 80).

The other assumption that is embedded in the idea of individual rights is that every individual has the right to maximize his or her potential. This is one of the premises on which the principle of *normalization* is based: providing opportunities to encounter the normal developmental experiences of the life cycle so that individuals with disabilities can learn about their abilities and potential and build their self-esteem (Wolfensberger, 1972). The ideal of maximization of potential is tied to the American values of occupational mobility, whereby people are responsible for constructing themselves as individuals in a multitude of alternative ways, as well as of freedom of choice, whereby people make active choices about who they want to be and how they want to live (Test, Fowler, Brewer, & Wood, 2005).

Valsiner noted, however, that the maximizing orientation may be antithetical to families who subscribe instead to what he called a "satisficing perspective" (1989, p. 74). Instead of linear, upward progression, success is measured in concentric, ever-broadening circles as individuals aspire to be the best at what they are; thus, a cobbler's son does not aspire to become a schoolmaster, which in his ascribed role as cobbler he cannot, but the best cobbler within the largest circle of community possible (Kalyanpur & Gowramma, 2007; Kalyanpur & Harry, 1997; Valsiner, 1989). This perspective ties in to a belief in hierarchical interdependence, whereby people with disabilities are not stigmatized because they are dependent because, in a way, everybody is dependent on each other and everybody has a social role no matter what one's status is (Kalyanpur & Harry, 1997). It also ties in to a belief in a hierarchical social order in which inequalities not only exist but are accepted as right, proper, and desirable (Kalyanpur & Misra, 2011). For instance, recent studies of perceptions of disabilities in Cambodia have found a definite social hierarchy among communities, where people with disabilities have lower status than individuals without disabilities and people or children with intellectual disabilities have the lowest status among people with disabilities (Ayala Moreira, 2011; Kalyanpur, 2011).

How, one might argue, is this perspective different from families accepting that their adolescent with disabilities will be trained to work at a fast-food restaurant or choosing to place their child with disabilities in a segregated environment? Two factors intrude: the ideal of upward mobility and freedom of choice. Although in reality many parents might indeed have few choices and many individuals with disabilities, along with other discriminated groups, may never move up a career ladder, the fact is that the milieu of individualism allows the possibility for social mobility and choice and thus for the maximization of potential.

By the same token, it might be easy to conclude that the satisficing perspective does not allow for self-determination. Indeed, it very well may not—and therein lies the argument. One must acknowledge that families' different social orientations and parental ethnotheories will have implications for their responses to the condition of disability, their perception of need for intervention, and the type of services that they might seek. An additional factor that often has an impact on families' expectations is the question of choice.

The Ideal of Personal Choice   Western society, asserted Friedman (1996), is characterized by freedom of choice and individualism. Indeed, so entrenched in the lives of Americans is the culture of choice, from the microlevel of personal choice to the macrolevel of political choice, by legal mandate as much as by collective social conscience, that it has become an integral component of developmentally appropriate practice in special education instruction. For instance, Japanese and Chinese preschool teachers, viewing the instructional practices of American preschool teachers on videotape, commented on what they thought was an extraordinary emphasis on giving such young children so many choices (Tobin et al., 2009). Similarly, a major component of self-determination and other empowerment strategies is the acquisition of skills that enable people with disabilities to maximize and expand their range of life choices and to decide on, maintain, and change their life choices when necessary (Renz-Beaulaurier, 2003). Conversely, families who believe in the predominance of group identity would not endorse the need for freedom of choice for individual members ("Hmong Family," 1991), much less concur with the professional emphasis placed on giving a child with disabilities choices.

The emphasis on individualism assumes that children with disabilities have rights and that they have the right to maximize their potential. These values are tied to the ideals of upward social mobility and freedom of choice. Educational programming for children with disabilities incorporates these assumptions by planning toward a normal routine of life including the same activities and developmental life-cycle experiences as are available to people without disabilities and by providing opportunities to children to make their own choices on these issues. Professional interactions that lack awareness of these cultural underpinnings have potential for conflict with families who may stress a satisficing perspective.

Work

In an analysis of the changing meanings and value of men's and women's work, Wheelock and colleagues (2003) have asserted that work is a socially constructed category because tasks are codified according to gender relations and prestige within specific cultures. In other words, work in different cultures has different meanings and value. This section pursues this thought.

Personal Value Judged by Economic Productivity   Productivity is a crucial characteristic of capitalist economies (Wheelock et al., 2003). In particular in Western society, human worth is measured in terms of economic productivity. As a result, economically "nonproductive" individuals, such as people with disabilities and older adults, often are devalued. Within this social orientation, work, skills, and competence are crucial factors in the construction of individual identity, and having waged or paid work is considered an important aspect of being an adult person. As the association of adult identity with one's occupation is based on the ideal of social mobility, within this framework in which all individuals are expected to work to acquire adult status, people with disabilities must have jobs if they are to be normalized. As Box 6.2 illustrates, the single factor of caste status among Indian families can override other considerations of competence and the need for having paid work when trying to find a job for a young adult with disabilities.

Definitions of Meaningful Work   Recognizing that work must be valued if it is to enhance the worker's societal worth, Brown and colleagues (1983) developed two criteria for meaningful work: 1) It should be essential in that if one individual did not undertake the task another person would have to, and 2) it should be paid. These precepts are underscored in the vocational option for people with disabilities—supported employment—which further emphasizes that the jobs be acquired through open competition.

As Harry and Kalyanpur (1994) pointed out, however, these criteria do not apply to all valued work even within the mainstream: work such as that of a housewife, "who performs needed work within the context of a reciprocal relationship based on a division of labor," and that of an entertainer or an artist, who "performs work which is, in fact, not necessary and would not have to be done by someone else" (p. 156). These criteria also do not apply to entrepreneurs who create new kinds of businesses for which there was no previous demand. Furthermore, the issue of competitive employment for young adults with disabilities becomes moot when levels of unemployment are high among able-bodied family members, a finding corroborated in studies of families from CLD families (Smith & Routel, 2010; Wilder, Jackson, & Smith, 2001). Working with families from CLD backgrounds on transition planning, Hasnain, Sotnik, and Ghiloni (2003) found that translation was an issue, not only because of the difficulty in identifying equivalent terms for "person-centered planning," "transferable skills," and "supported employment" in the families' languages but because the concepts themselves had little meaning and were unfamiliar and often confusing to the families.

Similarly, Rueda, Monzo, Shapiro, Gomez, and Blacher (2005) found that Latina mothers were more concerned that their young adults with disabilities become self-sufficient in terms of meeting their own personal needs than by becoming employed and also believed that marriage was a marker of independence and movement from the family home rather than the Anglo-American concept of independent living after high school. They noted that the mothers identified transition as a home-centered, sheltered adaptation as opposed to a model emphasizing independent productivity. Blacher (2001) suggests that values such as *familism* or interdependence among family

BOX 6.2 **An Appropriate Job in a Caste-Based Society**

How would a young adult with mild intellectual disabilities find a job if caste were a factor? When strictly observed, the caste system in India restricts job options for all its members so that a member of a low caste such as a shoemaker can only be a shoemaker and, by the same token, members of high castes would be considered "polluted" if they engaged in manual labor. A study on the concerns of the parents of young adults with mild intellectual disabilities in India found that the difficulties they faced finding jobs for their children were exacerbated by caste barriers (Kalyanpur & Gowramma, 2007). Even though jobs involving manual labor would have been much more suited to the abilities of these young adults, the parents could only consider jobs that were allowed by their upper caste status. Unfortunately, the appropriate jobs meant that the young adults had to have skills, at the very least, in money management and in negotiating public transportation. In addition, the parents worried about the safety of their daughters (e.g., "Only one lady works at the screen-printing institution; the rest are gents, so it is a risky place to send a girl") and sons (e.g., "It is very easy to exploit them; the auto rickshaw drivers... say, 'The money you have given is less [than the fare]' and drop them off in some very faraway places, even though he has enough money").

In the end, rather than depending on formal networks, the parents typically looked within their informal, family networks to find appropriate jobs. One mother found her 16-year-old son a job in her sister's factory where he would get the support he needed, be safe, and earn enough to be independent, whereas another mother said her family intended to open a shop where her son could be accommodated and supported. Similarly, Thressiakutty and Govinda Rao (2001), describing the efforts of professionals to develop a transition plan for a 17-year-old boy with mild intellectual disability and cerebral palsy, noted, "As the boy belonged to an upper middle class joint [or extended] family having a business background, the parents were keen that his job should suit their socioeconomic status" (p. 49). He was given the job of issuing receipts in his father's company using a billing machine that could be operated from a sitting position.

members lending support as well as family cohesion among Latino families make family- or group-oriented interventions more acceptable than individually oriented programs and transition programs, affecting the rate that Latino youth without disabilities are transitioning out of the family home.

Finally, Geenen, Powers, and Lopez-Vasquez (2001) found that both CLD parents and professionals described their participation in transition activities as low; however, whereas the professionals saw the parents' participation as being low overall on all activities, the parents themselves reported being significantly more involved than European American parents in talking to their children about transition, helping their children prepare for postsecondary education, teaching their children to care for their disability, teaching their children about their family's culture, and teaching their children how to use transportation independently. The authors suggested that defining "parental participation as being solely within the realm of school-based planning...creates a skewed picture of passivity among CLD parents" (p. 278).

In conclusion, this section examined areas of potential conflict in the partnered process of developing education goals as a result of incongruent values and belief systems between parents and professionals. While parents may want the same outcomes of independence for their child or young adult with disabilities, the meaning of independence and the milestones toward independence in adulthood may be different. Families that value cooperation and collectivism are unlikely to raise children who are mindful of their rights to self-determination. Expecting these parents to want their child with disabilities to make personal choices and acquire personal autonomy without an adequate understanding of their parental ethnotheory may alienate the family.

IMPLICATIONS FOR PROFESSIONALS

In this book, we have identified the core values of mainstream America that are embedded in special education policy and practice and described the multiple differences that can occur in how families of children with disabilities from CLD backgrounds understand disability and seek help. We examined the values of individualism, choice, and equity that underlie special education policy and the implications for families who may not believe in individual rights or choice. We analyzed the assumptions embedded in the clinical or medical model of disability—that disability is a physical and individual phenomenon, is chronic, and requires fixing—and the implications for families who come from contrasting traditions and hold opposite beliefs about disability. We investigated the implicit and contradictory expectation that professionals, as experts, have all the answers, even as they are required to seek parental input, and how this plays out in the use of professional language, communication styles, and the structure of IEP meetings. We studied how differences in family values, structures, interactions, and community identity influence parenting styles, looking particularly at the issue of disciplinary and healing practices. We presented differences in perceptions of independence that affect families' decisions about educational and transition goals for their children and young adults.

We hope that these depictions of families' alternative realities help the reader to understand where families may be coming from when he or she interacts with them. We would like to reiterate that although we have presented many of these differences in terms of various cultural groups to provide a point of reference, we do not wish to imply that all families belonging to a group that may share certain commonalities will share all of the same commonalities. In particular, the level of acculturation among immigrant families and the extent to which the family may have adapted to mainstream values are major factors in creating parental ethnotheories that are unique to each family. Our purpose was to give the reader an opportunity, like Lucy, the young Caribbean girl in Jamaica Kincaid's book (see Chapter 2), to see the field of special education as a "foreign country," to glimpse possible alternative realities, and to start to identify what might be taken for granted in professional practice. For instance, when reading that in some hierarchically structured societies, people who have lower status may not necessarily be devalued, does one wonder how that can be? If a person has lower status, then surely that means that they are less valued in society or, at the least, are stigmatized because they have lower status? Or, when one reads that immigrant Indian mothers want their daughters to grow up to be "responsible," "obedient," "respectful," "hospitable," "modest," and "nonargumentative," does one have difficulty understanding how these attributes relate to independence? In fact, we hope that this feeling of strangeness was experienced several times while reading this book! As we wrote earlier, perhaps the best way to understand one's own taken-for-granted beliefs is by discovering that other people may not take those same beliefs for granted.

At the same time, our intention is not to present these differences as something exotic and strange that creates or enhances a sense of "otherness" and the feeling that there are no commonalities between one's perspective and the families who might have different perspectives and no possibilities for compromise or a middle ground. Toward this, we presented the process of cultural reciprocity as an approach that professionals can apply in their interactions with families—any family—to develop an awareness of the cultural underpinnings of their professional recommendations to families, learn how the family's perspective may differ, and arrive at a common understanding. As Harry explained in her interactions with Silvia and her family (see Chapter 2), this process can be cyclical. Certain interventions to increase Silvia's independence, such as traveling by bus, were implemented with the family's input and consent and then evaluated jointly with the family. The sustained engagement with the family helped the research team to recognize that although the family appreciated both the strides Silvia was making in riding the bus and the team's efforts, their perception of independence for Silvia was that she have an independent source of income, however small, hopefully through SSDI, and that she read independently. We think it is important to emphasize that we are not advocating that families have to necessarily change their position or adapt their values to come to this middle ground. The best outcome we expect is one in which families build their cultural capital, gain an awareness of the expectations and values of the mainstream culture, and make an informed choice or decision based on this new knowledge.

Similarly, we are not suggesting that professionals adapt their values either. We anticipate that by applying cultural reciprocity professionals will become more aware of families' alternative realities in the differences in values, intercommunication styles, parenting styles, and goals for the future and that, rather than perceiving them as "different" or even as deficit and thereby possibly dismissing them, professionals will acknowledge them for what they are: the family's reality. By acknowledging the family's point of view, respect is shown, which will in turn gain the family's respect. Most significant, it creates a starting point for discussion to explain the mainstream perspective and how it differs from theirs. Families who are informed and make informed choices are in the best position to ensure that their child or young adult with disabilities is served effectively.

CLOSING EXERCISE: NILOUFER AND THE PROCESS OF CULTURAL RECIPROCITY

Throughout this book, we have described examples of interactions between parents and professionals illustrating a source of conflict based on differences in values and explained how the outcome might have turned out differently if the professionals had applied the process of cultural reciprocity instead. In Chapter 2, where we introduced the concept of cultural reciprocity, we also provided an extended description of Harry's application of the process in her interactions with Silvia's family. Here is a final story—that of Niloufer and her younger daughter, Nabeela. We encourage the reader to use this example to try out the process of cultural reciprocity. Using what has been learned from this book, apply the process of cultural reciprocity to develop some options for her daughter Nabeela's transition from school. We have provided some questions at the end of the vignette to help with this process.

Niloufer is a 49-year-old mother of two young adult daughters—Nabeela, 18, and Sandra, 20. When Nabeela was born after a prolonged labor, she was found to have severe gastrointestinal anomalies and was not expected to live beyond a few months. "That's my Nabeela, proving everybody wrong!" says Niloufer with a laugh. Nabeela has her mother's sense of humor, although she is more reserved. She manages her colostomy bag herself and enjoys music with the help of her hearing aids. She has a mild speech impairment and developmental disability and is in a special education classroom for part of the day.

Niloufer is tall, humorous, and speaks animatedly using many gestures. She is Muslim; her husband is Christian. Although religion is important to each of them, they decided that they would introduce their children to the best of both religions and allow them to choose when they were ready to do so. They compromised on their children's names by giving one daughter a Christian and the other a Muslim name.

The family had been living in India, but Niloufer's husband applied for an assignment abroad after Nabeela's birth to seek further medical help. They have been living in the United States ever since. With her advanced degrees, Niloufer taught at a university in India. In the United States, without U.S.-recognized degrees, she works as a teacher's aide in a special education classroom in Nabeela's school. Her usual optimism helps her to see the positive side of the situation: "I get to meet other parents in circumstances similar to mine, and I can share my story with them and learn from them too. I can also check in on Nabeela from time to time. I know all her teachers and can find out how she's doing. Maybe people think I'm being overprotective, but I want to know that Nabeela is safe."

Nabeela's safety is a primary concern for Niloufer. "Maybe it's related to my own upbringing (in India) where I wasn't allowed to go out anywhere on my own. I was always accompanied by a maid, my brother, or a friend. I never saw it as a restriction because I knew it was for my safety until I saw the kind of freedom that girls have here. It was difficult at first to let go with Sandra and to explain that my concern was not based in lack of trust of her but in lack of trust of the rest of society! But it's harder to explain this to Nabeela. You can see that she's interested in boys, and I'm always worrying that somebody might take advantage of her. I think she's safer because I'm in the same school. There was one time when I toyed with the idea of a tubal ligation for Nabeela and broached the subject with her teacher. My goodness! You'd think I had suggested decapitation!"

Although Nabeela has the option of staying in high school until she is 21, she would like to start attending the local community college after the summer. This would mean taking the public transportation system, which neither Sandra nor Nabeela have been allowed to do. Niloufer and her husband had given Sandra rides all through school. Only when she left for university had they consented to giving her a car as the safest mode of transportation. "Now Nabeela wants to do something with computers, and her school doesn't offer her the program. Her teacher says it'll be good for her to learn how to take the bus and get there by herself. But the thought terrifies me," said Niloufer. "It's not that she's not independent. She does a lot of things on her own. She comes home on the school bus before I do, lets herself in, and makes a snack for herself. She'll take the dog for a walk. She manages all her personal health care, her period, her colostomy bag, her hearing aids. That's a lot for any kid—and she does it all herself! It's not that I don't think she can do it. It's that I worry about her safety. What if she got off at the wrong stop, if she got lost? What if somebody followed her to the house?"

"If we were back at home in India, the teachers would have understood my concern and would never have suggested that she travel by bus alone. I don't know how to explain this to the teacher. At the same time, I realize that I'm living in America; I have to be willing to do things the way they are done here. And I—we—have adapted in so many ways. I hardly ever wear a salwar kameez because it makes me stand out and look more different than I am. I've learned to make eye contact when speaking to people, to call ahead before visiting, not to get upset when people say 'no' quite plainly to me, not to celebrate my festivals with much fanfare (especially after 9/11). Most important, I've learned to ask for things on behalf of Nabeela—what they call advocating."

"At first, at IEP meetings, I just sat there and accepted everything they said. And because we didn't have any other Indian friends in the same situation, I didn't think about it. Now, by meeting the parents of the students in my classroom, I've learned that parents have rights and that it's okay to ask for services. It's still very, very difficult," she added, with a wry smile, "so I take my husband along for support. Unfortunately, it just adds to the teachers' stereotype of the Muslim woman who can't do anything without her man."

When asked what she wanted for Nabeela's future, Niloufer answered, "I don't see her leaving this home. She hasn't asked to leave, and we know Sandra will come back to live with us when she finishes university. That would be fine with us. When she's closer to finishing her program in studies in computers at the community college, my husband plans to start a small company of his own. It may be from our garage, which we would convert into an office, or he might rent a small office space close to here. What we hope is that Nabeela can help him with his computer needs, you know, use her skills helping him set up his business."

REVIEW QUESTIONS

1. At what points in Niloufer's story did you experience a sense of strangeness? Why?

2. What is Niloufer's perception of independence? What is your perception of independence? What are some indicators of independence that you have achieved so far in your own life according to this definition, and what are some of your future aspirations for independence? Use your personal identity web to explore the source of this meaning to you. Has acculturation played a role in it?

3. What was your reaction when Niloufer talked about tubal ligation for Nabeela? Why?

4. To what extent do you think Niloufer's level of acculturation is influencing her goals for Nabeela? Consider issues like Niloufer's professional status in India and in the United States, her religion, and her ideas about a girl going out unaccompanied.

5. Based on your responses to these questions, what recommendations for Nabeela's future would you suggest to Niloufer that you think would respond to her values and the concerns she has for Nabeela?

6. Imagine that you are working with a family that believes that the only way they can be a fully functioning, "normal" family is by placing their child who has

severe disabilities in a group home or other institutional setting. Imagine also a family that believes that the best way to ensure the safety of their teenage daughter with a disability and reduce her vulnerability to sexual abuse or an unwanted pregnancy is through tubal ligation. Would you see these situations as ethical dilemmas? How would you respond to them? Do you think that professionals also have an advocacy role to play in working with families?

Cultural Reciprocity

Applications and Variations

In this second section, we have invited contributors who have applied the principles of cultural reciprocity in their own practice to describe their experiences. We believe that these three chapters illustrate the range of personalized interpretations that can be stimulated by immersion in the cultural reciprocity process. In keeping with our approach in Kalyanpur and Harry (1999), all authors introduce themselves to readers through a brief disclosure regarding their positionality as special education researchers. Davenia Lea describes the personal cultural transformative journey of her life, values, and belief systems through her relationship with adolescent mothers who have children with disabilities. Eva Thorp and Monimalika Day present their application of the cultural reciprocity process to engage early childhood special education graduate students in a process of critical reflection that enables them to identify and explore cultural dilemmas in their interactions with culturally diverse families. Shernaz B. García describes how, as a university professor who is ethnically, racially, linguistically, and culturally different from her special education preservice student teachers, she creates intercultural spaces in which cultural differences are negotiated collaboratively among them in order to be able to adopt a culturally informed philosophy of teaching and learning for all students.

Chapter **7**

Cultural Reciprocity as a Transformative Journey in Research and Practice

Davenia Lea

I do not want my house to be walled in on all sides and my windows to be stuffed. I want the cultures of all the lands to be blown about my house as freely as possible. And I refuse to be blown off my feet by any.

Mahatma Gandhi

The overarching goal of this chapter is to further expand the application of the processes for the development of cultural reciprocity. I will reveal how I—an African American mother, wife, researcher, and early interventionist—had to grapple with my own beliefs, values, and attitudes as a result of being immersed into the lives of six adolescent mothers who had children with disabilities (Lea, 2001). My intent is to help facilitate your personal transformation, similar to that which I experienced as a result of my relationship with these mothers.

Note my use of the term *immerse* as opposed to *examine*. To examine would imply that I simply looked at or watched from the outside as my relationship with the mothers unfolded while sorting through the layers of complexity in order to apply and/or affirm some theoretical construct or to develop new relational or instructional strategies. This type of examination has value, and I do recognize its importance and contribution to the development of significant theoretical frameworks that shape and guide research. In fact, it was this process that guided the formation, implementation, and investigation of my research and even became part of the title, *An Ethnographic Study Concerning the Perceptions of Adolescent Mothers' of Children with Disabilities Participation on Their Child's Early Intervention Team* (Lea, 2001). Important theories such as Bronfenbrenner's (1986) ecological model provided the conceptual framework: Four research questions were answered, additional questions were raised, and insights into the development of collaborative relationships were provided. What I did not expect, however, was a transformation of my own life, values, and belief systems. Not only did my research increase my knowledge of adolescent mothers and early intervention, but also it challenged and altered the way I thought; the way I interacted with others; my expectations of others; and my perceptions of race, class, gender, adolescence, and parenthood. I also discovered that once I stepped out of the role of researcher as someone who examines a phenomenon and allowed myself to experience the phenomenon, I was able to understand and apply the concepts and theories that I had studied. More specifically, I had to rely heavily on and ultimately live and internalize the processes of cultural reciprocity. In essence, this ethnographic study that examined the lives of six adolescent mothers of children with disabilities essentially became an autoethnography in which I immersed myself into the lives of these mothers, thus experiencing a personal and cultural transformation. And this, I realize, is the most critical finding of my study. The theories, strategies, and practical applications that emerge from research are important, but if one's practices and beliefs are not affected in a significant and meaningful way, then the theories, constructs, and proposed practical implications are meaningless.

I must confess that one of the stumbling blocks that I encountered while writing this chapter was determining the vehicle by which I could best engage you in this transformative process. How could I get you to experience what I experienced or feel what I felt—to discern the joys, the pain, the sorrow, or the depth of these mothers as I did? An additional challenge in writing this chapter was to concisely present the data in a manner that tells the stories of the adolescent mothers through my lens while maintaining the authentic voices of the mothers. One of the mothers from my study aided me in this thought process by sharing her opinion of my summary and analysis of her specific case study. She commented, "What da' fu-- does this mean?" After my explanation, she went on to say, "Well, this won't make nobody cry, and you know my story sad. It don't even sound like me. I guess you gotta dress me up so all those educated people can stomach me." After reflecting on her comments, I realized that their stories have to be shared so that you, the reader, can feel and be immersed in their lives—well, immersed into *our* lives actually, as I cannot tell their story without telling my story and the intertwining of two worlds. Consequently, I have chosen to share some of our experiences as small vignettes, each designed to explore the processes involved in the development of cultural reciprocity while attempting to capture significant interactions that served as pivotal moments along my journey. To write our stories in any other fashion would allow you to remain distant from the story and from true transformation. As I attempt to briefly immerse you into the lives of Veronica and Stacy in this chapter, I will also attempt to uncover in more detail the process of conducting qualitative or ethnographic research by not simply explaining or conveying what the researcher actually does but by allowing you to feel as I felt while providing the opportunity to get inside of my head and heart.

The vignettes are deeply rooted in my research concerning the lives of and interactions with six adolescent mothers who had children with disabilities (Lea, 2001). This larger study draws from interviews and observations regarding the mothers' perceptions of early intervention, their schooling experiences, interactions with their friends and families, and their personal and intimate relationships. The study was framed through research questions all related to a larger question: "How have the life experiences of adolescent mothers shaped their perceptions of and participation in early intervention?" A detailed account of the data collected and analyzed in my study is presented elsewhere and focuses on the interactions between the adolescent mothers and the service providers (Lea, 2006). This chapter focuses on my personal transformation as well as my practices as an early interventionist as a result of my interactions with the adolescent mothers.

Each vignette represents pivotal moments in my research and/or practices that either revealed new personal truths, inspired deeper understandings of others, provided opportunities to share meaningful cultural revelations, or allowed for collaborative discourse. To ensure confidentiality, I have changed names within each vignette. In addition to sharing how I came to understand and apply the tenets of cultural reciprocity, I demonstrate the cyclical nature of the process through examples of my interactions and conversations with and reflections of the adolescent mothers. Although each phase of the process is presented separately, it is important to note that the practice of cultural reciprocity is not a linear process but rather a process in which the steps intertwine, overlap, and depend on one another. The vignettes accentuate the depth of the investment in developing culturally reciprocal relationships for each phase of the process. Finally, I provide practical strategies and suggestions for comprehending and applying the theoretical underpinnings of the cultural reciprocity process in research and in practice.

UNDERSTANDING SELF

The researcher's role as the primary data collection instrument in qualitative research requires the researcher to identify personal values, assumptions, and biases at the outset of a study (Creswell, 1994, Geursen, de Heer, & Korthagen, 2010). This idea often is expressed in terms of the *Is*, or the identities of the researcher, and these identities influence all research decisions (Peshkin, 1988). The researcher's identity is fluid and dynamic throughout the research process (Thomson & Gunter, 2011). Lynch and Hanson (2011) suggested that the gendered and multiculturally situated researcher approaches the world with a set of ideas that assists in specifying a set of questions to be explored. According to Harry (1996), the challenge is not to eliminate these values but to document how they influence the researcher's behavior. Harry (1996) further contended that the researcher must attempt to study objectively the subjective nature of the participants. In other words, the researcher must transcend his or her own biases, recognizing that the goal is to add knowledge and not to pass judgment.

Best practice in qualitative research emphasizes the importance of identifying the worldview perspectives and identities of the researcher at the outset of the investigation. This self-reflection and self-disclosure provides for increased objectivity and gives the audience a broader understanding of the framework that shapes the researcher's analyses and interpretations of the phenomena being examined.

As I delved into the qualitative research of these mothers, I was cognizant of this issue concerning self-awareness and of my own various identities in addition to my role as a researcher. First, I had been working with families of infants and children with disabilities for 8 years as both an early intervention teacher and as a team leader for the infants and toddlers program. In alignment with the mission and vision of the infants and toddlers program, I believed that parents were and should be recognized as important and equal members of their child's early intervention team. I also believed that professionals should make it their responsibility to ensure that the family members felt empowered and were not made to feel insignificant by the use of the professionals' policies, words, or behaviors. My role as an early intervention teacher was to listen to the parents' concerns, share my knowledge with them regarding child development, and assist them in attaining their identified goals for their child as well as their family.

I also had the shared experience of being a young, single mother and had consequently formulated some beliefs about the challenges the young mothers that I was to study may have encountered. Because of the struggles that I had faced—financial concerns; conflicts with my child's father; the complexities of trying to juggle school, parenting, and friendships; and the struggle to redefine myself in my new role as parent—I presumed that the young mothers in my study might have faced similar difficulties.

I also shared with five of the mothers the experience of being a minority. As an African American woman, I have experienced both blatant and subtle prejudices. I have also felt, at one time or another, as if I have had to work harder than members from the dominant culture to accomplish my professional goals and be recognized for my achievements. Furthermore, I characterize myself as someone who has a flexible approach to the concept of time, who enjoys sharing stories with and hearing stories from others, and who uses and appreciates humor.

In other words, I did not enter the investigation as a totally impartial observer. I believed I already knew a great deal about the topic from firsthand experience as well as from talking to many parents over the years. I also approached my study with the assumption that young, poor, minority parents lacked the skills to participate in a collaborative manner and, as a result of my experiences and work in early intervention, I believed that early intervention professionals lacked specific training to work with adolescent parents.

Darling-Hammond (2002) suggested that professionals must develop an awareness of their own perspectives. It is a practice described in the process of cultural reciprocity as identifying one's cultural values that are embedded in the interpretation of an experience, thought, or feeling (Kalyanpur & Harry, 1999). Self-disclosure prior to the start of an investigation is important for a researcher as well as for the intended audience. However, through my research experience, as I was confronted with experiences that continually challenged, confirmed, confused, or canceled my perceptions, I realized that self-reflection needs to be ongoing throughout the entire research process.

The following vignette describes one of my reflective journal entries following my first visit with one of the mothers in my study:

My stomach is doing flips as I approach Baden High School. Although anxious to get started, I'm thankful for the morning stop-and-go traffic as students pile out of cars preparing for another day of summer school. The delays give me the opportunity to gauge the personality of Baden High, which is newly constructed and serves as home to approximately 1,800 students. The school sits on a major street surrounded by shopping centers, fast food restaurants, and office buildings. Baden High gives the appearance of a facility dedicated to scholarly undertakings. The large edifice constructed of red granite with windows that seem to span the length of the building stands strong as the school flag flaps in the slight morning breeze atop the school's dome. Oak trees line the walkway leading to the school's entrance. Splashes of color are sprinkled throughout the massive sea of green as small gardens of pink creeping phlox and blue forget-me-nots peek through the expertly manicured lawn. The school's marquee is huge, maybe even a little pretentious, with digital messages of the upcoming events scrolling by as the school mascot's paw lies draped across the top. Wow. This place is immaculate. This place is gorgeous. This place is…. Wait a minute. Is that graffiti I see? Please tell me that's not graffiti. As my mom would say,

"Niggas. You can dress 'em up but you can't take 'em anywhere." This is just a crude summary of the many contrasts that exist between the town's recent economic growth and the leadership's desire to create "Beautiful St. Bondiville." A great concept. Plant trees. Pick up the litter. A little paint here. A little paint there. And wham. A beautiful new city. Almost perfect. But they forgot one thing: What's the plan to "beautify" the citizens? How will the masses who have been plagued by crime, violence, drugs, and despair benefit from the city's transformation? Who sprinkles color in their lives and makes all anew?

As I enter Baden High, I'm briefly transported back to my high school days. I wish that I could say I have pleasant memories of high school or that Baden High differs from my alma mater—Halston High in New York. Although it's summer time, the halls are packed. A school of nearly 2,000 students and at least 1,000 of them are in summer school trying to pass one class or another. Lockers line the walls on either side. Music (or a facsimile thereof) assaults me from…well, I don't know from where. Nelly rapping about b-----s and "hos." Guys wearing white T-shirts and jeans that seem to be twice their size, Timberland boots, and baseball caps. Tattoos everywhere: arms, necks, belly buttons, backs, breasts, ankles. All kinds of tattoos: hearts, names, dragons, crosses. And with just as much effort as the guys seem to put into layering themselves in more clothing than needed, the girls seemingly go through just as much trouble to ensure that as much skin as possible is visible. Breasts spilling from tank tops and tube tops. Midriffs in full view. Belly buttons, noses, eyebrows, tongues, and ears pierced. Shorts that can be mistaken for underwear and skirts that are very short and very tight. Red hair, pink hair, blue hair, no hair. I feel as if I am in the middle of a Dr. Seuss story (the remixed version, of course). Yet the discomfort that I feel seems to be mine alone. Those around me move with ease, like a well-orchestrated dance. There is laughter, dancing, kissing, and hugging; and all of this seems to take precedence over the intended purpose of summer school. Classes, books, and learning don't appear to be as important as seeing and being seen.

Again, seeking to continually understand how one thinks, feels, or perceives every interaction and experience is critical as one works to engage in culturally reciprocal relationships in research and in practice (Ford, Moore, Whiting, & Grantham, 2008). For me, writing my reflections immediately following every interaction and experience afforded me an unedited, uncensored glimpse into my inner thoughts and feelings. Analyzing my reflections at a later time then made it possible for me to ask the tough and important questions. In elementary school, most children learn about the five *Wh-* questions—*who, what, when, where,* and *why.* These questions are the most important questions for a researcher, especially one who wishes to apply cultural reciprocity, to ask (Leech & Onwuegbuzie, 2007). Asking questions such as "Why did I feel X when Y occurred?" "Why did I respond the way that I did?" and "What past experience may be contributing to my feelings or perceptions?" can help a researcher understand his or her own biases.

Journaling is an excellent strategy for engaging in this process of self-examination (Kremenitzer, 2005). Journaling allows an individual to examine his or her actions embedded in the complex interactions between him- or herself and others and assists in making connections and in developing reflective practice by pushing one to discover meaning, gain perspectives of others, and reflect on his or her own behavior (Bogdewic, 1999). Journaling stimulates increased personal awareness regarding one's own beliefs, values, and practices as well as of those with whom one interacts (Tillman,

2006). Journaling allows a researcher to gain a better understanding of how the different contexts in which one lives his or her life, juxtaposed with the lives of those with whom one is building a relationship, come together (Banks-Wallace, 2008). Initially it may be very uncomfortable, and, to be honest, it may remain uncomfortable throughout the entire process. I have learned, however, that this discomfort is actually a good thing; it is this state of discomfort that prompts me to go deeper and to ask more questions. I have learned to identify my discomfort as a tightening in the center of my stomach; and that tightening signals me to question, requestion, and question some more. The most common reaction to being uncomfortable is to withdraw or to hide behind what is familiar and safe, but to truly and meaningfully examine oneself requires one to get uncomfortable. By examining my reactions, my feelings, and my thoughts regarding an experience, I became better equipped to honestly and sometimes brutally reveal aspects of myself that I do not like, that I have not thought of before, that I had forgotten, that are uncomfortable, or that actually make sense. Understanding my perceptions allowed me to engage in a deeper, more honest, and more significant relationship with the mothers from my study. As an illustration, a partial analysis of my self-reflection on the vignette describing my first impressions of Baden High follows:

What historical and/or political events may have contributed to my description of the school and the environment? I live in the county in which Baden High is located, and I have observed and been affected by the political climate. Crime is up 24%, many social services have been cut due to state budget deficits, and the county executive is in his last term of office and is looking to move into state government, hence the numerous initiatives to beautify the county. The county is one of the wealthiest majority African American communities in the United States, but there has been a continuous dichotomy between the black middle class—the "haves"—and the black poor—the "have-nots." The "have-nots" seem to be isolated to certain regions within the county, and these regions border a large urban district. The middle class appears to deny that another class of citizens even exists.

Over the course of my life, I have experienced being classified within both social statuses, the "haves" and the "have-nots." My childhood would most probably be characterized as upper middle class. Both of my parents worked—my father as a Methodist minister and my mother as a middle school teacher. Although we moved a lot, we always lived in a single family home, we vacationed annually, my siblings and I were provided with more than we needed, and my friends actually referred to us as the "Huxtables (an upper middle class family as portrayed in *The Cosby Show* during the 80s)." After I had my son, I was classified as what would commonly be perceived as poor: Because I was not able to work for a year as I was preparing to complete my student teaching (a requirement of my teaching program), I received public assistance consisting of supports for childcare, medical insurance, and food. I lived in an apartment in a lower-class section of town, and I had no support from my son's father. Currently I would be classified as upper middle class. After I graduated with my bachelor's degree, I got my first teaching job. Shortly thereafter, I got married, and my husband's and my incomes shifted us into the socioeconomic status of the middle class. These classifications, partly based on one's financial standing, carry with them social connotations as well. For example, when I was "poor" because of my financial situation, I resented being viewed as "one of those living off the system." I hated how people treated me when I used my food stamps. For example, I recall hearing statements such as "So this is what my tax dollars are being used for? They can buy steak and I can barely afford hamburger to feed my family and I have a job"; "Maybe if they stop having all these babies and get a job, they wouldn't have to be on welfare"; and, "What a shame. Our taxes support them from daycare to jail." Because I grew up and was socialized as middle class, I still had the values, beliefs, and practices of my middle-class upbringing. My temporary situation, however, afforded me the opportunity to experience life "on the other side" while being cognizant of the fact that I did not fit in nor did I want to. I longed to be viewed with the respect that I felt came with being "in" the middle class, and I worked hard to be viewed as someone from the middle class and as someone who was poor. My initial assumptions of the students of Baden High were that they were "poor;" thus I had immediately painted a picture of students that did not care about receiving an education; that many of them were probably poor, living in the projects; and that many of the boys sold drugs or were in gangs and that many of the girls had a child and were recipients of welfare or social services. These assumptions were based on my personal experiences as well as society's and the media's depictions of who the poor or the middle class are. What personal and/or cultural experiences have contributed to my description of the school, the students, and the environment?

Upon review of my initial writings, one of my first thoughts was, "Wow! Why was I so comfortable using the term 'niggas'? It is commonly used in my circle of friends and amongst those in my primarily African American environments. I use it like I would say 'those bamas,' meaning people who act country, or 'those idiots.' I used the term to mean blacks who don't care, are thug like, or are socially and culturally deviant. Should I have used the term? I only use the term around those who would understand the usage, but still, should I have used the term at all? Probably not, because then I perpetuate these stereotypes. But what was I feeling when I used the term? I was feeling anger, because I believe that we (as in African Americans) should have a beautiful school edifice (and typically we don't); but when we do get one, we destroy it, thus the stereotypes that we are ignorant, barbaric, uncouth, and so forth are seemingly perpetuated. And I was feeling sadness, because I don't think that they (the students) understand how hard we (as in African Americans) had to work to have the opportunity to even go to school. And I don't know how to get the message across to this generation of youth who don't seem to understand the struggle and don't seem to care.

Finally, I felt hopelessness, because I don't know how to make a difference in the lives of African Americans. I believe that the plight of the African American seems to have been forgotten as the plight of African Americans seems to be intertwined with the plight of all diverse cultures. For example, it used to be that affirmative action was specifically for African Americans as a result of the slavery and the Jim Crow era in the United States. However, with the civil rights movement now 50 years behind us and as our society has broadened its definition of diverse cultures, specific initiatives are no longer set aside for African Americans. For example, during the 1970s, a company would have to account for how many African Americans it employed and the resources it made available to support the African Americans. Now a company is asked how many employees from diverse cultures it has employed. If the company employs two Latinos, three women, one Native American, and two persons of Asian descent, then the company would be viewed as a diverse workplace despite the fact that not a single African American works there. I feel African Americans have lost sight of our continued plight (and, yes, we do continue to have a plight), we don't have a true leader anymore, we aren't united as a people, and we've been lulled into a false sense of complacency (Edney, 2003; McCray, 2007; Patterson, 2010). So, I feel discouraged. Maybe the students do too, and perhaps, like me, they don't know what else to do. Maybe we've both chosen to cope, just in different ways—I through research and social justice; they through artistic expression (I'm trying to see the graffiti in a different way and understand that to some it may actually be art) and self-destruction.

Why did I feel so uncomfortable walking the halls? Was I scared? Scared of what? I wasn't scared as in fear for my safety. I wasn't scared of the students themselves—well, maybe I was uncomfortable with the way some of the guys were looking at me. Not scared like they would hurt me, but uncomfortable. The way the guys seemed to leer at me and at the girls in the hall made me feel uncomfortable for us as women, but the girls didn't seem to mind. Did they welcome how the guys were looking at them? Did they actually listen to the words of the music playing? Did they think they were b------s and hos like the songs suggested? Did I feel out of place? Yes. Why? This was just like my high school. I guess I felt uncomfortable there too. I guess I never really fit in. I cared about books, learning, and making *A*s, and that wasn't the culture of my school. Maybe the girls I saw today were uncomfortable too. I wonder if the girls I saw in the hallway were trying to fit in or maybe they, too, were looking for excitement. Maybe they were comfortable in the role they were in. I don't know. I need to explore this further.

Your Story

Recall an experience from your youth. This could be a school experience, a social activity such as going to the skating rink or the movie theatre, or attending a sporting event. Return to a similar venue and observe the environment for at least 30 minutes. Observe the environment through the lens of your past experiences. Reflect on your thoughts, your feelings, and your reactions to the similar experience of your youth through journaling. Record your initial reactions to the following questions: "How did I feel when I used to _____?" "Why did I feel _____?" "What was going on politically, socially, or culturally that may have contributed to my perceptions at that time?" Then, reflect on your thoughts, your feelings, and your reactions to the current experience. "What is my initial feeling as I return to _____?" "Am I comfortable or uncomfortable in this environment?" "Why or why not?" "How have things changed or remained the same politically, socially, or culturally?" "What do I think of the people around me?" "Do I continue to fit in or not fit in?" After you have recorded your initial reactions, review your responses and delve in deeper. Continue to question, write, question, and rewrite. Be honest, get uncomfortable, and, in the words of one of the teenage mothers from my study, "be real" (Lea, 2001).

UNDERSTANDING OTHERS

The heart and soul of qualitative research is to attempt to describe and interpret human phenomena, often in the words of selected individuals (Lewis, 2009). To gain the perspective of others and to view the world through their lens, it is important to build relationships. At the onset of conducting my study, I had formulated the steps that I would take to collect the necessary data. I had determined the approximate number of interviews I would need to conduct with each participant, the number and types of observations I would need to make, and which documents I would review and analyze. My data collection methods were well triangulated, and these initial approaches to collecting data yielded good responses to my research questions. In

addition, although this is, indeed, extremely important, I found myself lost in technical details such as what interview questions I should ask and whether I had enough
tapes and batteries to record. When I interacted with the study participants from the
stance of the researcher, I was more concerned with what I could glean from the
mothers. I was attempting to make sense of their lives and experiences through the lens
by which I viewed the world. And because I was so focused on collecting data, I initially neglected to focus on how I might develop actual relationships so that I could
learn more about the cultural and social constructs that framed who they were. Furthermore, I was completely unaware of how these relationships would affect me personally and as a researcher. However, it wasn't until I began to immerse myself into
the lives of the mothers as opposed to solely examining their lives that I began to com-
prehend life from their perspectives more fully.

The following vignette provides an example of the importance of acquiring the
perspective of the "other party" in the reciprocal relationship:

Today I am outraged. I have been interviewing Veronica for the past 6 weeks and I discover that
she's been lying this whole time. I was so caught up in how well my themes were coming together and how my initial hypotheses were panning out as I had expected. I was thrilled that she
and I had developed this wonderful researcher–participant relationship. I asked questions and
she answered without reservation or trepidation, and I was sure that I could wrap up Veronica's
case study within a month. And today, as I'm conducting another interview, my well-packaged
study falls apart.

"So, Veronica," I ask, "you shared with me last week that Arial's father died. If it's not too
painful, would you mind sharing with me how he died?"

"Died?" Veronica chuckles. "Oh, my bad." She laughs a little harder. "I can't believe you be
believin' half the sh-- I say. He ain't really die. That nigga servin' life. So maybe I didn't lie 'cause
it's like he dead to me and Arie. He might as well be."

I'm dumbfounded. Was this a joke to her? If she lied about this, had she lied about other
things? What am I supposed to do with the data I've collected? How can I proceed if I can't trust
that the information provided is reliable and valid?

"Awww, you look mad. Don't be mad." More laughter. "I gave you what you wanted to hear
and you was eatin' that sh-- up. You got what you wanted, so why you mad?"

Inhale. Exhale. "Yes, Veronica, I'm upset, but not because I don't have a 'story,' as you put
it, but because you either don't take this seriously or you don't trust me enough to tell me the truth."

"Truth. You can't handle the truth." The laughter returns to a chuckle. "You know that movie?"
Veronica assumes a serious posture and imitates Tom Cruise's character, Lieutenant Daniel
Kaffee, from A Few Good Men while she repeats, "Truth. You can't handle the truth." "You know
I want to be an actress, right? Can't you see me up on the big screen, walkin' on the red carpet,
everybody shoutin' my name? Wearin' that fly sh--, drivin'–no, havin' somebody drive me
around–in my Escalade."

"So now you want to act?" I asked. "What happened to working in the hospital because you
thought you'd look cute in scrubs?"

"Yeah, yeah, that's what's up, too. I just wanna make money and live that dope life."

Heavenly Father, help me. I want to strangle her. "So, Veronica, how are we going to do
this? I thought you understood that I was interested in understanding more about you, your life

as a mom, and what you think of the education that Arial receives. I really want your story told your way. Your story uncut. The answer is out there, Veronica, and it's looking for you, and it will find you if you want it to. I'm a movie buff too."

"What movie is that?" Veronica asks.

"*The Matrix.*" I respond. "I know you've seen it."

"Yeah, that movie was bad."

"Well, do you remember the scene between Trinity and Neo?" I ask.

Veronica chuckles. "Yeah. I'm a have to watch that again just to listen for that part." Another chuckle. "Truth about my life. Nobody never really cared about my story. It's just easier to tell people what they want to hear. People say they want the truth, but they really don't. So it's kinda like a game. I try to figure out the other person and then try to come up with the story I think they want to hear. Like, I like tryin' to guess de answer and then I just keep makin' up sh-- and most times the script go just like I think it would."

"Maybe you should consider becoming a psychiatrist," I say.

"Right. That would be tight." Once again, she playacts, this time imagining a hospital scene: "Paging Dr. Harding." Reverting back to herself, she considers, "Yeah, I like that. Get all up in people's heads." We both chuckle. She continues, "Or maybe I should write movies and sh--. I could star in my own movie."

"So, you still didn't answer my question," I persist. "Where do we go from here?"

"Well, then, act like you wanna get to know the real me. Sittin' here in my motha's living room with a tape recorder ain't real. Or watchin' Arial and dem [referent?] play with blocks and sh-- ain't how we roll every day. So, if I put my sh-- out there, you sure you can handle it?"

"I asked, didn't I?" I respond. "I want to know you—not the you you think I want to know, but the real you. So if you are willing to share, then I'm ready to learn. School me."

"School you." Chuckle. "Ms. Dee down with the urban lingo." Pause. Chuckle. Pause. "Awright. Lesson one." Veronica's body moves in waves from her head down through her mid-section to her legs that open and close in a butterfly motion. All the while she's singing Lil' Kim's "Whoa". "So maybe you can come to work with me tonight?"

"You still a waitress?" I ask. "What restaurant? Should I come for dinner? What time?"

Another chuckle. I'm beginning to dread that chuckle. "Well, that wasn't all exactly true," she answers. "It's more like a club than a restaurant…and…well…I…I serve more than food." She begins to dance again. "I'm a stripper." More dancing. "I do lap dances too. But that's it. Dey can look, can't touch. Girl's gotta do what a girl's gotta do."

My turn to pause. Inhale. Exhale. I asked for honesty but perhaps I was more comfortable with the Veronica that was created for my comfort. Truth? Perhaps I can't handle the truth.

The process of understanding truth as understood by another requires us to be willing and able to handle the truth. So often, we mechanically go through the motions of conducting research or providing services and we neglect to remember that at the crux of both is the importance of the development of true reciprocal relationships. Although I had conducted a comprehensive review of the literature with respect to developing meaningful relationships (Bertacchi, 1996), working with persons from diverse cultures (Coll, 1993; Harry & Kalyanpur, 1994; Lynch & Hanson, 1998), and using family-centered practices (Bailey, McWilliam, & Winton, 1992; Beckman, 1996), I had not experienced as I had with Veronica and the other mothers what it meant to live what I had read about. The vignette presented provides a glimpse into my struggle to create meaningful, reciprocal relationships while maintaining the integrity of the research. As Veronica was one of the first of the mothers that I got to know, I had time to learn invaluable lessons from her that helped enrich my relationships with the other mothers.

The first lesson required an examination of those aspects of my way of relating with Veronica that served to distance me from her. It was important that I understood why she did not trust me enough to tell me the truth. Earlier, I revealed those aspects that I believed served to connect us. I believed that because I, too, had been a young, single mother and was also a person of color, these traits that we had in common would make it easier to connect. And, although these assumptions served to provide an initial framework for relating to the mothers, I soon realized that I needed to delve deeper. Initially, I had fully disclosed all that I thought was relevant to reveal about myself. In addition, I had studied the research regarding effective interviewing techniques, understanding diverse cultures, and working with families, yet I neglected to look beyond the surface of the similarities. For instance, although I too had been a young single mother, I had familial support, which a lot of these mothers did not have or at least not to the extent that I did. In addition, I had not been an adolescent mother, as I was 22 when I had my son. I was able to obtain a college degree while these young mothers were struggling to get a high school diploma or general equivalency diploma. I had the ability to support myself as well as my child and, although I had received public assistance, it was temporary for me and more long-term for them. In addition, with regard to the age difference between me and the mothers at the time of the study, although I was "young" in comparison to other service providers as well as to those in the doctoral program I was attending, I was still twice the age of many of the mothers. So while I thought I was young, in their eyes I was not. My role as a professional also presented a barrier to the formation of a reciprocal relationship. Although I had worked hard to distance myself from my role as an early interventionist and had worked to present myself as being fully interested in their lives and their perspectives, the mothers still viewed me as "one of them." Finally, although I, too, was a person of color, there were vast differences between our cultures.

As I diligently worked to understand the similarities and differences between us, I recognized the need not only to acknowledge them but also to view them, to the extent possible, through the lens of the mothers. I needed to be empathetic and attempt to understand how the mothers might view and receive me. Developing a posture of empathy required that I learn as much as possible about the psychology of adolescence, the Jamaican American and the French Guyanese–American cultures, the culture of poverty, the hip-hop culture, as well as the 21st-century high school culture. To become more empathetic, not only did I immerse myself in the literature, I also relied on varying forms of media. Reading works of fiction like *The Coldest Winter Ever* by Sista Souljah (2000) and *Makes Me Wanna Holler* by Nathan McCall (1995) and watching popular films such as *Save the Last Dance* (Cort & Madden, 2001) served to immerse me into unfamiliar worlds. These forms of media also gave the mothers and me common points of interest for discussion.

The second lesson I learned was that if I wanted the mothers to be authentic in their sharing, then I had to be more deliberate about creating an environment that was comfortable and familiar for them; this required viewing "comfortable and familiar" through their lens and not my own. For example, for most, being in one's home environment usually conveys a level of comfort; however, for the adolescent mothers, home usually conjured up feelings of discomfort because of tensions that existed between them and their guardians. I then had to identify places to meet outside of their homes, keeping in mind that most of the young mothers did not have transportation. I had to either arrange to meet in their neighborhoods or pick them up to take them to wherever we would meet. Meeting over meals seemed to be a viable option, but then I had to consider where we would eat. The first time I took one of the mothers out to dinner, I chose TGIFriday's, as I thought this was a casual atmosphere. I assumed that she had been there before and would actually enjoy it. Instead, her first reaction was "Wow! I've never been to a fancy place like this before." She was overwhelmed by the menu and the people; in fact, she was actually quite uncomfortable in the environment that I had chosen to facilitate comfort. Once again, I needed to view comfort through their lens and not my own; so, during the course of my study, I ate many value meals at McDonald's fast-food restaurants. I also had to consider things such as the car I drove and the radio station that I had playing when they got in the car. For example, Christian radio might convey that I was a religious zealot; conversely, hip-hop might have made it seem like I was trying too hard. So I settled on a neutral rhythm and blues mix of oldies but goodies and more current selections. I also had to consider the clothes that I wore as I didn't want to look too professional (I'd be too much like "one of them"), too casual (I might look like I didn't care), or too trendy (I'd look like I was pretending to be somebody I was not). I worked to maintain my identity while promoting a sense of comfort and familiarity, and I believe this served me well in the creation of a comfortable, safe space where the mothers could share.

Finally, to encourage a more reciprocal relationship with each mother, I had to be willing to enter their worlds no matter how uncomfortable that might have been for me. This meant that I attended baby showers, birthday parties, family dinners, places of employment, school, child care centers, and bus rides to doctors' appointments. Once the mothers believed that I was willing to step outside of my boundaries and become engaged with their lives, they were more trusting and more willing to share their innermost thoughts and feelings—their fears, joys, hopes, and dreams. I had moved from behind that impenetrable, thick, and obvious brick wall that typically serves as a barrier to reciprocal relationships, but I had to work purposefully at disintegrating a wall that still existed and continued to divide "us" and "them." The wall, which I later came to understand as "a thin layer of delicate glass" similar to a glass Christmas ornament, actually served as a greater barrier than the brick wall, because it gave the illusion that there was no barrier. From behind the glass wall, I had the illusion that we were building a reciprocal relationship, but it was not until I consciously and intentionally worked to understand myself and understand them that we were able to chip away at that wall to develop a significant and reciprocal relationship.

Your Story

1. View the movie *Losing Isaiah* (Koch & Foner, 1995). While viewing the film, document your initial thoughts and feelings. Be honest and candid. In order to delve deeper, answer questions such as the following: "How did I feel when I saw Kyla lighting up to get high?" "What do I think of Kyla as a mother?" "What do I think of Isaiah's future?" "What are my views on what it means to be a 'good parent'?" "How do my childhood experiences, my culture, and my values and beliefs contribute to

my feelings and my perspectives?" This process can be identified as *understanding self in the process of developing cultural reciprocity.*

Now, attempt to "walk a mile" in Kyla's shoes. She is a drug addict, she's young, she's abandoned her child, and she's attempting to recover and get her life back on track. What factors may have led her to a life of drugs and prostitution? Seek to explore cultures that may be unknown to you. The following is a list of cultures and titles of books and films that you may find helpful in understanding these cultures:

- Poverty
    - *A Framework for Understanding Poverty* (Payne, 2005)
    - *Savage Unrealities* (Gorski, 2005)
    - *The Other Wes Moore* (Moore, 2010)
    - *Waiting for Superman* (Chilcott, 2010)
- Hip-hop or urban culture
    - *The Hip Hop Generation: The Crisis in African American Culture* (Kitwana, 2002)
    - *Know What I Mean* (Dyson, 2007)
    - *Juice* (Dickerson, 1992)
- Drug use and addiction
    - *I Say a Prayer for Me: One Woman's Life of Faith and Triumph* (Anderson, 2002)
    - *The Life of Rayful Edmond: The Rise and Fall* (Fraser, 2005)
- Prostitution
    - *Working: My Life as a Prostitute* (French, 1997)
    - *Hope and Redemption: The Lena Baker Story* (Johnson, 2009)
- African Americans and the historical implications on today's African Americans
    - *Post Traumatic Slave Syndrome: America's Legacy of Enduring Injury and Healing* (Leary, 2005)
    - *Beyond the Color Line* (Hewes & Chinn, 2005)

This process of discovery would be identified as *understanding others in the process of developing cultural reciprocity,* and, as you can see, this process is time intensive, continuous, and in depth. It's like peeling back the layers of an onion; the more you learn, the more there is to discover. The readings and films highlighted are intended to give a glimpse into varying aspects of culture. Some are controversial; however, the primary intent is to provide more information, to generate more questions, and to broaden your perspectives.

2. To get to know another person more in depth, try writing a biographical sketch of a friend, colleague, or acquaintance whose culture differs from yours. Include information about the person's birth, family, lifetime achievements, and major life events as well as the effects on him or her of historical, cultural and/or societal events. Once you have documented these major facts, then delve deeper and seek to discover how the person views his or her role in society; how he or she believes society views him or her; and his or her perceptions of his or her education, religion, family, friendships, and so forth. Seek to know the person in a more meaningful and significant way, which might be accomplished through interviewing the person, conducting research with respect to the person's culture, and spending time with the person in his or her natural environments.

RESPECTING CULTURAL DIFFERENCES AND COLLABORATIVELY DEVELOPING COMMON GOALS

In addition to spending time with the mothers and engaging them in conversations, I also conducted observations of each mother and her child during early intervention sessions. My overall findings revealed that the majority of the service providers found it challenging to engage with the adolescent mothers primarily because their personal values and belief systems significantly differed from those of the mothers and the service providers did not attempt to or know how to reconcile these differences (Lea, 2006). However, there were a few providers who truly embodied cultural reciprocity in their engagement and interactions with the adolescent mothers. Their ability to form engaging relationships was not dependent on commonality of race, ethnicity, or culture but rather on their intentionality for developing culturally reciprocal relationships. The following vignette demonstrates this:

"I couldn't wait 'til y'all came. I wanna show you somethin'. Come in, y'all gonna be sysed [urban slang meaning excited]." This is the most excited I've seen Stacy since I've been working with her.

Stacy is 17; her daughter, Melina, is 3. Melina has been diagnosed with cerebral palsy, low vision, developmental disabilities, and gastroesophageal reflux. Because of difficulties coordinating her breathing and swallowing, she is fed through a feeding tube. Melina has been hospitalized over eight times, usually for asphyxiation, and her hospital stays have varied in length from 5–30 days. Stacy has had a difficult time adjusting to being a young, single mother of a daughter experiencing such significant medical and developmental challenges and, therefore, runs away often, sometimes for months at a time. Stacy is in the eleventh grade, has a diagnosed learning disability, and attends school inconsistently. Stacy and Melina live with Stacy's mother, who is seeking to gain custody of Melina. However, she does take Stacy back every time she returns from having run away.

Jean was Melina's initial teacher when services first began. She worked with Stacy and Melina for about 6 months and then, when Stacy left home the first time, Melina was reassigned to another teacher. Prior to Melina going to the toddler group, Jean worked with Melina and Stacy again for a couple of months, and I had the privilege of observing a couple of home visits before the toddler group teacher was to begin. Jean is approximately 50 years of age, is Caucasian, and has worked as an early interventionist for over 20 years. Jean's specialty is working with infants and toddlers with severe disabilities. Jean smiles as she responds, "Well, hurry up and let us in. Let's see the surprise." Jean and I follow Stacy into the house. As we enter, we both do a double-take as we are transported back in time to John Travolta's *Saturday Night Fever*. The living room has been transformed into a "discotheque." From the ceiling hangs a large, silver, mirrored disco ball. Streaks of color—red, blue, and green—dart vertically and horizontally across the room *and* the music is deafening! I can feel the floor vibrating from the thump of the bass. I'm thinking that I will surely have a seizure and I immediately look for Melina: Certainly she is being overstimulated and is near convulsions herself. Then I see Melina in the center of the room, seated in her tumble form floor sitter directly under the disco ball. She looks to be hyperextending and vocalizing what I perceive to be distress.

"Wow! This is really something." Jean shouts. Stacy turns off the lights and the music, and, with a grin as wide as the Sierra Desert, asks, "So what chu think? 'Member you told me since Melina can't see good, I should help her use her uva [other] senses. You said music and lights was good 'cause she might can see light. So me and Melina, we went to the circus last week and it was mad dope. She loved the music and the lights and the music was makin' the seats vibrate and sh--, and Mellie was dancin' and singin' and she was soooo happy. So when we left, I thought, "I want her to be like this all the time." So, I start thinkin', how I could do this at home. And look, I did it! See, how much Melina lovin' this sh--? So what chu think?" Stacy looks so happy and so proud and she seems to need approval desperately. As I stand here, I'm wondering how Jean will respond. As a fellow teacher, I recognize that Melina was more than likely experiencing overstimulation and possibly having petit mal seizures, yet I understand how difficult it can be to engage families, especially an adolescent mother.

The three of us sit down on the floor near Melina. Jean positions herself in front of Melina, gently rubs her arm, and speaks calmly. "Hi, sweet girl! I've missed you. You've got some Mamma! You know that, too, don't you?" Melina begins to relax visibly, and she coos. Jean continues providing mild pressure to her arms as she rubs them up and down. She continues to speak. "Yes, you agree. That's what you're telling me. 'I love my Mamma.' Yes, I know. She is really special, and she loves you too." Melina coos and her breathing is less labored. Jean begins to sing, "I love you. You love me." Jean continues to rub Melina's arm and then turns towards Stacy. "I'm so glad that somebody listens to me when I visit. I can see that you really want the best for Melina and that you went all out trying to make her happy."

"Yeah, that's my girl," replies Stacy. "She got it tough, and I just want her to be happy like uva kids. You not like everybody else. Da doctors always tellin' me what she can't do, what she can't have, and my motha she always tellin' me how f---ed up I am, but you show me how to make Mel happy. Mel like you, too, and she like dat song you was singin'. Where you know dat song from?"

Jean replies, "That's a *Barney* song. Barney is this big purple dinosaur. He's kinda dorky but kids like him. He drives me crazy, but I learn his songs and watch his show so I can reach the kids like Barney does." Jean reaches into her toy bag and pulls out a CD of Barney songs. "I can leave this for you and Melina if you want. You may not like the songs like me, but Melina will probably love it like the other kids and she loves you so much, she'll be in heaven havin' her Mamma sing them to her."

Jean hands the CD to Stacy, and Stacy asks, "So you like our circus at home? Maybe I can play that Barney music with the lights if she like that better."

Jean replies, "Yeah, I think that would work, and I do like the idea of a circus at home. That was very creative. You've been listening during our visits and then working with Melina during the week on the activities I leave. That's great. Now I have to apologize to you because during our last visit, I did share that music and lights would be good for Melina, but I should have given you more information. See, not all lights and music may be good for Melina. Yes, we do want to stimulate her, but we have to be careful not to *over*stimulate her. You know that she might suffer from seizures, right?"

Stacy responds, "Yeah, that's why she on all that medicine."

Jean replies, "Exactly. Well, the medicine keeps her from having seizures but there are some things that might cause a seizure. One of those things is certain types of lights."

Stacy's eyes widen and she replies, "Oh, sh--! So you think I gave Melina seizures?"

Jean is quick to reassure her. "No, I don't think that you gave Melina seizures, and I'm not saying that she's having seizures. We would have to have her doctor tell us that. But what I'm saying is that I need to look into the kinds of light that would work best for Melina in order to stimulate her and make her happy, like you do so well, without overstimulating her. The lights that you have are probably fine, but maybe we should try just one at a time and see how Melina responds. That way we can tell which one she likes or doesn't like. Also, we should take some time to learn what Melina is telling us. Remember I told you that, although she can't talk now, she does communicate."

Stacy responds, "Yeah, that's cool. That way I can know what light she like and den the ones she don't like I can throw away. I know she like the lights 'cause she get so happy and she had fun at the circus wit' the other kids. I just want her to have fun and be happy too."

Jean asks, "Why don't we dim the overhead lights and let's just try the disco ball light and see what happens?" Stacy jumps up, turns off the overhead light, and then turns on the disco ball. Everyone watches Melina for about 30 seconds.

Jean then quietly asks, "So what do you think?" to which Stacy replies, "I think she likes it. Maybe she likes quiet stuff. She seem like she chillin', not all spazzed out like before."

Jean smiles and responds, "Cool. Hey, where did you get that cool disco light? I might get me one to use with some of my other kids. We can also think about other places that you can take Melina so she can have fun with her cousins but not get overstimulated so she won't end up in the hospital again. I know how hard that is for you when she's away." Jean places her hand on Stacy's, and Stacy replies, "Yeah, dat sound good."

Working with Stacy as a researcher as well as a service provider was challenging at best because of her complex past, her chosen coping mechanism of running away, and the complexities which surrounded the care of Melina (Lea, 2006). Yet, Jean was able to interact with Stacy in a culturally reciprocal way. Through interviews with Jean, I learned of the varying strategies and techniques that she used to engage Stacy in the process. For example, she shared her beliefs about children with such significant disabilities needing more intensive services and therapy while also valuing family-centered service provision. She shared her experience of being a grandmother wanting what's best for her grandchild as well as her experience of trying to balance discovering herself as a single mother against being supported by her own mother. Jean also sought to understand Stacy's perspectives, her world, and her past. For example, the first goal on Melina's IFSP was to build a relationship with Stacy, Melina, and Stacy's mother. Jean indicated to me that she values this and that this is usually the first goal of every IFSP she develops. Jean utilized this time to get to know Stacy through conversations and makes this a goal with all of her clients' families because she believes that it helps her be intentional and accountable about developing relationships (understanding others in the process of developing cultural reciprocity). The vignette demonstrates how Jean so delicately and admirably validated Stacy's beliefs and needs while sharing her beliefs and then working to collaboratively generate a mutually agreed-upon goal. Jean recognized how important it was to Stacy for Melina to "be happy" and to have experiences like other children. She also realized that Stacy was trying and wanted to do what was best for Melina, yet Jean realized that this was challenging given the complexities of Melina's disabilities (which would be challenging for most parents) and Stacy's limited capacity to fully understand given her age as well as her own learning disability.

One of the strategies that Jean used to respect and share cultural differences and to then collaboratively develop a common goal included praising Stacy's strengths. Jean worked to affirm Stacy for listening during the sessions and for being creative in the follow-through. Jean also modeled the behavior that she hoped Stacy would emulate, such as singing "I Love You" to Melina while gently rubbing her arms. This provided Stacy with an example of how she should interact with Melina without criticizing Stacy's approach. In addition, Jean was willing to accept responsibility for not providing Stacy all the information that perhaps she could have used when creating the in-home circus. Jean's actions communicated that this was in fact a partnership and further communicated that "professionals can make mistakes." Asking Stacy where she got the disco ball also validated Stacy as a partner who had pertinent information to bring to the table. Finally, Jean shared her beliefs in a nonjudgmental manner while validating Stacy's desires for Melina to be happy and like other children her age, which could be considered a characteristic of the "culture of parenthood" or perhaps the "culture of adolescence."

Your Story

Let's return to our analysis of the film *Losing Isaiah* (Koch & Foner, 1995). The previous two "Your Story" exercises asked you to perform the first two steps of the process of cultural reciprocity. Now, to engage in Steps 3 and 4, rewrite the ending of the movie to include scenes between Kyla, Isaiah's mother, and you, as Isaiah's teacher. The scenes should depict meetings with Kyla to discuss strategies to assist Isaiah in class and should reflect your perspectives and collaborative efforts toward understanding the following hypothetical positions of Kyla: 1) spanking is a valid form of discipline; 2) there is a distinct division between the role of the teacher and the role of the parent, and parental involvement is limited to sending the child to school fed, clothed, and rested; and 3) assessment is just another way to label and track black boys into special education where there is no return. Your dialogue should reflect a sharing of your values and beliefs, an acknowledgment of Kyla's values and beliefs, and a collaborative exchange in which you reach mutually agreed-upon goals. Be mindful of your responses in the previous "Your Story" section with respect to your values, beliefs, and experiences in relation to all that you felt about and have uncovered about Kyla historically, culturally, and experientially.

SUMMARY

A human being is a part of the whole that we call the universe, a part limited in time and space. He experiences himself, his thoughts and feelings, as something separated from the rest—a kind of optical illusion of his consciousness. This illusion is a prison for us, restricting us to our personal desires and to affection for only the few people nearest us. Our task must be to free ourselves from this prison by widening our circle of compassion to embrace all living beings and all of nature.

Albert Einstein

The intent of this chapter was to provide you, the reader, with insights into my transformational journey as I sought to develop culturally reciprocal relationships with adolescent mothers whose values, beliefs, and experiences differed significantly from my own. By sharing my experiences, it is my hope that you recognize and understand that the development of a posture of cultural reciprocity is more than a tool or strategy that is applied to a given situation; it is an attitude or a way of being. Each vignette and my subsequent analysis of it reveals the intentionality and the depth required in formulating culturally reciprocal relationships. Understanding self, seeking to understand others, explicitly respecting and explaining cultural differences, and then working collaboratively to adjust and adapt recommendations requires a commitment to the process; a willingness to be vulnerable and honest; and an investment in the time required for effective implementation. Every relationship and interaction should be a personally transforming journey that transcends research and practice. I encourage you to immerse yourself completely as you work toward the development of culturally reciprocal relationships.

Chapter 8

Stories of Transformation

Eva Thorp and Monimalika Day

I have always felt that the action most worth watching is not at the center of things but where the edges meet. I like shorelines, weather fronts, international borders. There are interesting frictions and incongruities in these places, and often if you stand at that point of tangency, you can see both sides better than if you were in the middle of either one. This is especially true, I think when the apposition is cultural.

Anne Fadiman

We, the authors of this chapter, both teach in an early childhood special education program at a university located near a large metropolitan city in a mid-Atlantic state. The population in this area is very diverse, and we have a strong emphasis on preparing professionals and teacher candidates in the field of early childhood and early childhood special education to serve families and children from diverse cultural and linguistic backgrounds. As a part of that emphasis, since the beginning of our collaboration in 2005, we have both spent much time exploring ways to teach these preservice professionals the cultural reciprocity process.

The cultural reciprocity process is a relationship-based approach initiated by special educators to develop collaborative relationships with families (Harry, Kalyanpur, & Day, 1999). In our experience, the fact that cultural reciprocity is a process rather than a set of well-defined strategies holds great promise but is also challenging for students, because most of them are drawn toward strategies that appear to be more straightforward. As teacher educators, we have struggled with this problem and have sought ways to engage students in the critical thinking, self-reflection, and cultural discourse that prepares educators to implement the process of cultural reciprocity. Harry and colleagues (1999) have explored in great detail the importance of using case studies to engage students in a discussion of cultural reciprocity. One variation on the use of case studies is the use of students' own life experiences, particularly those they have found perplexing. We refer to these experiences as *cultural dilemmas*. Cultural dilemmas emerge from cultural discontinuities that come from interactions with those whose culture or language is different from one's own. As in the Fadiman quote, cultural dilemmas occur at the "point of tangency," when individuals from two cultures interact and friction or incongruity occurs. Cultural dilemmas indicate that one's cultural beliefs, values, or assumptions have been challenged

137

(Sánchez & Thorp, 2008; Thorp & Sánchez, 1998). Our research suggests that cultural dilemmas can be a powerful strategy to engage students in exploring the cultural reciprocity process, providing them with sustained opportunities to focus on the self-awareness (Step 1) and perspective-taking (Step 2) aspects of cultural reciprocity.

OUR CONTEXT

Because our approach to teaching this process is anchored in our own experiences, it is essential that we begin by reflecting on our own stories. In this section, we describe our personal stories, the setting for our work, and the need for a focus on both cultural reciprocity and the use of cultural dilemmas.

Our Journey

Monimalika, who goes by Moni, identifies herself as an immigrant from India, who has developed strong connections with her students and colleagues in the United States. She grew up in a family in which both of her parents were committed to exploring social justice issues but in somewhat different ways. Whereas her father approached it more from a sociopolitical perspective, her mother approached it from a spiritual perspective grounded in the key principles of Hinduism. Moni developed a strong commitment to working with families of children with disabilities during her training as a doctoral student, when she had the opportunity to work closely with Harry and Kalyanpur to coauthor the book on case studies in cultural reciprocity (Harry, Kalyanpur, & Day, 1999).

Eva identifies herself as a Caucasian American with roots in the United States' Midwest. Like Moni, she grew up with parents who shared a commitment to social justice. She benefited from many interactions with individuals from different cultural communities who early on challenged her to reflect on her own relative privilege and to be aware of the different lenses people bring to the same experiences. She is strongly committed to preparing early childhood educators to work effectively with children and families from various backgrounds. Along with Dr. Sylvia Sánchez, Eva established the Unified Transformative Early Education Model program, which was the nation's first preservice program integrating the perspectives of bilingual education, multicultural education, early childhood special education, and early childhood education. Drawing on the principles of reflection outlined by Brookfield (1995), they used cultural dilemmas to explore different dimensions of culture when working with families. Eva feels that her own development has benefited from co-teaching with faculty whose diverse backgrounds differed from her own.

Description of the Program

Since 2007, we, Eva and Moni, have worked collaboratively on the Special Educators Entering a Diverse Society project, a personnel preparation grant funded by the Office of Special Education Programs to prepare early childhood special educators to work effectively with children and families from diverse cultural and linguistic backgrounds. We also attempt to recruit students who themselves come from diverse cultural experiences. Our students come to the program with an understanding that

Table 8.1. Assignments on cultural reciprocity

Steps of cultural reciprocity	Assignment	Courses
Step 1: Self-awareness Step 2: Learning about other cultures	Family story project	Families of children with special needs
Step 1: Self-awareness Step 2: Learning about other cultures	Dilemma narratives	Field experience and internships
Step 1: Self-awareness Step 2: Learning about other cultures Step 3: Explaining recommendations Step 4: Collaborating	Cultural reciprocity project (developing a culturally responsive plan with a family)	Early intervention
Step 1: Self-awareness Step 2: Learning about other cultures Step 3: Explaining recommendations Step 4: Collaborating	Teacher action research with a component on addressing families' needs	Special education research
Step 1: Self-awareness Step 2: Learning about other cultures Step 3: Explaining recommendations Step 4: Collaborating	Journals	Internships

culturally and linguistically diverse young learners are the focus of the program; however, we recognize that each student brings his or her own cultural lens and that that lens may support or impede the individual in his or her efforts to engage in collaborative interactions with families. Often, students learn about best practices in university settings but have a difficult time implementing them. For example, merely reading about family-centered practices, which is a cornerstone of early intervention, does not prepare students for the real work involved in collaborating with families from other cultures. We have developed a program structure that embeds several assignments on cultural reciprocity in different courses or internships in an integrated manner for a period of 2 years. During these assignments students interact with families from other cultures and often experience a discontinuity; that is, their new learning from interactions with a family does not fit their existing ways of thinking, and they have difficulty making sense of these experiences (Thorp & Sánchez, 1998).

The program intentionally uses a multipronged approach to enable our students to internalize cultural reciprocity: 1) Throughout the program, we scaffold students' conceptual understanding of culturally responsive teaching through a sequence of courses grounded in multicultural theory, responsive pedagogy, and evidence-based approaches to teaching young children with disabilities and their families (refer to Table 8.1 for an overview of these course experiences); 2) we directly teach the cultural reciprocity approach in the context of a course on culturally and linguistically diverse families of young children with disabilities; 3) we integrate an assignment into an early intervention course in which students are asked to apply cultural reciprocity in their interactions with a family with whom they are working; 4) we teach students about the use of critical reflection and ask them to consider their interactions with families in the light of the concept of cultural reciprocity; and 5) we introduce students to the power of cultural dilemmas and provide instruction on how to use the strategy of cultural dilemmas to address more explicitly elements of their interactions with families that they have found to be perplexing or challenging.

The Need

Our university is located close to a major metropolitan city where, since the 1990s, there has been a dramatic influx of immigrants, particularly from Latin America, Asia, and Africa. This shift in the population has heightened some students' awareness of the need for cross-cultural work but has prompted others to take a more defensive posture as they feel that their European American cultural identity is being threatened. Also, as is true throughout the country (Kushner & Ortiz, 2000), the service providers in many school districts are primarily from European American backgrounds, whereas many of the families they serve are Latino, African, or Asian.

Gay (2010), Gonzalez-Mena (2008), and other scholars have noted that mainstream educators often view the parenting practices of non-mainstream cultures as inappropriate. Traditionally, children with special needs and their families have been marginalized by the mainstream society. All too often, faculty who prepare early childhood special educators find that teacher candidates view families of children with disabilities from a deficit perspective. This view is manifested in blaming parents for the children's developmental delays, judging parents as being overprotective, and labeling parents as being "in denial" (Gallagher, Fialka, Rhodes, & Arceneaux, 2002). Professionals in the field of special education frequently use the term denial, which is essentially a psychiatric label, when there is a disagreement between the family and the providers (Gallagher et al., 2002; Harry, 1997). This may reflect providers' lack of understanding of the sociocultural context in which disabilities are defined, specifically that special education labels are socially constructed rather than fixed and that they reflect the cultural values of a society (Harry, Kalyanpur, & Day, 1999; Howard, Bicard, & Cavanaugh, 2007; Shapiro, 2003; Skrtic, 2004). In this manner, educators begin to dehumanize (Freire, 2006) parents of children with special needs. It is our view that this posture of labeling the parents relieves the provider from the responsibility of collaborating with the parents to engage in authentic dialogue regarding the disability and the child's needs. Parents of young children with special needs are especially vulnerable to being labeled, as many of them are just learning about the diagnosis and are in the process of understanding the child's disability. As demonstrated in the scenarios described later in this chapter, early childhood special education candidates sometimes develop these biases from subtle and sometimes not-so-subtle messages from professionals in special education programs.

As teacher educators, we are often perplexed by the frequency with which we encounter these deficit perspectives. Rather than blaming our students, we are motivated to create a learning space where they can struggle with conflicting messages, reflect on their own cultural lenses, deconstruct mainstream social biases, and finally engage in a conscious effort to explore new ideas and processes.

CULTURAL DILEMMAS

Thorp and Sánchez (1998) define cultural dilemmas as "a perceived discrepancy that occurs in the experience of a student when applying university coursework to work with children and families" (p. 20). The fact that the discontinuity emerges from the direct experience of the student is central to the power of using cultural dilemmas when compared to the use of case studies, as students see the dilemmas as their own and are motivated to work through them. The cognitive dissonance experienced by the students when they perceive a conflict between their own values and assumptions and the behavior and attitudes of the families with whom they are working may cause them to hastily seek congruence with a quick solution. As teacher educators, our goal is to help them pause and avoid making quick decisions; instead, we encourage students to stay in this state of discontinuity (Brookfield, 1995; Day, DeMulder, & Stribling, 2010). We do so by requiring students to document the dilemma as a structured narrative, using a form that clearly describes the key elements. In doing so, the students name the dilemmas and acknowledge ownership of them, recognizing that others might not share their perspective.

Using Cultural Dilemmas to Practice Cultural Reciprocity

We view cultural dilemmas as opportunities that allow students to recognize situations for which they might need to implement the process of cultural reciprocity. The use of cultural dilemmas as an instructional strategy can have a powerful impact on learning. As Brookfield (1995) notes, dilemmas are everpresent in the daily practice of teachers, presenting ethical and methodological challenges. When students do not consciously analyze dilemmas, they risk experiencing disparate feelings of discomfort: 1) a sense of isolation, as in "I am alone in this. Everyone else seems to understand"; and/or 2) a sense of judgment, as in "What is wrong with these families? Why don't they do, believe, and/or behave in the way that I think is right?" Later in this chapter, we describe a process of systematically addressing dilemmas, which we term *choreographing*. When students systematically address dilemmas, they come to realize the power of multiple perspectives and approaches and, as a consequence, are able to link the theory learned in coursework to actual practice. Ultimately, it is our view that in dealing with dilemmas, we enable the students to deeply engage in the first two steps of the cultural reciprocity process and to begin to consider how their new understanding of dilemmas might provide guidance for Steps 3 and 4 in subsequent interactions with families.

The cultural dilemma strategy has multiple goals: Broadly, the goal is to assist the student to enter a "3rd space." According to Barrera, Corso, and Macpherson (2003), the "3rd space focuses on creatively reframing contradictions into paradoxes. As such, it invites practitioners to make a fundamental shift from dualistic, exclusive perceptions of reality and to adopt a mindset that integrates the complementary aspects of diverse values, behaviors, and beliefs into a new whole" (p. 75). Applying the cultural dilemma strategy allows students to address the discontinuities they experience; reframe situations and view them from multiple perspectives; negotiate two or more cultural realities; move from dualistic thinking to identifying multiple possible responses to a dilemma; and recognize that "staying in" a dilemma results in avoiding judgment, thus promoting moral professionalism and ethical decision making in the service of cultural reciprocity with families (Brookfield, 1995; Day et al., 2010).

The cultural dilemma strategy can be used both in group settings and with individual students. When addressed in a group setting, using the dilemma strategy brings benefit to the individual student whose dilemma becomes the focus of discussion. At the same time, the types of dilemmas students experience may have some similarities. As a result, each member of a group of students may resonate with one student's particular dilemma and, through processing that dilemma together, develop new skills that he or she can apply to better understanding his or her own dilemmas. It is the role of the instructor to identify quickly those dilemmas that might have the potential for the highest degree of transformation among the group members. We call these powerful dilemmas. Powerful dilemmas have multiple attributes. They come from deeply felt personal experience. Often, it is the dilemma that is the most painful and about which the student may feel the most isolated or embarrassed that has the most potential for transformation. Powerful dilemmas tap into cultural biases. For example, a student once described a dilemma she had with a family. In describing the family, she said, "All four children share one bedroom. They don't have their own rooms for reading and doing homework like we all did." In that statement, she demonstrated her assumptions about what children need to succeed academically. By exploring this dilemma it became possible for her to recognize her cultural bias and to recognize that, even among her classmates and her instructors, there were varied meanings attributed to the situation. Thus, she was able to become less ethnocentric in her approach.

Preparing for Dilemma Work

As mentioned earlier, the use of dilemmas is woven into an intentional sequence of courses and assignments that support the development of cultural reciprocity (again, see Table 8.1). Direct dilemma work occurs in the context of students' field experiences. These include two field-based assignments in which students learn directly from a family from a culture other than their own, and two internships, one with infants and toddlers with disabilities and their families and one in preschool classrooms providing services to young children with disabilities. As students undertake their field experiences, they also participate in structured group meetings during which they can share their dilemmas and engage in a variety of activities to support perspective taking and problem solving.

Quite simply, we ask students to briefly describe an interaction that has been perplexing or confusing to them. They are given a form (Thorp, 2009) on which they describe the setting, the people involved, and the details of the dilemma. They do not write a detailed analysis nor are they asked to come up with any possible course of action. In fact, we call this "Just the Facts, Ma'am," to remind them that it is the dilemma itself that provides the meat for the hard work of reflection and application to cultural reciprocity.

Although this seems straightforward, we have learned that it does not come naturally. Several aspects need to be addressed to ensure that the dilemmas we receive are meaningful and lend themselves to critical reflection. First, students need to be reminded to describe a single event that presented itself as a dilemma to them. We have found that when students do not write about a single event, they may start to generalize and become judgmental. We point out to the students that when they generalize a situation, they lose the opportunity to explore alternate situation-specific courses of action. For example, consider a student's description of a particular home visit during which a mother appeared unprepared for the visit although the appointment time had been agreed upon: "Mrs. Nguyen and I had scheduled the home visit for 2:00 Monday, but when I got there, she wasn't home. I waited, and she showed up at 2:30." Contrast that description to a student describing a series of such events: "Mrs. Nguyen is never ready for home visits. We call and call, and we give her an appointment card, but still she seems surprised when we show up." In the first instance, the student can begin to think about how it felt for her, the student, to arrive and feel that the family was unprepared as well as to wonder what might have been the parent's understanding of the appointment or what might have prevented the parent from being there at the appointed time. In the second instance, the student has already begun to generalize about this family and, in fact, judge them, despite the complete lack of information regarding how often this has happened or why, and the student's view of the family may have become firmly calcified as resistant or uncooperative.

In preparing their dilemma narratives, we also remind the students to avoid the use of any judgment words, such as *never* or *always*, or assumption phrases, such as *families like this* or *families from that country*. This is critical for entering the 3rd space. It is extremely challenging to recognize a dilemma without beginning to jump to judgments and conclusions. The degree to which we can stay with the dilemma creates a space for looking for multiple interpretations, and, in the case of cultural reciprocity, to deeply explore the attitudes and assumptions one brings to the dilemma and to begin to wonder what one needs to understand about the family to better make sense of the dilemma and identify possible responses. Thus, the student can spend time reflecting on the meaning of appointment and being ready as well as her own attitudes about time and timeliness and begin to wonder what these mean for the family.

CATEGORIES OF DILEMMAS IN SPECIAL EDUCATION

We have found that cultural dilemmas fall into several broad categories. As students prepare to become culturally responsive early childhood special educators, many specific dilemmas arise related to interactions with children and families from diverse cultural communities. In this chapter, we focus on dilemmas related to goals, roles and relationships, and intervention approaches to service delivery. It is important to note that although some of these dilemmas emerge from interactions with families, others may include interactions with staff members whose views challenge what the student has already learned about culturally responsive practices.

Goals for the Child

When collecting data for their longitudinal study on families, Harry and colleagues (1999) came across several instances during which, in keeping with the requirements of IDEA, professionals asked parents what their goals were for the IFSP or IEP but were then unable to explore the goal collaboratively when the parents' expectations did not match their own. In the early intervention course, we have embedded an assignment on cultural reciprocity during which students have to interview a family, find out its goals for the child, and develop a responsive plan for the next home visit. Next, Carmen reports her dilemma as one father shares his vision for his daughter:

> An important dilemma that I faced was when the father expressed his expectations for Emma as she grows up. As I heard these parents' expectations for their daughter with Down syndrome that included Emma becoming a writer, I could not avoid feeling sad and worried because, somehow, I think some of their expectations are idealistic. During this part of the conversation, I experienced some sort of difficulties that relate to the second and third cultural reciprocity steps concerning the family's assumptions and beliefs about the child's disabilities and those of the special education program.

Having learned about the process of cultural reciprocity and the sociocultural perspectives on disability, Carmen does not simply dismiss the parents' view as "denial," as many professionals would do under the circumstances (Gallagher et al., 2002). Here, Carmen recognizes the discrepancy of her view of the child's ability and the parents' view of the child's ability and phrases it as a dilemma. This alerts her that she needs to apply the process of cultural reciprocity, and she begins by reflecting on her own perspective. Moreover, she recognizes her bias (Step 1) and identifies her struggles using the cultural reciprocity process. She states clearly that she finds it difficult to engage in Step 2, which requires her to engage the family in a dialogue to get a better understanding of their perspective. She also has difficulty with moving to Step 3, which requires her to explain the cultural underpinnings of her own view on this issue. In the following quotation, Carmen demonstrates an understanding that she needs to pause and reflect, as her own expectations are grounded in the cultural assumptions regarding disability in the field of special education.

Nevertheless, I felt comfortable taking a few seconds to think about what they were saying. After this, I commented that parents always want the best for their children and that all children (typically and atypically developing) show diverse skills and difficulties that need to be addressed as they go through the school years. And, just like their other three children might struggle in school and in life with different issues, Emma will also have to deal with her own issues. One way or the other, I know they will realize with time the implications of Down syndrome on their daughter's life."

During class discussions, Carmen revealed that she used a strategy that we call "That Reminds Me Of…" to bring the two perspectives together and create some congruence before responding to the parents. She mentioned that as she recognized the dilemma and stopped to reflect on it, she thought of her own experience of being a parent of two teenage sons and the uncertainties about their futures. This allowed her to connect with the parents' hopes and dreams and respond to them in an empathic way.

Views of Family Roles and Relationships

Views of what is considered to be a "normal" family as opposed to one that is deemed strange or dysfunctional often are grounded in an individual's own early experiences. The notion of a two-parent family with a father and a mother is often viewed as normal in the mainstream United States; however, family composition and responsibilities differ based on cultural backgrounds and sexual preferences (Turnbull et al., 2011). Many professionals struggle to understand same-sex parents and form relationships with them. In a course on families, Amanda, an early childhood special educator, shared her discomfort in working with Tom's family, as both parents were male and the child referred to one of them as "Mommy." She was puzzled by the situation and wondered how she could respond in a supportive way. In this situation, the advice from her colleagues further complicated the situation. After listening to her, we encouraged her to work with this family on the family story assignment, which provides an opportunity for students to practice the first two steps of cultural reciprocity. We had several discussions in class regarding this dilemma, and the whole class benefited much from this experience. Next is an excerpt from Amanda's first reflective paper, in which she clearly delineates how she is perplexed by her own re-action to this situation and is experiencing a cultural discontinuity.

> *The most uncomfortable part of this process for me has been putting thought into why I have such a strong reaction and aversion to acknowledging that Tom calls his parents "Mommy and Daddy." I felt placed in the middle of an uncomfortable situation and controversy when fellow staff members indicated that they thought I should broach the issue with the parents and have them change the name for "Mommy."*

Through class discussions and comments on her papers, we encouraged Amanda to recognize that she was dealing with two dilemmas. First, she was struggling with her own reaction to the same-sex family structure and, second, she was dealing with expectations from her colleagues that she tackle the issue in a specific manner. In such a situation, when facilitating the discussion, we ask students to separate out the different dilemmas and begin to explore each separately. Following class discussions, Amanda was able to separate the two dilemmas. She also reflected on her own experiences and early memories to identify what she defined as a normal family. As she began to understand that her definition of a normal family was grounded in her own cultural experiences and assumptions, she began to accept the family structure and the roles assumed by Tom's parents. Amanda visited the family twice for her assignment and had extensive conversations regarding the child's special needs. As she interacted with the parents, she became comfortable with their lifestyle. This excerpt was taken from her third reflective paper and explains her journey from experiencing the discontinuity to moving toward continuity.

> *One main reason I was so uncomfortable addressing the issue of what the child calls his parents is that I felt pressure from other staff members to fix something that, in my opinion, may not be broken. By addressing the parents' names with the family, we are placing one huge judgment on them that what they are doing is wrong. That is not our job. I have become more comfortable with the parents' names despite how different it is from my own upbringing. My question to myself then became, "If I am just being judgmental of the parents, is there any other reason why I need to be concerned with what Tom calls his parents?"*

Amanda worked through the first dilemma and clearly identified her biases, which allowed her to question her own perspective and the suggestions of her colleagues. At this point, she began to question her colleagues' suggestions and wondered whether she needed to intervene in any way to change how the child addressed his parents. She turned to her readings (another component of the cultural dilemma strategy) to clarify her role in this situation as a culturally responsive provider.

> *I referred to my class readings and, as Turnbull and colleagues (2011) note, although adoptive parents on the whole have similar coping skills as birth parents, many children of same-sex marriages are likely to be bullied. My obligation to [the parents] now becomes putting thought into how I should and can deal with possible future bullying.*

Based on the readings, Amanda decided that she needed to find ways to discuss how children of same-sex parents may be teased or bullied in schools. She became interested in finding out if Tom's parents were aware of this issue and, if so, how they planned to address it. Furthermore, she became curious about how she could support the parents to prepare and protect Tom. Thus, from feeling that she needed to correct how the child addressed his parents to wanting to intervene and protect the child from bullying in school, Amanda was able to work through her dilemma by applying the process of cultural reciprocity and develop a more supportive role with the family.

Intervention Approaches to Service Delivery

IDEA recommends that early childhood special educators serve children in their natural environments using the resources available to the family in that environment and building on the strengths of the family's natural ways of interacting and playing with its children. The effectiveness of this approach has been clearly established. However, when students and professionals enter families' homes and notice a lack of toys and books in the child's environment, they often are tempted to bring in a bag of toys. We, the authors, have encountered this dilemma on several occasions and refer to it as the "toy bag dilemma." It is important to note that this dilemma is quite prevalent even though early intervention programs have adopted a policy that instructs service providers not to bring in toy bags during home visits. Nicole encountered this dilemma as she conducted home visits with her cooperating teacher in an early intervention program during her first internship and explored it through journal entries and class discussions.

> I struggled with this situation since I know that it is not the practice of this agency to bring a toy bag into the home of a family. We have also discussed this in class with regard to how this might make the family feel and how the child might feel when it is time for the educator to leave with the toys. It was upsetting for me to see that these children had so few materials to play with. I was having a hard time considering how the children could play without toys. Their environment was so sparse in comparison to how I live and that caused me some distress—my assumption was that the family was "needy" and that the children did not have enough. I also had a dilemma about the fact that the educator I am shadowing brought a toy bag into the house anyway. She stated that she is not sure "if the mom believes in toys."

Nicole, who is genuinely committed to working with families from diverse cultures and was willing to reflect on her own background, shared this dilemma in a class on child development. She did not need much help from us to realize that her judgment of the family being "needy" stemmed from the privileges she enjoyed as a child and an adult. We introduced the concept of *developmental pathways* (Weisner, 2002) and discussed how some families value interdependence rather independence, which was new to her. We had lengthy discussions on how the use of tools is valued in the mainstream U.S. culture and is rooted in the value of independence. Toys are primarily tools to engage children in their play, and not all societies view their importance in the same way. For example, many societies in which children care for their younger siblings do not care as much about playing with dolls (Rogoff, 2003). As a result of this conversation, Nicole became more open to exploring the possibility of not bringing in a bag of toys and grew rather angry when a special educator suggested otherwise. The following is a journal entry from her second internship. It also serves to describe how the dilemmas that students encounter with families are complicated by the dilemmas that emerge from their interactions with co-workers.

> *I was really surprised at some of the things she said to me. She said that they tried to plan with families and not bring materials with them but "it just didn't work." That seemed like such an out [meaning that this was a way to ignore the responsibility to collaborate with the family]—I couldn't understand what she meant. She also said something about the fact that "You know, we are working with the population on Route 1"—how on earth could you possibly generalize about an entire group of people just based upon their geographic location? It really made me kind of mad and made me feel defensive for the families we are working with. It seemed like such an "us" vs. "them" way of thinking—the haves and the have-nots. This journal entry is full of things she said because they had such a strong impact on me and I wrote things down as soon as she walked away from my desk. And then, finally, when I was talking to her about working in natural environments, she said, "I know it's best practice...." But she told me to at least "bring a little bag of tricks." She just wouldn't let it go.*

The anger reflected in the entry suggests that Nicole's perspective had shifted and her dilemma now was to work with professionals who believed she needed to bring a bag of toys and find ways to be an ally with families and an advocate for them. Nicole continued to explore this dilemma over many months and through different assignments. In a course focused on special education research, she worked with immigrant families from low-income neighborhoods for her action research project.

> *I worked with a family during my internship that did not have ready access to more than a few children's books—the mother was very skilled at teaching her child but could benefit from more resources. During conversations with the mother, I learned that they would be interested in obtaining a library card, and we agreed to investigate the library system together. We took two visits to the library together during [home] visits, and the family was able to get a library card and access literacy materials on its own to facilitate working with the child on identified goals. Helping to empower this family would provide the child with the most benefit, and I feel that this project with this family was one of my greatest accomplishments during my internship.*

Similar to the previous situation, Nicole felt that this family did not have adequate books at home. However, instead of bringing in books, she responded by introducing the family to some of the resources in the community, thus empowering the family. Currently, she is working as a special educator in an early intervention program, and we recently invited her to share her dilemmas with the students in the program. Indeed, it was very rewarding to hear that an important principle for her is to never bring a toy bag into any family's home. For situations in which she feels a child may benefit from a certain toy, she plans with the family to address that need. It was a real joy to hear that she was preparing to present a workshop on how to conduct home visits without a toy bag at a state conference. We have asked her to write a journal article on this topic to support her efforts to advocate for families and inspire other professionals by sharing her story.

Here we have focused primarily on discussing dilemmas that emerge from differences in perspectives between the early childhood special educator and the family. It is important to note that dilemmas also may emerge from interactions with colleagues (such as occurred with Nicole). It is important to acknowledge these as well, because students will be entering a service delivery culture that may challenge their use of culturally responsive practices and will need to find productive ways to engage in dialogue with colleagues in the same ways they practice culturally responsive dialogue with families. In addition, the dilemmas reported by Amanda and Nicole illustrate how multiple dilemmas may be embedded in one dilemma. When this happens, faculty members can play a critical role to help students identify the various dilemmas and work through each of them separately.

CHOREOGRAPHING DILEMMAS

In many ways, we find assisting students to make meaning of their dilemmas to be like a dance; therefore, we describe what we do once students have described their dilemmas as "choreographing dilemmas." Students come to class with dilemmas from their lived experience, and we want each student to have a chance to describe his or her own dilemma. Then, as mentioned earlier, we need to quickly decide if, among those, there are one or more dilemmas that lend themselves to specifically enhancing the students' skills of cultural reciprocity. As students become more experienced with the dilemma approach, they become a part of this process of selecting a dilemma for group work. Having identified one or more dilemmas for deeper work, we select a strategy for addressing the dilemma from which the entire group can benefit. Finally, we provide opportunities for each student to return to his or her own dilemma and reflect on how that strategy might assist him or her in reframing or addressing his or her own dilemmas.

According to Sánchez and Thorp (2008), the primary goals in this process are to assist students to 1) identify and acknowledge dilemmas and remain in a state of discontinuity rather than jumping to solutions, 2) describe dilemmas from a cultural perspective in ways that ensure that they see themselves at the center of the dilemma, 3) interpret personal and professional meanings of the dilemma through interpersonal dialogue and systematic problem solving, and 4) practice applying their new understandings to deepen relationships with families.

We use the different steps of the cultural reciprocity process to pose questions and scaffold the students' learning by analyzing the dilemma in depth. Because the students are bringing their dilemma narratives to class, we are able primarily to scaffold an intensive focus on self-awareness (Step 1) and perspective-taking (Step 2). It is our goal that students are able to use what they learned from the process of analyzing the dilemma in class to plan for how they would proceed to Step 3 (discussing their different perspectives) and Step 4 (moving forward collaboratively) in subsequent interactions with a family. However, we also recognize that in some instances, the dilemma may only be experienced by the student and not by the family; therefore, the work to be done is that of the student exploring why it is a dilemma for him or her. Having discovered that, there may be no need to intervene and dialogue with the family. Rather, the student's changed perspective likely will create a more productive space for future interactions with families as the student becomes more alert to his or her assumptions and biases.

Step 1: Self-Awareness and Discussion of Personal Meanings

According to Harry (1992a), self-awareness is an essential step in the process of forming collaborative relationships. To work through this step, we ask students to identify the values (the importance or worth), beliefs (what is regarded as truth), and assumptions (a working hypothesis based on prior experience) that contribute to how they view the situation. Focusing on these three aspects of culture provides practitioners with a framework to identify their cultural lens and not be overwhelmed by the complex definitions of culture. We also ask students to reflect on their early experiences to identify the roots of their cultural beliefs. The goal is to move students from an overt or covert level of self-awareness to more subtle levels of self-awareness (Kalyanpur & Harry, 1999).

These are the questions that are really at the heart of Step 1 of cultural reciprocity. What we hope is that the students will look closely at their dilemmas to discern the hidden meanings they hold that made the dilemma a dilemma for them in the first place. One of the beautiful outcomes of this process is that students see that not everyone (even among their peers) experiences the same event as a dilemma.

How Did the Dilemma Make You Feel?   Recognizing that there are feelings associated with a dilemma seems obvious but is often missed in the moment. Students can set their feelings aside by merely identifying them. Sometimes, we ask the student to imagine placing their feelings on the table or crumpling them up and throwing them away. The students' feelings are acknowledged, but they can be set aside long enough for the students to move on to wondering about other elements of the dilemma.

Can You Think of a Time Early in Your Life When You Felt the Same Way?   Sometimes, a student experiencing a dilemma is, in truth, reexperiencing a feeling from earlier in life. A student angry at a parent who has missed an appointment may, in fact, be recalling his or her own parent who was chronically late and missed an important event. Recognizing that feelings may come from a student's early experience enables the student to recognize that "that was then, but in this moment I can see that I don't have to worry about that anymore. My feelings are from another time."

What Beliefs, Values, and/or Assumptions About Children and Families May Be Influencing Your View of the Dilemma?   This question allows students to look beneath the dilemma to explore what their discomfort says about what they hold to be "truths" about children and families. We ask the students to explore what beliefs led to a concern about a child not having enough toys or whether children have their own bedrooms or how and when children are fed. Many people hold strong beliefs about child-rearing practices. When we assume the role of teacher in an institutional setting, one grounded in the beliefs of the dominant culture, all too often these beliefs take on the aura of "truth" (Gay, 2010). Exploring beliefs, values, and assumptions allows us, as faculty members, to assist students to begin the arduous task of separating beliefs from truths. Without being forced to let go of their beliefs or assumptions, they can begin to see that other views exist. Ideally, this begins to happen just in the process of sharing dilemmas with other students.

How Might Others in Your Family View This Dilemma?   Sometimes, we call the activities organized to address this question "Wisdom of the Elders." We ask students to examine whether the beliefs, values, and assumptions about children and families may have changed even in their own family culture. One way to do this is to have students think about sayings they heard from their grandmothers that were intended to guide behavior. Students can then be asked whether they would still agree with the sayings or how things might have changed. Another way to guide more flexible thinking about child-rearing truths is to have students think about how previous generations or even relatively close generations in their own family culture have approached things such as behavior and punishment, sleeping in a family bed, or extended breastfeeding. In addition, students may share how these practices vary within their own group. One student brought a dilemma about what she perceived to be a family's chaotic meal patterns with "no limits set for the children" and "children being allowed to carry their food around the house." Another student challenged her peer, describing her own upbringing in an immigrant Italian family home. She reported, "My mother followed us around with a spoon in her hand, saying, 'Eat. Eat.' It was just important to her that we eat. She didn't require us to eat only at the table at a particular time."

It can be seen that these questions around personal meanings are all addressed without even addressing what might be going on for the families or others in the dilemma. Instead, these questions give students the time to look at who they are in the dilemma, what they bring to the situation, and how that colors their experience of the dilemma. As such, these questions are critical to Step 1 of cultural reciprocity.

Step 2: Preparing to Learn from Families by Engaging in Perspective Taking

Because it is our hope to support student transformation to a reciprocal stance, we have developed multiple questions that are associated with Step 2 of cultural reciprocity that allow the student to look more deeply at the perspectives of the other people in the dilemma.

What Might the Family's Perspective Be on the Very Same Dilemma?
Several activities may help students think about this question and help them ponder whether, in fact, the other person in the dilemma even experienced the situation as a dilemma. One very telling approach is to have the student step into the same event but in the role of the parent or family member with whom he or she experienced the dilemma. You may ask the student to turn over his or her dilemma sheet and write it as if the parent had been asked to write it. Or, ask the student to do a role play in which another classmate plays the student and the student with the dilemma plays the family member. In both instances, advise the student to stay only with the event as described and not to add any more detail or interpretation—just turn the lens in another direction. Doing either of these activities should allow the student to begin to see the richness of the story he or she had first experienced as so straightforward and, it is hoped, begin to appreciate the many ways people interpret the very same shared event.

What Are Some of the Beliefs, Attitudes, and/or Assumptions that the Parent or Family Member Might Hold?   In this instance, it is very important to stress the word *might*. That is, the student does not yet know, with certainty,

what those beliefs, attitudes, and/or assumptions might be, but we can begin to ask the student to wonder about some possible deeply held beliefs or truths that could account for the behavior the student found disconcerting. In that regard, it is also important to make sure that the student avoids going to any previously held stereotypes; for example, "I know that families from that culture don't believe in independence." Although the student may have learned something about another culture's beliefs or values, he or she cannot know with certainty what this family believes. Rather, we encourage the student to identify possible interpretations from the perspective of beliefs and values. This approach can also help him or her to interpret challenging actions from a strengths perspective. One way to encourage this is to have the student write down the specific behavior that was difficult to understand and then complete the following sentences: "When the parent did that, it may mean that she believes _____ about children. This might be a strength because _____."

As an example, we offer a story about a dimension of culture that frequently comes up with our students—that of time. Little seems to be more frustrating to them than a family who has come late for an appointment. They take it personally. They feel that they are not valued. They may even think that this parent does not care about his or her child. Eva shares a story about a friend visiting from South Africa. One day, he accompanied her to work, and she was rather hurriedly walking across campus for a meeting. En route, her visiting companion greeted each and every person, individuals unknown to Eva and definitely unknown to her visitor. Upon arriving at their destination, the visitor commented on the fact that Eva did not seem to stop to greet everyone. He noted that it was his belief that everyone was important and that one never knew when one might meet that person again in a different circumstance. When using this story, Eva now asks students to think about how a deeply held belief about the value of each person might conflict with someone else's deeply held belief about timeliness.

Preparing for Steps 3 and 4: Thinking About the Dilemma in New Ways

When students identify and analyze their dilemmas, their intense dialogue and inner reflection is done with faculty and peers, which gives them space to consider multiple interpretations and perspectives. By heightening students' awareness of the cultural underpinnings of their reactions to families, the structured conversation assists them to shift their beliefs away from a deficit perspective. In some instances, this prepares them for Steps 3 (explaining their perspective and recommendations) and 4 (moving forward collaboratively) in their future interactions with families. To engage in the third step of cultural reciprocity, we encourage students to present the dilemma to the family by acknowledging the family's perspective first and then explaining their own perspective. The intense work they have done in the first two steps plays a crucial role in preparing students to converse with the family and explain the cultural basis of their recommendations. At this stage, we may use role plays to find ways the student can present the dilemma to the family. We try out scripts such as "On the one hand, I understand why you want _____; on the other hand, my experience with _____ tells me _____." However, we make it clear that the purpose is to explore the dilemma with the family and not to tell the family what members should be doing differently.

In other instances, the students' analysis of their reactions may result in the realization that there is no need to make recommendations or to intervene. For example, when Nicole realized that her view of toys was culturally based and that she did not need to provide additional toys, she no longer felt an urgent desire to explain to families why toys were so important. The dilemma process interrupted her initial reaction and allowed her to join with the family rather than be at odds with them about how to carry out IFSP goals in the natural environment.

Sometimes, students feel "paralyzed" or stumped when they find out that the family's view is different from their own, and they become unable to figure out how to move forward. To prepare them for future dialogue directly with families outside the university classroom, we ask students to consider what additional information they would need from the family or from other sources such as books, journal articles, and so forth to develop a deeper understanding of the family's perspective on the dilemma. We also ask students to rephrase the dilemma with statements such as "On the one hand, I think _____; on the other hand, I understand _____." At this stage, we often ask students to continue writing in their journals about their dilemma, and we respond to the journal entries to continue the dialogue on the dilemma.

We make it very clear to our students that the purpose of dilemma work is to stay in the dilemma to make as much sense of it as possible and not to come to quick solutions. Thus, in any given class session or supervision session, we may not even get to a solution in the way that students may have felt about it—that is, a fix for the feelings of discomfort. However, we do use several guiding questions to help students think about their dilemmas in new ways. And, it is our view that these questions can be addressed most effectively when students have spent sufficient time exploring their own meanings and those of the other individuals in the dilemma. Exploring the following questions helps students prepare to move into deeper dialogue with families. We pose these questions to guide the individual work that occurs after shared group discussion of a dilemma.

How Might You Create a Reframed Problem Statement from the Dilemma?
A student often presents the dilemma as a problem statement or as a cultural conflict. After engaging in initial reflection and perspective taking, most of the students reach a state in which they are able to view the situation from multiple perspectives. At this point, it is important to ask students to restate the dilemma from the point of view of one or more participants, as this forces the student to move away from dualistic thinking. According to Darling-Hammond (2002), recognizing that there may be other culturally constructed views different from one's own significantly enhances a professional's ability to engage in an authentic dialogue.

What Additional Information About Yourself Might Help You Better Understand the Situation?
The process of reflecting on one's own experiences does not stop with simply identifying the bias but requires the student to identify the source of his or her bias and gain a deeper understanding of the dilemma. As a student explores a dilemma through discussions or journal entries, teacher educators can encourage him or her to engage in dialogues with family members, reflect on some of the significant events in his or her own life, or consider the sociopolitical climate in which he or she grew up or the institutional biases he or she may have adopted

through participation in different cultural groups. For example, a student who was deeply concerned about gender roles in a family with whom she was working realized later that some of her reactions stemmed from the fact that she felt marginalized in her family growing up and actively fought against the gender roles that were imposed on her. Her ability to identify her feelings allowed her to engage in a dialogue about the decision-making roles in the family.

What Additional Information About the Family Might Help You Better Understand the Situation?
As students engage in the process of reflection and develop a newer understanding of their cultural lens, they become more curious about the family's perspective. Teacher educators can play a critical role in helping students identify the questions they need to consider as well as the methods they can use to seek information. Often, students fail to consider the fact that observation is just as important as interviews when considering child-rearing practices. For example, posing a question such as "What is your cultural perspective on toilet training?" may not yield a valuable response because this implicit aspect of culture may be difficult for parents to articulate. However, if the student says, "Show me how you toilet train your 6-month-old child," the student will have an opportunity to observe the practice. Then, he or she can have a productive dialogue regarding the practice by saying, "I observed you doing _____. Why is it important?" At other times, the student may need to read about the history of a group or speak to a cultural informant to understand the family's practices or preferences.

What Other Experiences Might Help You Understand This Situation?
This question is connected to the previous one. In addition to direct interactions, other experiences may help students gain a deeper understanding of the family's perspective. Visiting the family's neighborhood often helps students understand the challenges and resources of the community in which a family resides. Attending key events in the community provides a similar benefit. Dialogues with community members such as pastors, health workers, or translators can yield valuable information. Sometimes, it is helpful for students to read or watch a film that provides valuable insight into a family's journey. For example, the story of a Hmong family seeking medical help for their child with epilepsy often helps students to understand that cultural misunderstandings can occur even when professionals are committed to serving a child (Fadiman, 1997).

What Resources Are Available to Help You Better Understand This Situation?
Analyzing a dilemma involves intense work and can be emotionally draining for the students. To motivate them to stay on the path and continue to seek a solution, it is important for them to realize the internal and the external resources that are available to them. It is essential that teacher educators recognize and point out the courage, insight, and dedication that students may have demonstrated in articulating the dilemma, thus supporting the students to be aware of the internal resources they bring to this situation. When considering external resources, we focus on both social and material resources. As graduate students, the students have access to their peers and faculty members. Through a focused discussion on allies, they are able to identify a group of people who can support them as they grapple with a dilemma. In addition, they systematically identify the resources that are available in

the university, community, and county as they seek information and explore alternatives.

Having addressed these questions, students are enabled to identify a new view of the dilemma and possible next steps in their journey with a particular family. As we get to this final piece of the process, at the end of each session in which dilemmas have been addressed as a group, we ask each individual student briefly to reflect and write about any new lens he or she now has related to his or her own dilemma. We ask students to continue writing in their journals about their dilemma, and we respond to the journal entries to continue the dialogue on the dilemma.

CONCLUSION

We find that by identifying and working through cultural dilemmas, students are able to pause and deliberately work through Steps 1 and 2 of the cultural reciprocity process and, when appropriate, to plan for Steps 3 and 4 in their future interactions with families. In many situations, the students are able to engage in perspective taking, viewing the situation from multiple points of view, and become less judgmental and more willing to explore the family's viewpoint. It seems to us that the cultural dilemma method of exploring cultural reciprocity provides a definite, confined space to have a focused discussion and practice the flexible thinking required for a true process of cultural reciprocity. We find that students are much more willing to find options and develop imaginative alternatives when they have the opportunity to work through a dilemma. Ultimately, we feel this leads students to the possibility of rich, reciprocal, collaborative interactions with families.

Chapter 9

The Preservice Classroom as an Intercultural Space for Experiencing a Process of Cultural Reciprocity

Shernaz B. García

Shernaz's Story

I grew up in Pune, India as part of a large, close-knit extended family that gave me a very strong sense of belonging and fostered a strong ethnic identity as a Parsi and as a Zoroastrian. Although individual family members varied widely in the strength of their religious beliefs and practices, this was and continues to be an integral part of my individual and group identity. Growing up in a recently post-British, independent India, I also was aware of the tensions between generations: my grandmother and her friends fondly recalling a British India where Parsis had enjoyed a favored sociocultural and economic status at the same time that I was learning about colonialism and India's struggle for independence in my Indian history classes in school, which, ironically, was a private school run by English, Anglican nuns. Even as a teenager and later in college, I found myself identifying much more strongly with the latter. To this day, this duality of being Indian as well as Parsi centers me as I navigate intercultural borders as an immigrant in the United States.

How I am perceived by others in the U.S. context does not always fit with my identity: I have been viewed as Asian (not Indian) or informed that India is not part of Asia; in addition, I often have been mistaken as being Hispanic or Mexican American. Because García is my last name (my husband is from Venezuela), I have been asked by some why I don't speak Spanish; others have expressed surprise that I speak English "without an accent" (even as my family in India comments on my "American accent"). When I am dressed in my Indian attire, my Asian origins are more visible, but no less controversial (eliciting remarks ranging from, "You just can't give it up, eh?" to "Asians have a strong work ethic and value education"—i.e., the model minority stereotype). Even though I have resisted being defined by these perceptions, it is impossible not to be affected by them. The experience of being positioned as an outsider has challenged, frustrated, and angered me and, at times, has been alienating and painful. Simultaneously, it continually serves as a source of reflection and introspection and, ultimately, has supported a much deeper understanding of the complexities and contradictions involved in crossing socio-cultural and linguistic boundaries and how these experiences contribute to identity formation.

As I reflect on my journey and experiences in my personal and professional life that have contributed to my development as a multicultural teacher educator, I find myself thinking about my multiple identities and roles and their consequences on my professional identity as an Asian Indian, bilingual/multicultural special education researcher and teacher educator in a predominantly white university. What links these characteristics together is that they have all required me to become very conscious and keenly aware of how I communicate and interact with others who are different from me; to question my own assumptions about race, ethnicity, and so forth; and to learn to field others' assumptions about me that are based on their perceptions of my race, ethnicity, and nationality. Having entered the field of bilingual special education early in its development and without much formal academic preparation in cultural studies, I had a great deal of on-the-job learning to do.

CONTEXT: NEGOTIATING IDENTITIES AS A TEACHER EDUCATOR

As I began to teach my first courses in multicultural special education, I remember being extremely upset about what I perceived to be my students' ethnocentrism, racism, bias, and resulting deficit orientation toward difference. As the mother of a young daughter at the time, I questioned whether I would want them to be her teacher; as a teacher educator, I questioned the feasibility of trying to foster intercultural competence in the short span of one semester; and as a learner myself, I sought answers to many questions about the most essential content, the most effective theoretical frameworks to guide my instruction, and the most appropriate pedagogy to achieve these goals. Over time, my initial perceptions, frustration, hurt, and—occasionally—anger, gave way to the realization that many of my young, white, mostly middle class, female students had experienced very little contact with diversity and few intergroup interactions that might foster a deeper understanding or appreciation of difference. Given my own dual identity as Indian and Parsi, I remember thinking it was inconceivable that the majority of students self-identified as "just white" or "American." Finally, I was puzzled and disconcerted by course-instructor evaluations that simultaneously described me as the best and the worst instructor that students had ever had: How I could have earned such accolades and intense criticism for the same course? Confronted with these experiences, I had to acknowledge that I needed to reexamine my teaching if I wanted to be more effective in reaching all of my students.

The most important insight that I believe I came to is that I needed to view my own classroom as an intercultural space; that is, given the cultural differences between instructor and students, my own pedagogy had to be guided by principles of intercultural communication (ICC) (Brislin & Yoshida, 1994; Gudykunst & Kim, 2003). Only then could I support their ability to adopt a similar perspective in their own teaching. Eventually, with the publication of *Culture in Special Education* (Kalyanpur & Harry, 1999), I expanded my framework to incorporate the construct of cultural reciprocity. Given my realization that I needed to view my students as learners on a cultural journey (rather than focus primarily on their whiteness and/or deficit views of the "other"), I realized that the steps of cultural reciprocity offered a way to foster a culturally responsive teacher education pedagogy. Ultimately, I wanted them to move away from associating culture with being nonwhite to understanding culture as the context in which we *all* operate (García & Guerra, 2006) so that they could begin to develop a culturally informed philosophy of teaching and learning for all students. As a result of this transformation in my own thinking as a teacher educator, I began to revisit my assumptions and expectations related to the preparation of predominantly white, middle-class preservice special educators to work in diverse settings, to search for theoretical principles to support my goals, and to develop effective ways to measure learning outcomes (Betsinger, García, & Guerra, 2000; García & Schaller, 1999).

CONTEXT: SITUATING MY LEARNING IN THE TEACHER EDUCATION PROGRAM DESIGN

Although teacher preparation occurs primarily at the undergraduate level, my department also offers postbaccalaureate certification in conjunction with a master's degree in special education. Because each has contributed in different ways to the framework that emerged from my experience, I provide a brief overview.

Undergraduate Preservice Teacher Education

My university's current program is guided by a standards-based approach to curriculum design, with state (Texas State Board of Educator Certification) and professional standards (Council for Exceptional Children, 2009) providing the primary impetus for learning outcomes related to culturally and/or linguistically responsive special education practice. Preservice teachers complete a special education section of a course that provides an introduction to social and cultural factors that contribute to children's development and learning. This section also specifically addresses the complex, dynamic interrelationships among culture, language, and disability as the basis for culturally and linguistically responsive practice. A primary goal of the course is to provide the requisite knowledge and skills to build preservice teachers' cultural self-awareness and knowledge. In their final semester, preservice teachers enroll in a second course in conjunction with student teaching, which provides the field-based setting for them to apply the theory. Through course assignments, preservice teachers develop and utilize culturally and linguistically responsive inclusive practices, engage in "family dialogue" and "paraeducator dialogue" projects, and collaborate with student teachers in the bilingual/bicultural education program to develop academic and social interventions for English language learners in a bilingual education classroom who are either struggling and/or receiving special education services.

Graduate-Level Preservice Teacher Education

Graduate students who wish to add a certification in special education to an existing teaching credential in general education have the option to fulfill these requirements as part of their master's degree. The department has offered a graduate specialization in bilingual special education since the 1980s (the department has one of the longest standing programs in this area in the country). In the 1990s, a core course was added to the master's degree plan. This foundations course provides an overview of issues and emerging practices surrounding the education and transition of students from diverse sociocultural and linguistic backgrounds in special education. The goal is to increase students' understanding of the history and significant events that have impeded or promoted the acceptance of diversity within the educational system.

Given my experiences with teaching undergraduate courses, I had recognized that dynamics of ICC were reflected in my own teaching. Simultaneously, I had begun to conceptualize teaching and learning in schools characterized by student diversity as a form of ICC. To explore the relevance of these concepts for graduate students, I offered an elective course, the primary goal of which was to promote students' ICC skill development by increasing their knowledge of basic principles of ICC and providing a nonjudgmental, nonthreatening environment in which to experience the process. The current version of this course reflects refinements and incorporation of new topics and content in response to the growing body of literature on the sociocultural foundations of disability. Equally, these changes document my own growth in creating a pedagogy for diversity education that would be responsive to my students' professional development needs as well as the intercultural dynamics of my classroom.

Writing this chapter has given me the opportunity to articulate, refine, and formalize these aspects of my instruction into an intercultural framework that simultaneously serves to structure course content as well as pedagogy. I begin by presenting this framework, in which I have integrated principles of ICC competence with cultural reciprocity as a way to foster students' development of these complementary skills. Next, drawing from my collective experiences and personal learning, I describe how the very principles that comprise my curriculum have become a part of my diversity pedagogy, given the uncertainty and anxiety associated with the controversial nature of course topics as well as the collective social and personal identities of students and instructor. Using incidents from my courses that depict the tensions and conflict that arise, I identify features of ICC and cultural reciprocity that support my efforts. I use the term *diversity pedagogy* to refer to courses and pedagogical approaches that are expressly designed to foster participants' cultural understanding and skills. From this perspective, courses that include some readings about culturally responsive pedagogy or cultural reciprocity would be considered to employ diversity pedagogy only if they also support participants' development of ICC competence. Principles of diversity pedagogy are equally relevant when instructors and students are members of different sociocultural, racial, ethnic, and/or linguistic communities because the intercultural nature of setting demands requires instructors to pay simultaneous attention to their own ICC effectiveness.

TOWARD AN INTEGRATED FRAMEWORK FOR COURSE DESIGN

Although specific course content varies by level (undergraduate versus graduate), the framework and related guiding principles presented in the remainder of this chapter are reflected across levels and courses and serve as guideposts for ongoing course revisions. Figure 9.1 depicts my conceptualization of the relevance of ICC competence (Gudykunst & Kim, 2003; Column 1) for the key features of a posture of cultural reciprocity (Kalyanpur & Harry, 1999; Column 2). Together, they mutually support the successful implementation of the steps in Column 3. I begin by defining key constructs related to ICC competence.

CULTURAL RECIPROCITY

Step 1
Identify cultural values embedded in professional interpretation of the student's difficulties or recommendations for services.

Step 2
Find out whether the family recognizes and values these assumptions and, if not, how their view differs from that of professional.

Step 3
Acknowledge and give explicit respect to any cultural differences identified, and fully explain the cultural basis of professional assumptions.

Step 4
Through discussion and collaboration, determine the most effective way of adapting professional interpretation or recommendations to the value system of the family.

	Components of intercultural communication effectiveness/competence (Gudykunst & Kim, 2003)	Foundation for cultural reciprocity (Kalyanpur & Harry, 1999)
Motivation	• Desire to communicate effectively in intergroup interactions • Assumptions, perceptions, beliefs about intergroup differences and similarities • Need to reduce anxiety and uncertainty, to increase predictability, and to sustain self-concept	• Internalized values of respect, reciprocity, and collaboration (universality of posture) • Awareness of subtle layers of culture
Knowledge and awareness	Understanding of components of effective and appropriate intercultural interactions: • Dimensions of cultural variability • Cultural influences on socialization, cognitive development, and identity formation • Patterns of verbal and nonverbal communication • Sources of and response to intercultural conflict • Strategies for gathering cultural information • Strategies for conflict management • Barriers to communication, including sociopolitical factors that mediate responses to difference	• Cultural self-awareness (personal and professional) • Social, professional, and personal identities • Cultural foundations of the educational and legal system • Clinical and social systems perspectives about disability
Skills	• Mindfulness • Emotional resilience • Flexibility • Ability to make accurate predictions and explanations • Creation of 3rd space • Management of intercultural conflict	• Avoid stereotyping. • Accurately identify underlying values, based in deeper, subtle levels of culture. • Explain and verbalize cultural differences and similarities. • Adapt to the value system of the family.

Figure 9.1. Integrated framework for intercultural communication competence to support the posture of cultural reciprocity.

Intercultural Communication

Although the characteristics and features of ICC overlap with those involved in interpersonal communication, the central difference lies in the salience of cultural group
membership on communication. Because the process is interdependent and transac-
tional in nature and involves the attribution and negotiation of meaning between
people from different cultural communities (Gudykunst & Kim, 2003; Ting-Toomey
& Chung, 2007), it is likely that these interactions will be influenced by people's perceptions of each other's cultural identities. In addition, the reduction of anxiety and
uncertainty has also been identified as a major function of communication when
interacting with strangers (Gudykunst, 2005). "*Strangers* represent the idea of near-
ness because they are physically close and the idea of remoteness because they have
different values and ways of doing things" (Gudykunst & Kim, 2003, p. 23, emphasis
added). Viewing stranger status as a figure-ground phenomenon, the authors argue
that anyone can be a stranger: "When members of other groups approach our groups
in our environment, they are the stranger. When we approach other groups in their
environments, we are the strangers" (p. 24). This concept of stranger is particularly
relevant for the various ways in which professionals experience their roles. From the
perspective of special educators interacting with students and families from nondominant sociocultural and linguistic communities, the students and families may be
viewed as the strangers; however, when special educators approach general educators to collaborate in creating inclusive classroom environments for students with
disabilities, they may be perceived as strangers by their general education colleagues
depending on the contexts and purposes for the interaction.

In my own classroom, the notion of *stranger* has been a valuable lens through
which to anticipate and interpret my interactions with my preservice teachers: As a
nonwhite faculty member whose ethnic and cultural identities are often unclear to
others, I realize that, for many of my students, I am the stranger. This status can be
somewhat mitigated for some students, particularly nonwhite students, as they see
cultural similarities in our value systems and communication styles in spite of ethnic
and/or racial differences. Conversely, at various points in any given semester, I find
myself viewing my students as strangers, as we work through misunderstandings or
their perceived lack of clarity in my instructions for assignments, evaluation criteria,
or group activities. At these times, I am keenly aware that their uncertainty and anxiety are heightened by differences in our value orientations (mine leaning toward collectivism) and communication styles. In spite of my efforts to be responsive to their
preferences and expectations for direct, explicit, succinct instructions, I must continuously be mindful of my tendency toward indirect, high-context, and elaborated communication styles, with a preference for mutual-face negotiation (Ting-Toomey &
Chung, 2007; i.e., interactions in which self-worth, interests, and identities are upheld
for all parties involved, including self).

Intercultural Communication Competence

In thinking about the concept of competence, or skill, I find it useful to consider
Gudykunst & Kim's (2003) distinction between *effectiveness* and *competence*. Whereas
effectiveness generally refers to one's ability to minimize misunderstandings and to
send and receive messages as intended (fidelity), two views of competence are presented in the literature. It is viewed either as an individual's capacity to facilitate the

process or as a contextual (situational) judgment made by one individual about another's communication behavior (Spitzber & Cupach, 1984, as cited in Gudykunst & Kim, 2003). Judgments about competence cannot be understood, however, without knowing the criteria being applied and are prone to error, bias, and subjectivity. In educational settings, even as special educators may judge the communication competence of families or general educators through their cultural and professional lenses, their own competence is being evaluated, often using a different set of norms and expectations. Because each group relies on a set of implicit criteria that are influenced by its respective professional and cultural norms and assumptions, an accurate judgment about intercultural competence also requires an adequate and accurate cultural understanding of self and others. Focusing on effectiveness and competence as related constructs allows consideration of all these aspects of our communication, with the ultimate goal of preventing or reducing misunderstandings and conveying meaning. Together, these concepts support the development of a "third-culture perspective" which acts as a psychological link between one's cultural frames of reference and those of the other party involved (Gudykunst, Wiseman, & Hammer, 1997, as cited in Gudykunst & Kim, 2003). These perspectives are also congruent with the notion of 3rd space (Gutierrez, Baquedano-Lopez, & Tejeda, 1999), which acknowledges the validity of multiple and alternate frames of reference and worldviews and is characterized by respect, reciprocity, and responsiveness (Barrera & Kramer, 2005). Both support the ability of professionals to implement the four steps of cultural reciprocity. As Harry and colleagues (1999) argued, "professionals [must] initiate a two-way process of information sharing and understanding—a process that can be truly reciprocal and lead to genuine mutual understanding and cooperation" (p. 7).

Components of Intercultural Communication Competence   Based on their synthesis of the ICC literature, Gudykunst and Kim (2003) identified three essential components of perceived competence: motivation, knowledge, and skills (see Figure 9.1). This model also identifies the underlying cultural, sociocultural, and psychocultural dimensions of ICC competence. In turn, it guides my selection of learning outcomes, course topics, readings, assignments, and activities as well as evaluation criteria. In the ICC context, *motivation* refers to an individual's desire to engage in intergroup interactions and can influence or mediate the development of competence as well as the goals and outcomes sought by each party. For example, when motivated by a desire to manage stress and increase predictability in interactions, an individual may initiate contact in order to increase his or her *cultural knowledge* about other groups. In this process, he or she also becomes more aware of his or her own cultural worldviews and may find him- or herself reframing his or her prior understanding of intergroup dynamics, sources of potential conflict, as well as strategies for effective communication. The individual may experience more effective interactions when these cultural insights lead to ICC *skills* such as greater openness and flexibility, a willingness to suspend judgment, and an enhanced ability to make more accurate predictions. On the other hand, when difficulties in making accurate predictions raises one's anxiety and uncertainty to stressful levels, a person may be motivated to withdraw from or avoid future interactions. Or, if an individual is motivated by a need to sustain his or her self-concept (e.g., as a nonracist, unbiased person), his or her actions to seek greater knowledge and awareness and the quality of his or her interactions with cultural strangers may focus on sustaining his or her self-concept more than on improving the actual quality and appropriateness of his or her interactions with members of other groups. At all times, the process is facilitated by opportunities to examine one's emotions and beliefs about culture and difference to ensure that unexamined belief systems do not hinder activation of newly acquired understandings and skills (Brislin & Yoshida, 1994). I am making a distinction here between a culture-specific or *emic* approach to studying culture, and a culture-general or *etic* approach, which focuses on identified dimensions of cultural variability that exist in every culture, and understanding how groups are similar or different along these dimensions (Gudykunst & Kim, 2003; Hollins, 2008).

Integrating Cultural Reciprocity into the Intercultural Communication Framework

In their discussion about the universal applicability of the process of cultural reciprocity, Kalyanpur and Harry called for professionals to "internalize the values of reciprocity, respect, and collaboration," and to adopt this reflective practice as "a way of life" rather than "an 8-hour syndrome" (1999, p. 121). However, although the four steps of cultural reciprocity provide a clear sequence of actions that can be taught and incorporated into my own pedagogy, the strategies or skills needed to implement them successfully, even using the key features of cultural reciprocity as a guide, were beyond the scope of their book. For example, although my students and I discussed the importance of avoiding stereotypes or the need to accurately identify a family member's underlying values and even the strategies for obtaining this information, I was left with questions about how best to foster the underlying skills to achieve these desired outcomes. The complementary nature of the cultural reciprocity model and the ICC competence literature suggested that my goal could be addressed by integrating them into a single, unified framework. Given limited attention in the ICC literature on educational contexts in the United States, another benefit of this integration would be the inclusion of applications in special education. For instance, the case studies and scenarios involving interactions between professionals and families from diverse sociocultural communities (Harry et al., 1999; Kalyanpur & Harry, 1999) could be used to illustrate how intercultural conflict may occur in special education contexts. These examples not only provided professionally relevant examples for analysis using principles of ICC theory but could be used to demonstrate the use of ICC knowledge and skills in the application of the four steps of cultural reciprocity. Although my initial focus in creating this framework was on the development of my preservice teachers' ICC competence, it is equally relevant to the intercultural context of my own university classroom practice.

The specific components of this integrative framework are organized in Figure 9.1, in accordance with the three components of ICC competence (motivation, knowledge, skills). I began by classifying the key features of cultural reciprocity into each of these categories (Column 2); for example, "internalized values of respect, reciprocity, and collaboration" was placed under *motivation* because an individual's desire to engage with families using cultural reciprocity may or may not support the internalization of these values. Kalyanpur and Harry's (1999) analysis of the cultural foundations of IDEA was categorized as cultural knowledge because it broadens students' understanding of culture as a system of embedded beliefs and connects values such as choice and equity with individualism. Next, I identified discrete knowledge and skills from each of the three components of ICC competence (Column 1) that I associate with, and have found to scaffold implementation of the four steps of cultural reciprocity. Taken together, the knowledge and skills reflected in these two columns support the adoption of the process of cultural reciprocity. This relationship is not sequential or linear in the sense that a given skill may be required at more than one step. The organization of concepts in this figure reflects the ways in which these elements work together given my identity and the student, classroom, and university contexts in which I operate. To the extent that readers find elements that are transferable to their own contexts, the framework may offer a useful way to conceptualize their pedagogy. However, their frameworks can be expected to—and should—vary based on the contexts in which their work is situated.

Interface Between Intercultural Communication Motivation and Cultural Reciprocity

The motivation component of ICC competence supports development of critical characteristics associated with cultural reciprocity, including internalized values of respect, reciprocity, and collaboration as well as awareness of the subtle levels of culture fostered by a willingness to go beyond visible, more easily discernible aspects of culture by asking "why?" The development of these attributes presupposes a desire to engage successfully with families with diverse worldviews, especially about [dis]ability (motivation), even as the ability to identify the embedded values of one's professional practice as well as those of families (Steps 1 and 2 of cultural reciprocity) assumes willingness on the part of professionals to acknowledge and be open to any differences that may exist (attitudes, beliefs). This component of Figure 9.1 guides the design of course activities and experiences that provide opportunities for students to reflect and become more aware of the influence of motivation in adopting the process of cultural reciprocity. It also serves to remind me that there are varying levels of willingness and/or motivation among my preservice teachers to engage in course assignments and activities and that it is equally incumbent upon me to learn about the influence of their cultural upbringing and life experiences on their values, beliefs, and perceptions about difference.

Inherent in the successful implementation of all four steps of the process of cultural reciprocity is the assumption that professionals know how to manage any anxiety, tension, or uncertainty resulting from cultural differences (perceived or actual) and any conflict resulting from these differences and that they have the appropriate tools for managing their emotions (emotional resilience, tolerance for ambiguity). Although increased cultural knowledge and understanding are necessary, they may not be sufficient in instances in which emotions related to uncertainty or anxiety trigger a desire to avoid interactions. As a teacher educator who is likely to be viewed as a cultural stranger by many of my students, I must not only foster my students' emotional resilience for their future interactions in multicultural settings, but both they and I must find ways to manage and reduce uncertainty, anxiety, and conflicts that may emerge and possibly be detrimental to teaching and learning. In such instances, our success relies on our ability to manage uncertainty and anxiety in order to create a 3rd space for intercultural learning in the classroom.

Interface Between Intercultural Communication Knowledge and Cultural Reciprocity

In order to implement all four steps of cultural reciprocity successfully, professionals need a framework of cultural knowledge from which to operate: Kalyanpur and Harry's (1999) analyses of the cultural and epistemological sources of professional knowledge and expertise lay the foundation for building professionals' understanding of the cultural bases of legal, organizational, and societal systems of embedded beliefs and practice. This institutional knowledge is coupled with an awareness of one's personal, social, and professional identities as well as the socialization experiences that contribute to his or her development. These understandings foster a deeper awareness of the complex ways in which one's multiple identities interact with the assumptions, expectations, and practices espoused by educational, legal, and societal value systems.

The knowledge component of ICC competence also delineates specific types of cultural knowledge required to experience successful interactions. For educators, these include an understanding of the deep meaning of culture (e.g., Hollins, 2008) and its influence on teaching, learning, and interactions with families. Rather than adopt a culture-specific or emic approach to studying culture, the cultural knowledge in this framework relies on a culture-general or etic approach, which focuses on identified dimensions of cultural variability that exist in every culture and on understanding how groups are similar or different along these dimensions (Gudykunst & Kim, 2003; Hollins, 2008). Students develop this knowledge base by learning about dimensions of cultural variability, patterns of communication, and conflict management as well as barriers to intergroup communication (e.g., stereotypes, prejudice, deficit views about difference, forms of social privilege). They are also exposed to an array of strategies for gathering cultural information about self and others to increase the likelihood of gathering accurate cultural information and avoiding stereotypes. Using the dimensions of cultural variability offers a culture-general approach to understanding how communication differs across cultures even when culture-specific information about a group is not available or feasible to expect, as when teaching in multicultural, multiethnic, multilingual communities. It also provides a foundation of cultural understanding from which preservice teachers can learn to gather culture-specific information about individual students and families (e.g., through dialogue). Adopting a culture-general approach also provides a foundation of cultural knowledge that can be applied in any cultural context, which is an important consideration when preparing preservice teachers for settings and communities that are yet undetermined.

Interface Between Intercultural Communication Skills and Cultural Reciprocity

Successful application of the process of cultural reciprocity relies heavily on effective ICC. For example, in order to engage effectively in dialogue with family members, professionals must be mindful of the responses of family members, adjust their verbal and nonverbal communication styles, as necessary, when explaining the values guiding their professional practice, and elicit relevant cultural information from families using strategies that are respectful of culturally influenced differences in communication, self-disclosure, and conflict management. Ultimately, they must be able to engage with families to determine how services may need to be adapted to be congruent with the value system of the family.

The skills component of the ICC competence framework emphasizes several cognitive skills that support accurate interpretation and appropriate actions for interacting with strangers. These include mindfulness, emotional resilience, flexibility, empathy, and an ability to make accurate predictions and explanations. These skills are particularly relevant when dealing with intercultural conflict, defined as "the implicit or explicit emotional struggle or frustration between persons of different cultures over perceived incompatible values, norms, face orientation, goals, scarce resources, processes, and/or outcomes in a communication situation" (Ting-Toomey & Chung, 2007, p. 259). Effective conflict management involves mindful listening and reframing skills, which are also central to gathering accurate cultural information and increasing the accuracy of one's predictions. The ability to act mindfully (Langer & Moldoveanu, 2000) calls for increased attention to one's own thoughts and actions and for being aware of one's tendency to interpret strangers' behavior from his or her own cultural frames of reference. Defined by Langer & Moldoveanu as "the process of drawing novel distinctions" (2000, p. 1), *mindfulness* "keeps us situated in the present" so that we rely less on rules and routines derived from past experiences and avoid mindless behavior, also defined as acting on *automatic pilot* (Gudykunst & Kim, 2003). Acting mindfully results in greater perceptual acuity, increased openness to new information, creation of new categories for organizing one's perceptions about others, and greater awareness of alternate approaches or perspectives (Langer & Moldoveanu, 2000). It also reduces stereotyping by moving away from broad generalizations about others to more refined, narrower social categories derived from a greater use of personalized information, greater awareness of subtle differences or nuances, and awareness of more than one perspective to explain or understand our interactions with others.

When the potential for misunderstanding is high, mindfulness facilitates greater attention to the communication process, calling for all parties to seek clarification of meaning and to engage in conversation repair as needed. Learning to calm oneself and developing a higher threshold of tolerance for ambiguity are effective tools for managing anxiety and uncertainty, which then supports the ability to adapt one's behavior and goals and to adjust to communication demands across varying contexts. When employed effectively, all these skills can result in more effective interactions.

In summary, the integrated framework in Figure 9.1 provides an organizational schema from which to consider the critical elements of effective communication between educators, students, and their families because it draws attention to the *cultural* elements that are likely to influence these interactions. The framework guides the development of course content as well as instructional practices that support preservice teachers in their ability to communicate effectively and to employ cultural reciprocity while simultaneously utilizing the intercultural elements of the classroom as spaces for intercultural learning. In the next section, I turn to these pedagogical implications.

INTERCULTURAL COMMUNICATION AND CULTURAL RECIPROCITY AS PEDAGOGICAL TOOLS

As adult learners, preservice teacher candidates enter the preservice program with a fairly well-established (but often unexamined) worldview, acquired through their childhood socialization and life experiences including school, community, peers, media, and technology. In order to communicate effectively and successfully adopt the process of cultural reciprocity with individuals whom they may view as strangers, they need opportunities to compare and contrast their values and beliefs with those of others; to identify potential cultural differences, tension, and/or conflict; and to reflect on the likely impact of these differences on their motivation and ability to successfully engage in interactions. Given the range of sociocultural beliefs and values reflected in a preservice classroom, courses must create a learning environment in which students can examine and deconstruct their existing worldview, identify the influence of these beliefs on intergroup interactions, and, where necessary, reconstruct their understanding of effective communication to support cultural reciprocity. Mezirow's (1997) theory of transformative learning as "a process for effecting change in a *frame of reference*" [italics in original] (p. 5) highlights the cultural, social, educational, and political sources of an individual's frames of reference. Mezirow posits that changes in the ways that other groups are viewed are generally more difficult to achieve, "as long as what we learn fits comfortably in our existing frames of reference" (p. 7). To be effective with adult learners, pedagogy must promote critical reflection and "actively resist[ing] social and cultural forces that distort and delimit adult learning" (p. 11). This point is clearly relevant to developing ICC competence given the potential for cultural dissonance between students' worldviews and the content and goals of the course. Less clear, however, are the implications for teacher educators in terms of strategies to achieve transformational outcomes.

The formal use of transformative learning theory in my thinking is relatively recent and resulted from research that investigated the characteristics of my university classroom to which some students (especially white students) have attributed a transformative shift in their own intercultural thinking and growth (Dray, 2005; Dray, García, Tackett, & Smay-Ashton, 2007). The results of this study revealed that participants' life experiences and sociocultural characteristics were significant in reconstructing their understanding of difference in education, and mindfulness served to facilitate their thinking and engagement in the course. These students identified three characteristics of my pedagogy to which they attributed their ability to reframe their thinking about difference: "meeting people where they are at, having to think about it, and another way of looking" (Dray, 2005, p. 207).

As I suspect is true for many of my teacher educator colleagues, my own development as a teacher educator has intuitively reflected aspects of transformative learning. Confronted by unsettling instructional dilemmas, I have had to process my own assumptions as well as emotional responses to the course content and to my students' reactions, have tried different approaches, and have sought professional development to acquire the knowledge and skills to support their implementation. A significant aspect of my early growth as a diversity educator was the realization that, as an Asian Indian faculty member in a large, predominantly white, research-intensive university, I needed to constantly check my assumptions about my students, about my instruction, and about myself as their instructor. In retrospect, this allowed me to see how my assumptions could be influencing our perceptions and expectations of each other and consequently mediating (or even limiting) my ability to effectively prepare my preservice teachers to be culturally and linguistically responsive educators. I had to be willing to entertain the possibility that I could be a source of anxiety and uncertainty (albeit unintentional) that heightened my students' emotional filters to levels that interfered with the teaching–learning process. In considering potential intercultural dissonances in our classroom as a source of their anxiety and stress, I found myself struggling with my own emotions. Significantly, it led me to another realization that has influenced the way I approach my instruction: If I didn't find ways to diffuse my students' anxiety as well as my own, our emotional states were likely to polarize our communication and therefore limit the students' opportunities to learn and mine to teach effectively.

Drawing on Intercultural Communication Competence and Cultural Reciprocity to Mediate Emotional Filters in the Intercultural Classroom

In this section, I describe how the very principles of ICC competence and cultural reciprocity that comprised course content came to serve simultaneously as pedagogical tools to manage anxiety and uncertainty in my own classroom.

Accepting the Inevitability of Intercultural Conflict and Discomfort

The very nature of ICC makes it likely that conflict will result during intergroup interactions. Many of these conflicts are likely to be "well-meaning culture clashes" (Brislin, 1993); that is, they reflect misunderstandings or disagreements between well-intentioned individuals from different cultural groups acting from their own frames of reference for what is appropriate. To the extent that each party's cultural norms for appropriate and effective communication differ, one or both parties may experience tension. Rather than view this tension negatively, it is more productive to focus on understanding how cultural factors may be contributing and to learn to use effective approaches to manage conflict. Engaging in rigid or inappropriate methods is more likely to result in polarized communication than the conflict itself (Ting-Toomey & Chung, 2007).

Not only will preservice teachers encounter intercultural conflict in their future practice, they also experience it in my classroom, albeit to varying degrees. I have found it helpful to apply my understanding of intercultural conflict to identify how our respective cultural lenses (individualistic or collectivistic) are influencing how the conflict is being perceived, the sources of the conflict (e.g., content, relationship, identity), and the specific conflict style reflected in our responses (e.g., avoiding, obliging, accommodating, dominating, collaborating). Because these concepts are part of the course content, they are readily available to students in their readings (Ting-Toomey & Chung, 2007). The purposeful debriefing and deconstruction of selected incidents through class discussion has sometimes served as a teachable moment regarding course concepts while simultaneously diffusing anxiety or clarifying meaning, although this is not always the case.

In their student teaching semester, preservice teachers in my course are paired with bilingual education student teachers to collaborate on designing and implementing interventions for an English language learner in the bilingual education partner's classroom. Each partner has specific roles and responsibilities based on her or his areas of expertise: The bilingual education preservice teachers identify the focus student and compile academic, social-emotional, linguistic, and sociological data to guide instructional planning. In turn, my preservice teachers conduct one classroom observation and bring these data to an instructional planning seminar. Together, teams use these data to identify one academic and one social skills goal designed to support the focus of the student's learning and design an intervention plan to be implemented by the bilingual education partner. As part of this process, special education preservice teachers offer recommendations for specific academic and social skills interventions and take the lead in designing systems for data collection and monitoring student progress. Once implementation begins, partners are required to communicate regularly (via e-mail, phone, text, and/or team blogs) in order to support implementation fidelity. In addition, partners meet face to face at midpoint to review student progress and modify the interventions if necessary. Their final report includes an analysis of student outcomes in the context of the collaborative process. They are expected to draw from course readings about collaboration (Friend & Cook, 2010) and ICC to reflect on the successes and challenges they experienced, identify factors that may have contributed to these outcomes, and identify implications for their future practice.

The assignment generates anxiety at several levels: The partners are placed at different schools; my preservice teachers must observe in classrooms where instruction is provided in Spanish—a language in which most are not proficient; and they must negotiate their own cultural, ethnic, and racial identities (whereas my students are predominantly white, the majority of their partners are Hispanic). In the 2 years that this project has been implemented, several variables have contributed to conflict and discomfort. In some dyads, my students have expressed frustration at having to relinquish control of the interventions, even as their bilingual partners have viewed them as "dominating," "bossy," or "arrogant." When there are communication breakdowns over meeting schedules or project reports, my preservice teachers have complained about their partner's silence or delayed response. In spite of being assured that the collaboration *process* rather than student *outcomes* would be the basis for evaluating their learning, their anxiety and uncertainty about project grades has resulted in frustration and resentment, contributing to polarized communication between partners as well as with me.

Living with Discomfort   Discomfort is a predictable consequence of experiencing conflict or dissonance and can be expected to disrupt teaching and learning, if ignored. Like conflict, it is usually viewed as something to be avoided, presenting a cultural dilemma when interacting with strangers, given the inevitability of both conditions. Consequently, part of my role in the classroom is to scaffold my preservice teachers' acceptance of discomfort as well as their ability to manage their emotions so they can analyze, reflect, and develop appropriate responses to a given situation. Also, there is a delicate balance to be achieved between adequate discomfort to produce insights and new learning and too much discomfort, which impedes the process. My example reflects both ends of this spectrum. When confronted with differences between their expectations (e.g., response time for e-mails or text messages, division of work load, roles for data collection) and the responses of their bilingual education partners, my preservice teachers experienced frustration, anxiety, and uncertainty about how to proceed. Despite exploring alternate explanations such as differences in role definitions, the bilingual preservice teachers' limited knowledge of special education interventions, and the theoretical differences in the preparation of general versus special educators, some of my students' reactions remained emotional and judgmental. They maintained that differences in the respective instructors' expectations for each cohort explained their bilingual education peers' lower engagement in the assignment. These strong emotions on all sides necessitated temporary disengagement to allow the instructor and students to calm themselves. Some eventually realized that their preferred patterns of communication (and resulting expectations based on these norms) might have contributed to the conflict. A student's final reflection, written at the end of the semester, captures this realization:

> As the project progressed, communication became less frequent.... As my attempts at communication were denied, I began to hold animosity towards my partner, which led

to a break in communication. I felt like I was not being listened to... Additionally,
we continued to use impersonal communication channels such as text messages and
emails; we were talking to computers—not one another. When we did speak face to
face, it was very stiff and awkward. I tried being polite and gave substantial wait time
for responses from my partner but was unsuccessful. Maybe if I would [sic] reach out
daily for the first few weeks I would find more success... I would also be more diligent
in requesting data and interpreting results.... In the future, I would even take some of
that data collection responsibility if possible so as not to burden my partner with data
collection, progress monitoring, and instruction.

The limited success of my efforts to calm some students' anxiety and to successfully reengage them in considering alternative explanations is a constant reminder of the delimitations of my own communication style and approaches to conflict management and of the importance of mindfully evaluating the quality of their learning outcomes.

On a much lighter note, increasing the level of unpredictability in classroom routines can also serve as opportunities to be "desensitized," provided it is used judiciously and sparingly. For example, noticing that many students prefer to sit at the same table every week and usually with the same group of peers, I now routinely encourage the class to vary their choice of location in the room as well as their table partners. Their varied professional interests and specializations also offer a basis for groupings. When planning small-group exercises, I may create homogeneous groups (e.g., all preservice teachers who are student teaching in life skills settings) if the assignment requires this background knowledge. Or, I may create heterogeneous groups (e.g., group members represent different communication styles) if divergent perspectives are relevant to the task. At other times, I have used varied strategies for randomly assigning students to group work (e.g., by alphabetic order, birthday, height). If students seem reluctant to move, as some are, I gently nudge them with a reminder of the benefits of "becoming comfortable with being uncomfortable." Although these types of grouping strategies are commonly used in educational settings, I have employed them purposefully to foster emotional resilience.

Practicing Mindfulness, Respect, and Reciprocity   Cultivating mindfulness during my instruction has helped me to better understand my students and their responses to course content. Particularly when a student appears to disengage or resist, I have learned to withhold judgment based on my assumptions and to seek an understanding of the reasons for the behavior; that is, to ask "why?" The search for explanations may take many forms, including e-mails, face-to-face meetings, and analysis of the student's assignments, especially personal reflections and responses to readings. At all times, these efforts require a willingness on my part to identify and respect the student's reasons for disengagement and to be open to the possibility that I may need to adjust aspects of my instruction to support the student's emotional state. By being responsive to his or her current levels of ICC effectiveness and competence, I am better able to tailor assignments to his or her zone of proximal development (Vygotsky, 1978), thereby increasing the probability of reengaging.

Many of the reasons I have discovered through this process now replace assumptions with initial hypotheses to be explored. They include 1) the perceived irrelevance of culturally and linguistically responsive practice to future goals and preparation for the settings in which these will be achieved (often influenced by perceptions of self as nonracist and/or nonbiased); 2) life experiences that may have exerted a strong impact on their desire to live and work in multicultural settings; 3) the reason for enrolling in the course (required versus voluntary); 4) assumptions about what will be expected of them (e.g., being culturally competent implies giving up one's values and beliefs); and 5) the consequences of reframing existing views and beliefs for the student's identity and continued acceptance in her or his reference groups, including family, friends, and workplace colleagues. When students are affected by one or more of these variables, the emotions generated by course content and activities can be heightened to levels that can make it difficult, at best, for them to engage meaningfully or appropriately.

Over time, I have utilized various strategies to explicitly scaffold my own use of ICC skills and cultural reciprocity in my classroom. Because an exhaustive review is beyond the scope of this chapter, I have selected two of these strategies to illustrate the process: respecting personal and cultural variations in norms regulating communication and conflict management and acknowledging students' multiple identities. The first is salient to the communication dilemmas described herein; the second illustrates how my own ICC skills continue to grow.

Respecting Personal and Cultural Variations in Norms Regulating Communication and Conflict Management
The interactive, experiential format of the course and each class meeting provides routine opportunities for debriefing the outcomes of small- and large-group activities. Students are invited to share their responses to a given activity or task and to consider the attributions influencing their interactions with each other. In my intercultural classroom, effective use of debriefing requires mindfulness on my part. As students are engaged in activities, I have found it essential to monitor their engagement in the task as well as the quality of their interactions with each other. Mindful attention to communication breakdowns between students, and between instructor and students, serves to bring to my attention students who may be struggling with their emotions so that I may respond appropriately. As I consider the response options available to me, I have found that I must weigh each option against what I know about the sources of the conflict, the identities of the students involved, and, ultimately, the most appropriate ways to communicate when debriefing the situation while respecting each individual's respective needs for face negotiation.

On the last class day of a recent semester, students were working in small groups to review key concepts we had covered in the course and to convey their understanding of assigned terms through a performance before the rest of the class. To actively engage the rest of the class, other teams received points for each concept they identified accurately. Concepts had been randomly drawn by each team, but it became apparent as I listened to group conversations that one team in particular was working with concepts more challenging to dramatize. As other teams struggled to identify these concepts, a few students commented and joked about their peers' "failure." Although the remarks were good-natured in tone, it was evident that they had upset the team in question. Amidst the laughter that followed, the team members remained silent, and the offending students appeared to be unaware of their impact. Based on what I had learned from the "failing" team members' reflective essays about their cultural identities, values, and communication styles, I realized that this interaction might reflect aspects of a well-meaning culture clash. Fully aware of my own preference for saving face for both parties, I chose to respond by e-mailing the team after class:

> In class today, right after your second performance, I noticed that some of you were visibly upset, so I'm touching base to make sure that all is well. You didn't seem to have a very positive experience with either concept that your table drew, which is unfortunate, as our goal was to end the semester on a positive note for everyone. It also makes me wonder if my very brief explanation about "natural growth" had created some misunderstanding about its meaning, which was then reflected in your performance. If that's the case, then please accept my apologies, as that was certainly not my intent.

Two of the five students assured me that they were not upset but thanked me for my e-mail. The responses of the two students who had seemed the most upset are excerpted (identifying information has been removed to protect confidentiality and privacy):

> I must admit that I was upset about my group's performance in class today but in no way was my frustration aimed toward you. I felt like we were getting picked on by our classmates for "missing the boat" on the activity, although, I promise that my group and I know a lot more about the terms we went over in class today than it showed. There is no need for you to apologize but thank you so much for e-mailing to check up on us. I greatly appreciate it. . . . Today's mishap did not affect the positive feelings I have about this class.

> I think more than anything, [peer]'s comment really upset us. All of us actually had a really clear understanding of what you meant when you explained natural growth to us, but I suppose our skit did not convey our understanding.... I'm sure all the other girls grasped that as well, and probably because [team member] was the only person of a non–face-saving culture, she was the only one who actually said something in our defense, but I'm pretty sure no one heard her above the laughter.... But no worries, Dr. G. We had a really good last class, and it was a lot of fun!

Based on their responses, I would like to think that that my follow up e-mail had helped to alleviate any negative impact of this incident for these students. However, the effectiveness of my decision remains an open question for one student who did not respond at all.

Acknowledging Students' Multiple Identities   Research on multicultural teacher education has been dominated by a discourse on whiteness and white teachers and has mainly documented their attitudes and their limited understanding of diversity (Sleeter, 2001). Although these studies address an important problem in teacher education, analyses about white teachers have seldom been disaggregated by other possibly salient variables such as social class, life experience, the amount and quality of prior intercultural experience and contact, and so forth. The resulting monolithic depiction of white teachers has influenced my classroom discussions about these topics in a variety of ways:

1.   Some white preservice teachers have rejected or discounted research in which they did not see themselves "fairly" represented, thereby missing its relevance to their own practice.

2. Their nonwhite counterparts have tended to be silent or silenced by their peers' reactions.

3. I have wondered if they are tacitly developing simplified and unexamined over-generalizations about their white peers or reinforcing existing stereotypes.

4. The preponderance of whiteness in discussions about sociopolitical factors such as power, privilege, and institutional discrimination has often maintained a focus on race, which has not been conducive to a *cultural* analysis of the ways in which even teachers of color may be privileged through their professional socialization to think and teach from a monocultural norm.

These factors also contribute to the emotional climate of the classroom and can mediate our collective ability to engage in a critical dialogue about the ways in which systemic policies and practices serve to marginalize students and families in classrooms staffed by caring and well-intentioned teachers. Two classroom incidents illustrate these phenomena.

In the first incident, students had read McIntosh's (1989) article about white privilege and had watched a YouTube video (http://www.youtube.com/watch ?v=DRnoddGTMTY) in which McIntosh describes the events that precipitated her research on white privilege. As is often the case when the topic involves race, the conversation was initially awkward and one sided (my prompts to elicit responses punctuated by silence). Eventually a student blurted out that, although white, she did not feel privileged because she was a single parent and struggling financially to support herself and her child. Consequently, she did not see how this article applied to her. Although the room became quiet, I sensed that her remarks resonated with a few other students. In the second instance, students had been asked to share their reactions to an article about deficit thinking (García & Guerra, 2004). This time, a white student from a middle-class suburban community voiced feelings of helplessness and seemed overwhelmed by the documentation of limited educational opportunities for nonwhite and poor students in an educational system in which she had been successful.

In both situations, it was clear that I needed not only to ensure that students would leave with a more complete and accurate understanding of the complexities reflected in these topics but also to address the tension and discomfort in the room. A considerable amount of debriefing time was devoted to listening to the students' reactions, acknowledging and validating their emotions, and encouraging them to seek individual meetings with me or the teaching assistant should they desire a more private space for reflection and debriefing. Even as we engaged in these conversations, I found myself noticing the silence among the nonwhite students in the room and wondered how I might elicit their responses to these articles without contributing to the dichotomous thinking about privilege that I was trying to disrupt. I also was held back by ethical considerations related to bringing such a complex discussion to an acceptable level of closure in the time remaining (Brislin & Yoshida, 1994) and a reluctance to promote some students' learning at the risk of violating my other students' norms for privacy and self-disclosure as well as possibly causing some students pain in retelling their stories.

Acknowledging the complex ways in which peoples' multiple identities interact has allowed me to circumvent the limitations noted previously and contributed to richer discussions about privilege and oppression. Because students are encouraged to identify the multiple ways in which they may experience various forms of social privilege (Black & Stone, 2005) rather than focus solely on white privilege (McIntosh, 1989), they are able to consider factors that mitigate white privilege (e.g., poverty, sexual orientation) while also acknowledging other forms of social privilege that can be experienced by nonwhites (e.g., social class, professional expertise). As a result, more members of the class have participated in these conversations, and tensions that might have previously constrained dialogue seemed to diffuse. These more complex and multivocal conceptualizations of the concepts also seem to contribute to transformative learning that extends beyond the semester, as suggested by the following comment in Dray's 2005 study by a participant who took a multicultural counseling course after she had completed mine:

> *This class is nothing like [Dr. García's] class, and I will tell you why (and why I am upset about it).... NOT ONCE has Dr. Fuentes [pseudonym] discussed anything having to do with socioeconomic status, disability, religion, cultural competence, etc. The only two things that she has focused on have been race and ethnicity, preferably how white privilege and white oppression have affected America and people's definition of "Americans." Now, I agree with a lot of the material that we are reading, ... HOWEVER, these two fundamentals of multiculturalism (racism and ethnicity in regards to white oppression) have been the ONLY things Dr. Fuentes has focused on (and continues to focus on.) ALL of our readings and journal articles for the semester are tied to these two ideals, and do not incorporate any of the other elements of multiculturalism that [Dr. García] found so important to include in her lectures (pp. 254–255)*

The use of intersectionality as a conceptual tool for processing emotions has expanded the possibilities available to me. First, although discussions about privilege and multiple identities have been included in my curriculum for many years, only more recently have I begun to pair them. When students write about the development of their personal and various social identities (e.g., race, class, gender, ability, religion, geographic region, nationality, ethnicity, language), they are simultaneously assigned readings that serve as explicit illustrations of within-group diversity among different groups, including their own. To date, these readings have addressed interrelationships between race and class (Lareau, 2003); immigrant histories and marginalization experienced by Appalachian white communities (Bauer & Growick, 2003; Heilman, 2004); religion, race, and ethnicity (Britto, 2008); and race, class, gender, and learning disabilities (Ferri & Connor, 2010; Oswald, Coutinho, & Best, 2005). Introducing [dis]abilities into these analyses is particularly important for the preparation of special educators: For example, linking discussions about privilege and deficit thinking to the ways in which individuals with disabilities may be viewed as an oppressed group (disability studies perspective) or to factors that privilege special educators when interacting with families is particularly relevant to fostering the underlying values of respect as well as increased awareness of attitudes and beliefs about difference (in this case, based on varying abilities). As future professionals, irrespective of their other social identities, all preservice teachers must be able to engage in discovering how professional language and expertise may create barriers to communication just as they must understand the impact of a clinical perspective on the judgments about alternate cultural views and traditions related to disability. Only then can they develop strategies that will support their ability to adopt a more respectful, accepting stance from which to interact. When discussions about multiple identities are integrated with these topics, students can also be challenged to consider how their special education expertise is likely to be mitigated by the fact that the majority of them are not parents, much less parents of a child with special needs.

Finally, I have built on these concepts during the remainder of the semester by reinforcing them during debriefings and by drawing students' attention to the importance of making finer distinctions in their categorization of themselves and others. In turn, my ability to view each student in the context of his or her multiple identities allows me to respond more mindfully, with respect and appreciation. Over time, these activities are likely to promote the use of more refined categories in students' thinking, an essential skill associated with reducing stereotypes through mindfulness (Gudykunst & Kim, 2003).

LOOKING AHEAD: THE ONGOING JOURNEY

With every new group of students, the process of negotiating my own identities and interaction style while teaching course material brings new nuances and challenges. Given the intercultural spaces we occupy in my classroom, I am the students' instructor but inevitably become part of the intervention: In order to learn (and teach) about ICC and culturally responsive pedagogy, my students (and I) must be able to engage with each other successfully in spite of elements of our identities that position us as strangers. My presence in the classroom can be an opportunity for students to learn from their intercultural experience only if we can keep our collective uncertainty and anxiety at manageable levels. Although my stranger status is dynamic, it can surface at any time and can have consequences for both parties, albeit in different ways. For students, instructional experiences designed to prepare them to teach in culturally diverse settings can be compromised. In turn, their uncontrolled uncertainty and anxiety resulting from studying about diversity can give rise to negative judgments about my teaching effectiveness and be attributed to my "ineffective" or "confusing" communication. Ironically, I have been criticized by some of my white students for not being culturally responsive to them! Although the identities and roles of the players are reversed, the political discourse in teacher education resembles the discourse about diversity in the public schools. A key difference, however, lies in the ways that culture and race come together to privilege members of the dominant groups: No matter whether I am the student or the instructor, I am the stranger. Nonetheless, the professional and ethical commitment to ensure equal educational opportunity applies equally to us all, so the journey continues. As I tell my students, learning to communicate effectively in intercultural settings is a lifelong journey. Although we may each enter at a different point on the road, forge our own path, and occasionally take the wrong turn, it is the process—not the destination—that matters, because the destination is but an idealized vision that can show us the way.

References

Adam, B. (1995). *Timewatch: The social analysis of time.* Cambridge, England: Polity Press.

Ahluwalia, H.P.S. (2004). Future challenges in rehabilitation of persons with disabilities. In C.S. Mohapatra (Ed.), *Disability management in India: Challenges and commitments* (pp. 3113–3118). Secunderabad, India: National Institute for the Mentally Handicapped.

Albrecht, G.L., Seelman, K.D., & Bury, M. (2001). *Handbook of disability studies.* Thousand Oaks, CA: Sage Publications.

Algozzine, B. (1977). The emotionally disturbed child: Disturbed or disturbing? *American Journal of Abnormal Child Psychology, 5,* 205–211.

Al-Jasser, M., & Al-Khenaizan, S. (2008). Cutaneous mimickers of child abuse: A primer for pediatricians. *European Journal of Pediatricians, 167*(11), 1221–1230.

Anderson, S. (2002*). I say a prayer for me: One woman's life of faith and triumph.* Peabody, MA: Walk Worthy Press.

Apple, M. (2003). Patriotism, religion, and the struggle over knowledge in schools. *Educational Policy, 17,* 385–391.

Apple, M.W., & Beane, J.A. (Eds.). (1995). *Democratic schools.* Alexandria, VA: Association for Supervision and Curriculum Development.

Artiles, A.J. (1998). The dilemma of difference: Enriching the disproportionality discourse with theory and context. *Journal of Special Education, 32,* 32–36.

Ayala Moreira, R. (2011). *Intellectual disability in rural Cambodia: Cultural perceptions and families' challenges.* Phnom Penh, Cambodia: New Humanity.

Bailey, D., McWilliam, P., & Winton, P. (1992). Building family-centered practices in early intervention: A team-based model for change. *Infants and Young Children, 5*(1), 73–82.

Ball, E., & Harry, B. (2010). Assessment and the policing of the norm. In C. Dudley-Marling and A. Gurn (Eds.), *The myth of the normal curve,* pp. 105–122. New York, NY: Peter Lang.

Ballenger, C. (1994). Because you like us: The language of control. *Harvard Educational Review, 62,* 199–208.

Ballenger, C. (1999). *Teaching other people's children: Literacy and learning in a bilingual classroom.* New York, NY: Teachers College Press.

Banks, J.A., & McGee Banks, C.A. (Eds.). (1997). *Multicultural education: Issues and perspectives* (3rd ed.). Hoboken, NJ: John Wiley & Sons.

Banks, J.A., & McGee Banks, C.A. (Eds.). (2010). *Multicultural education: Issues and perspectives* (7th ed). Hoboken, NJ: John Wiley & Sons.

Banks-Wallace, J. (2008). Eureka! I finally get it: Journaling as a tool for promoting praxis in research. *Association of Black Nursing Faculty Journal, 19*(1), 24–27.

Barrera, I., Corso, R.M., & Macpherson, D. (2003). *Skilled dialogue: Strategies for responding to cultural diversity in early childhood.* Baltimore, MD: Paul H. Brookes Publishing Co.

Barrera, I., & Kramer, L. (2005). *Skilled dialogue: Guidelines and strategic questions for ensuring respectful, reciprocal and responsive assessment and instruction for students who are culturally/ linguistically diverse.* Denver, CO: University of Colorado at Denver, National Institute for Urban School Improvement.

Barth, R.P. (2009). Preventing child abuse and neglect with parent training: Evidence and opportunities. *Preventing Child Maltreatment, 19*(2). Retrieved from http//futureofchildren .org/futureofchildren/publications/journals/article/index.xml?journalid=71&articleid =513&sectionid=3497

Barton, E.L. (2007). Disability narratives of the law: Narratives and counternarratives. *Narrative, 15*(1), 95–112.

Bauer, W., & Growick, B. (2003). Rehabilitation counseling in Appalachian America. *Journal of Rehabilitation, 69*(3), 18–24.

Bean, G., & Thorburn, M. (1995). Mobilising parents of children with disabilities in Jamaica and the English speaking Caribbean. In B. O'Toole & R. McConkey (Eds.), *Innovations in developing countries for people with disabilities* (pp. 105–120). Chorley, England: Lisieux Hall, in association with AssociazioneItaliana Amici di Raoul Follereau.

Beck, M. (2000). *Expecting Adam: A true story of birth, rebirth, and everyday magic.* New York, NY: Berkeley Books.

Beckman, P. (1996). *Strategies for working with families of young children with disabilities.* Baltimore, MD: Paul H. Brookes Publishing Company Co.

Behr, S.K., & Murphy, D.L. (1993). Research progress and promise: The role of perceptions in cognitive adaptation to disability. In A.P. Turnbull, I.M. Patterson, S.K. Behr, D.L. Murphy, J.G. Marquis, & M.J. Blue-Banning (Eds.), *Cognitive coping, families, and disability* (pp. 151–163). Baltimore, MD: Paul H. Brookes Publishing Co.

Bennett, A.T. (1988). Gateways to powerlessness: Incorporating Hispanic deaf children and families into formal schooling. *Disability, Handicap, and Society, 3,* 119–151.

Bernheimer, L.P., & Keogh, B.K. (1995). Weaving interventions into the fabric of everyday life: An approach of family assessment. *Topics in Early Childhood Special Education, 15,* 415–433.

Berry, J.W., Phinney, J.S., Sam, D.L., & Vedder, P. (2006). Immigrant youth: Acculturation, identity, and adaptation. *Applied Psychology: An International Review, 55*(3), 303–332.

Bertacchi, J. (1996). Relationship-based organizations. *Zero to Three, 17*(2), 1–7.

Bérubé, M. (1996). *Life as we know it: A father, a family, and an exceptional child.* New York, NY: Pantheon.

Betsinger, A., García, S.B., & Guerra, P. (2000). *Organizing for diversity: Final report.* Austin, TX: Southwest Educational Development Laboratory (ERIC Document Reproduction No. 449 260).

Biklen, D. (1974). *Let our children go: An organizing manual for advocates and parents.* Syracuse, NY: Human Policy Press.

Blacher, J. (2001). Transition to adulthood: Mental retardation, families, and culture. *American Journal on Mental Retardation, 106*(2), 173–188.

Black, L.L., & Stone, D. (2005). Expanding the definition of privilege: The concept of social privilege. *Journal of Multicultural Counseling and Development, 33*(4), 243–255.

Blasco, P.M., Falco, R.A., & Munson, L.J. (2006). Project SELF: Preparing professionals to facilitate self-determination. *Journal of Early Intervention, 29*(1), 63–79.

Blue-Banning, M.J. (1997). *The transition of Hispanic adolescents with disabilities to adulthood: Parent and professional perspectives.* (Unpublished doctoral dissertation). University of Kansas, Lawrence, KS.

Bogdan, R., & Knoll, J. (1995). The sociology of disability. In E.L. Meyen & T.M. Skrtic (Eds.), *Special education and student disability: An introduction. Traditional, emerging,* and *alternative perspectives* (4th ed., pp. 609–674). Denver, CO: Love Publishing.

Bogdewic, S.P. (1999). Participant observation. In B.F. Crabtree & W.L. Miller (Eds.), *Doing qualitative research* (2nd ed., pp. 47–69). Thousand Oaks, CA: Sage Publications.

Bowers, C.A. (1984). *The promise of theory: Education and the politics of cultural change.* New York, NY: Longman.

Bowers, C.A. (1995). *Educating for an ecologically sustainable culture: Rethinking moral education, creativity, intelligence, and other modern orthodoxies.* Albany, NY: State University of New York Press.

Bowles, S., & Gintis, H. (1976). *Schooling in capitalist America: Educational reform and contradictions of economic life.* New York, NY: Basic Books.

Bowles, S., & Gintis, H. (2002). Schooling in capitalist America revisited. *Sociology of Education, 75*(1), 1–18.

Boyd, B.A., & Correa, V.I. (2005). Developing a framework for reducing the cultural clash between African American parents and the special education system. *Multicultural Perspectives, 7*(2), 3–11.

Brantlinger, E. (2003). *Dividing classes: How the middle class negotiates and rationalizes school advantage.* New York, NY: Routledge.

Brantlinger, E. (2006). *Who benefits from special education? Remediating (fixing) other people's children.* Mahwah, NJ: Lawrence Erlbaum Associates.

Brislin, R. (1993). *Culture's influence on behavior.* Fort Worth, TX: Harcourt Brace Jovanovich.

Brislin, R.W., & Yoshida, T. (1994). *Intercultural communication training: An introduction.* Thousand Oaks, CA: Sage Publications.

Britto, P. (2008). Who am I? Ethnic identity formation of Arab Muslim children in contemporary U.S. society. *Journal of the American Academy of Child and Adolescent Psychiatry, 47*(8), 853–857.

Bronfenbrenner, U. (1986). Ecology of the family as a context for human development: Research perspectives. *Developmental Psychology, 22,* 723–742.

Brooker, L. (2003). Learning how to learn: Parental ethnotheories and young children's preparation for school. *International Journal of Early Years Education, 11*(2), 117–128. doi:10.1080/0966976032000116176

Brookfield, S. (1995). *Becoming a reflective teacher.* San Francisco, CA: Jossey Bass.

Brown, L., Shiraga, B., Ford, A., Nisbet, J., Van Deventer, P., Sweet, M., et al. (1983). Teaching severely handicapped students to perform meaningful work in non-sheltered vocational environments. In R. Morris & B. Blatt (Eds.), *Special education: Research and trends* (pp. 131–189). New York, NY: Pergammon.

Bruininks, R.H., & Lakin, K.C. (1985). *Living and learning in the least restrictive environment.* Baltimore, MD: Paul H. Brookes Publishing Co.

Bullivant, B.M. (1993). Culture: Its nature and meaning for educators. In J. Banks & C. McGee-Banks (Eds.), *Multicultural education: Issues and perspectives* (2nd ed., pp. 29–47). Needham Heights, MA: Allyn & Bacon.

Burchinal, M., Skinner, D., & Reznick, J.S. (2010). European American and African American mothers' beliefs about parenting and disciplining infants: A mixed-method analysis. *Parenting Science and Practice, 10,* 79–96.

Buriel, R., Mercado, R., Rodriguez, J., & Chavez, J.M. (1991). Mexican-American disciplinary practices and attitudes towards child maltreatment: A comparison of foreign- and native-born mothers. *Hispanic Journal of Behavioral Sciences, 13*(1), 78–94.

Carpenter, B. (1997). Empowering parents: The use of the parent as researcher paradigm in early intervention. *Journal of Child and Family Studies, 6,* 391–398.

Ceballo, R., & McLoyd, V.C. (2002). Social support and parenting in poor, dangerous neighborhoods. *Child Development, 73*(4), 1310–1321.

Chilcott, L. (Producer) & Guggenheim, D. (Director). (2010). *Waiting for Superman* [Motion picture]. United States of America: Electric Kinney Films.

Cho, S.J., Singer, G., & Brenner, B. (2003). A comparison of adaptation to childhood disability in Korean immigrant and Korean mothers. *Focus on Autism and Other Developmental Disabilities, 18*(1), 9–20.

Cianciolo, A.T., & Sternberg, R.J. (2004*). Intelligence: A brief history.* Malden, MA: Blackwell Publishing.

Cloud, N. (1993). Language, culture, and disability: Implications for instruction and teacher preparation. *Teacher Education and Special Education, 16,* 60–72.

Coleridge, P. (2000). Disability and culture. Special issue: CBR in Transition. *Asia Pacific Disability Rehabilitation Journal, 18*(1), 9–20.

Coll, C.G. (1993). *Cultural diversity: Implications for theory and practice.* Wellesley, MA: The Stone Center.

Collins, R., & Camblin, L.D. (1983). The politics and science of learning disability classification: Implications for black children. *Contemporary Education, 54*(2), 113–118.

Connor, M.H., & Boskin, J. (2001). Overrepresentation of bilingual and poor children in special education classes: A continuing problem. *Journal of Children & Poverty, 7*(1), 23–32.

Conrad, P. (1976). *Identifying hyperactive children.* Lexington, MA: D.C. Health.

Cooney, M.H. (1995, Spring). Readiness for school or for school culture? *Childhood Education,* 164–166.

Coots, J.J. (1998). Family resources and parent participation in schooling activities for their children with developmental delays. *Journal of Special Education, 31,* 498–520.

Correa, V.I. (1989). Involving culturally diverse families in the educational process. In S.H. Fradd & M.J. Weismantel (Eds.), *Meeting the needs of culturally and linguistically different students: A handbook for educators* (pp. 130–144). Boston, MA: College-Hill Press.

Correa, V.I. (1992). Cultural accessibility of services for culturally diverse clients with disabilities and their families. *Rural Special Education Quarterly, 11*(2), 6–12.

Cort, R., & Madden, D. (Producer), & Carter, T. (Director). (2001). *Save the last dance* [Motion picture]. United States of America: Paramount.

Council for Exceptional Children. (2009). *What every special educator must know: Ethics, standards, and guidelines* (6th ed.). Arlington, VA: Author.

Creswell, J. (1994). *Research design: Qualitative and quantitative approaches.* Thousand Oaks, CA: Sage Publications.

Cross, T. (1995). Developing a knowledge base to support cultural competence. *Family Resource Coalition Report, 14*(3 & 4), 17–18.

Cutler, B.C. (1993). *You, your child, and special education: A guide to making the system work.* Baltimore, MD: Paul H. Brookes Publishing Co.

Danseco, E.R. (1997a). *Building bridges: African-American mothers' and teachers' ethnotheories on child development, child problems, and home–school relations for children with and without disabilities.* (Unpublished doctoral dissertation). University of Maryland, College Park.

Danseco, E.R. (1997b). Parental beliefs on childhood disability: Insights on culture, child development, and intervention. *International Journal of Disability, Development, and Education, 44*(1), 41–52.

Darling-Hammond, L. (2002). *Learning to teach for social justice.* New York, NY: Teachers College Press.

Das, M. (1995). Tough decisions: One family's experiences crosses cultures and continents. *Volta Voices, 2*(3), 5–7.

Davis, L.J. (Ed.). (2006). *The disability studies reader* (2nd ed.). New York, NY: Routledge.

Davis, R.E. (2000). Cultural health care or child abuse? The Southeast Asian practice of Cao Gio. *Journal of the American Academy of Nurse Practitioners, 12*(3), 89–95. doi: 10.1111/j.1745-7599.2000.tb00173.x

Day, M., Demulder, E.K., & Stribling, S.M. (2010). Using the process of cultural reciprocity to create multicultural, democratic classrooms. In F. Salili & R. Hoosain (Eds.), *Democracy and multicultural education* (pp. 237–262). Charlotte, NC: Information Age Publishing.

DeGangi, G., Wietlisbach, S., & Royeen, C. (1994). The impact of culture and socioeconomic status on family–professional collaboration: Challenges and solutions. *Topics in Early Childhood Special Education, 14,* 503–521.

Delpit, L.D. (1995). *Other people's children: Cultural conflicts in the classroom.* New York, NY: New Press.

Delpit, L., & Dowdy, J.K. (Eds.). (2002). *The skin that we speak: Thoughts on language and culture in the classroom.* New York, NY: The New Press.

Dentler, R.A., & Hafner, A.L. (1997). *Hosting newcomers: Structuring educational opportunities for immigrant children.* New York, NY: Teachers College Press.

Devlieger, P. (1995). Why disabled? The cultural understanding of physical disability in an African society. In B. Ingstad & S.R. Whyte (Eds.), *Disability and culture* (pp. 94–106). Berkeley, CA: University of California Press.

Dickerson, E. (Producer and Director). (1992). *Juice.* United States of America: Island World.

Dinnebeil, L.A., & Rule, S. (1994). Variables that influence collaboration between parents and service coordinators. *Journal of Early Intervention, 18,* 349–361.

Donovan, S., & Cross, C. (2002). *Minority students in special and gifted education.* Washington, DC: National Academy Press.

Dorris, M. (1989). *The broken cord.* New York, NY: Harper Collins.

Dray, B. (2005). *A collaborative inquiry with white women about our understanding of difference in education.* (Unpublished doctoral dissertation). The University of Texas, Austin, TX.

Dray, B., García, S.B., Tackett, K., & Smay-Ashton, R. (2007, April). *Working together to reflect on our beliefs: Researcher, teacher educator, and participant perspectives.* Paper presented at the annual convention of the American Educational Research Association, Chicago, IL.

Dudley-Marling, C., & Gurn, A. (2010). *The myth of the normal curve.* New York, NY: Peter Lang.

Dunst, C.J. (2002). Family-centered practices: Birth through high school. *The Journal of Special Education, 36*(3), 139–147.

Dyson, M. (2007). *Know what I mean?* New York, NY: Westview Press.

East, P.L., Weisner, T.S., & Reyes, B. (2006). Youths' caretaking of their adolescent sisters' children: Its costs and benefits for youths' development. *Applied Developmental Science, 10*(2), 86–95.

Edgerton, R.B. (1970). Mental retardation in non-Western societies: Toward a cross-cultural perspective on incompetence. In H.C. Haywood (Ed.*), Sociocultural aspects of mental retardation* (pp. 523–559). New York, NY: Appleton Century-Crofts.

Edney, H.T. (2003). Urban League report outlines plight, progress in state of black America. *New York Amsterdam News, 94*(31), 10.

Edwards, C.P., Gandini, L., & Giovaninni, D. (1996). The contrasting developmental timetables of parents and preschool teachers in two cultural communities. In S. Harkness & C.M. Super (Eds.), *Parents' cultural belief systems: Their origins, expressions, and consequences* (pp. 270–288). New York, NY: Guilford Press.

Edwards, M.L. (1997). Constructions of physical disability in the ancient Greek world: The community concept. In D.T. Mitchell & S.L. Snyder (Eds.), *The body and physical difference: Discourses of disability* (pp. 35–50). Ann Arbor, MI: University of Michigan Press.

Erwin, E.J., & Brown, F. (2003). From theory to practice: A contextual framework for understanding self-determination in early childhood environments. *Infants & Young Children, 16*(1), 77–87.

Fadiman, A. (1997). *The spirit catches you and you fall down: A Hmong child, her American doctors, and the collision of two cultures.* New York, NY: Farrar, Straus, & Giroux.

Falicov, C.J. (1996). Mexican families. In M. McGoldrick, J. Giordano, & J.K. Pearce (Eds.), *Ethnicity and family therapy* (2nd ed., pp. 169–182). New York, NY: Guilford Press.

Falicov, C.J. (2005). Emotional transnationalism and family identities. *Family Process 44*(4), 399–406. doi:10.1111/j.1545-5300.2005.00068.x

Fass, P.S. (1989). *Minorities and the transformation of American education.* New York, NY: Oxford University Press.

Feeney, S., Christensen, D., & Moravcik, E. (2005). *Who am I in the lives of children? An introduction to teaching young children* (7th ed.). Upper Saddle River, NJ: Prentice Hall.

Ferguson, P.M. (1994). *Abandoned to their fate: Social policy and practice toward severely retarded people in America, 1820–1920.* Philadelphia, PA: Temple University Press.

Ferguson, P.M., Ferguson, D.L., & Jones, D. (1988). Generations of hope: Parental perspectives on the transitions of their children with severe retardation from school to adult life. *Journal of The Association for Persons with Severe Handicaps, 13*, 177–187.

Ferri, B.A. (2011). Undermining inclusion? A critical reading of response to intervention (RTI). *International Journal of Inclusive Education,* 1–18. First published on 17 June 2011 (iFirst).

Ferri, B.A., & Connor, D.J. (2010). "I was the special ed. girl": Urban working-class young women of colour. *Gender and Education, 22*(1), 105–121.

Filmer, A. (2003). African-American vernacular English: Ethics, ideology, and pedagogy in the conflict between identity and power. *World Englishes, 22*(3), 253–70.

Fine, M. (1993). [Ap]parent involvement: Reflections on parents, power, and urban public schools. *Teachers College Record, 94*, 682–711.

Fong, R. (2004). *Culturally competent practice with immigrant and refugee children and families.* New York, NY: The Guilford Press.

Fontes, L.A. (2002). Child discipline and physical abuse in immigrant Latino families: Reducing violence and misunderstandings. *Journal of Counseling and Development, 80*, 31–40.

Ford, D., Moore III, J., Whiting, G., & Grantham, T. (2008). Conducting cross-cultural research: Controversy, cautions, concerns, and considerations. *Roeper Review, 30*(2), 82–92.

Forjuoh, S.N. (1995). Pattern of intentional burns to children in Ghana. *Child Abuse and Neglect, 19*(7), 837–841.

Foster, K.M. (2004). Coming to terms: A discussion of John Ogbu's cultural-ecological theory of minority academic achievement. *Intercultural Education, 15*(4), 369–384. doi:10.1080/1467598042000313403

Fraser, K. (Producer), & Elmalem, M. (Director). (2005). *The life of Rayful Edmond: The rise and fall* [Motion picture]. United States of America: Liaison.

Frattura, E.M., & Topinka, C. (2006). Theoretical underpinnings of separate educational programs: "The social justice challenge continues." *Education and Urban Society, 38*(3), 327–344.

Freire, P. (2006). *Pedagogy of the oppressed* (30th anniversary edition). New York, NY: Continuum.

French, D. (1997). *Working: My life as a prostitute*. London, England: Trafalgar Square Publishing.

Friedman, L.M. (1990). *The republic of choice: Law, authority and culture*. Cambridge, MA: Harvard University Press.

Friedman, L.M. (1996). Are we a litigious people? In L.M. Friedman & H.N. Scheiber (Eds.), *Legal culture and the legal profession* (pp. 53–78). Boulder, CO: Westview Press.

Friend, M., & Cook, L. (2010). *Interactions: Collaboration skills for school professionals* (6th ed.). Boston, MA: Pearson.

Gallagher, P.A., Fialka, J., Rhodes, C., & Arceneaux, C. (2002). Working with families: Rethinking denial. *Young Exceptional Children, 5*(2), 11–17.

García, S.B., & Guerra, P. (2004). Deconstructing deficit thinking: Working with educators to create more equitable learning environments. *Education and Urban Society, 36*(2), 150–168.

García, S.B., & Guerra, P. (2006). Conceptualizing culture in education: Implications for schooling in a culturally diverse society. In J. Baldwin, S. Faulkner, S. Lindsley, & M. Hecht (Eds.), *Culture [re]defined: Analyzing culture from diverse viewpoints* (pp. 103–115). Mahwah, NJ: Lawrence Erlbaum Associates.

García, S.B., & Schaller, J.L. (1999). *Effect of graduate instruction on preservice special educators' intercultural communication skills* (Unpublished paper). The University of Texas at Austin, Austin, TX.

Garlington, J.A. (1991). *Helping dreams survive: The story of a project involving African-American families in the education of their children*. Washington, DC: National Committee for Citizens in Education.

Garn, G.A. (2000). Arizona charter schools: A case study of values and school policy. *Current Issues in Education* [On-line], 3(7). Retrieved from http://cie.asu.edu/volume3/number7/

Gay, G. (2010). *Culturally responsive teaching: Theory, research, and practice* (2nd ed.). New York, NY: Teachers College Press.

Geenen, S., Powers L.E., & Lopez-Vasquez, A. (2001). Multicultural aspects of parental involvement in transition planning. *Exceptional Children, 67*(2), 265–282.

Geursen, J., de Heer, A., & Korthagen, F. (2010). The importance of being aware: Developing professional identities in educators and researchers. *Studying Teacher Education, 6*(3), 291–302.

Gibbs, B. (1993). Providing support to sisters and brothers of children with disabilities. In G.H.S. Singer & L.E. Powers (Eds.), *Families, disability, and empowerment: Active coping skills and strategies for family interventions* (pp. 343–363). Baltimore, MD: Paul H. Brookes Publishing Co.

Gibson, M.A. (1987). Punjabi immigrants in an American high school. In G. Spindler & L. Spindler (Eds.), *Interpretive ethnography of education: At home and abroad* (pp. 281–310). Mahwah, NJ: Lawrence Erlbaum Associates.

Giroux, H. (2006). *America on the edge: Henry Giroux on politics, culture, and education*. New York, NY: Palgrave Macmillan.

Gona, J.K., Hartley, S., & Newton, C.R.J. (2006). Using participatory rural appraisal in the identification of children with disabilities in rural Kilifi, Kenya. *Rural and Remote Health, 6*, 553.

Gonzalez-Mena, J. (2008). *Diversity in early care and education: Honoring differences*. New York, NY: McGraw Hill.

Gorski, P. C. (2005). *Savage unrealities: Uncovering classism in Ruby Payne's framework*. Retrieved from http://www.EdChange.org

Gould, S.J. (1981). *The mismeasure of man*. New York, NY: Norton.

Green, P.E. (2003). The undocumented: Educating the children of migrant workers in America. *Bilingual Research Journal, 27*(1), 51–71. Retrieved from http://ks-idr.org/resources/ems/educating_children_migrant.pdf

Groce, N.E., & Zola, I.K. (1993). Multiculturalism, chronic illness, and disability. *Pediatrics, 91*, 1048–1055.

Grossman, J.L., & Friedman, L.M. (2011). *Inside the castle: Law and the family in 20th century America*. Princeton, NJ: Princeton University Press.

Gudykunst, W.B. (Ed.). (2005). *Theorizing about intercultural communication*. Thousand Oaks, CA: Sage Publications.

Gudykunst, W.B., & Kim, Y.Y. (2003). *Communicating with strangers: An approach to intercultural communication* (4th ed.). Boston, MA: McGraw-Hill.

Guerreiro, L.A. (1987). An exploratory study of home–school relations among Portuguese immigrants having handicapped children. *Contemporary Education, 58*(3), 150–154.

Gutierrez, K., Baquedano-Lopez, P., & Tejeda, C. (1999). Rethinking diversity: Hybridity and hybrid language practices in the Third Space. *Mind, Culture, and Activity, 6*(4), 286–303.

Hadaway, N., & Marek-Schroer, J.F. (1992). Multidimensional assessment of the gifted minority student. *Roeper Review, 15*(2), 73–77.

Hall, E.T. (1981). *Beyond culture*. Garden City, NY: Anchor Press/Doubleday.

Hall, E.T. (1983). *The dance of life: The other dimension of time*. Garden City, NY: Anchor Press/Doubleday.

Harkness, S., & Super, C.M. (1996). Introduction. In S. Harkness & C.M. Super (Eds.), *Parents' cultural belief systems: Their origins, expressions, and consequences* (pp. 1–26). New York, NY: Guilford Press.

Harkness, S. & Super, C.M. (2006). Themes and variations: Parental ethnotheories in Western cultures. In K.H. Rubin & O.B. Chung (Eds.), *Parenting beliefs, behaviors, and parent–child relations: A cross-cultural perspective* (pp. 61–80). New York, NY: Psychology Press.

Harland, K. (2002). *A will of his own: Reflections on parenting a child with autism*. Bethesda, MD: Woodbine House.

Harry, B. (1992a). Developing cultural self-awareness: The first step in values clarification for early interventionists. *Topics in Early Childhood Special Education, 12*, 333–350.

Harry, B. (1992b). An ethnographic study of cross-cultural communication with Puerto Rican-American families in the special education system. *American Educational Research Journal, 29*, 471–494.

Harry, B. (1992c). Making sense of disability: Low-income, Puerto Rican parents' theories of the problem. *Exceptional Children, 59*, 27–40.

Harry, B. (1992d). Restructuring the participation of African-American parents in special education. *Exceptional Children, 59*, 123–131.

Harry, B. (1994). *The disproportionate representation of minority students in special education: Theories and recommendations*. Alexandria, VA: National Association of State Directors of Special Education.

Harry, B. (1996). These families, those families: The impact of the researcher identities on the research act. *Exceptional Children, 61*(4), 364–377.

Harry, B. (1997). Leaning forward or bending backwards: Cultural reciprocity in working with families. *Journal of Early Intervention, 21*, 62–72.

Harry, B. (1998). Parental visions of "una vida normal/ a normal life": Cultural variations on a theme. In L.H. Meyer, H.-S. Park, M. Grenot-Scheyer, I.S. Schwartz, & B. Harry (Eds.), *Making friends: The influences of culture and development* (pp. 47–62). Baltimore, MD: Paul H. Brookes Publishing Co.

Harry, B. (2008). Collaboration with culturally and linguistically diverse families: Ideal versus reality. *Exceptional Children, 74*(3), 372–388.

Harry, B. (2010). *Melanie, bird with a broken wing: A mother's story*. Baltimore, MD: Paul H. Brookes Publishing Co.

Harry, B., Allen, N., & McLaughlin, M. (1995). Communication versus compliance: African-American parents' involvement in special education. *Exceptional Children, 61*, 364–377.

Harry, B., Allen, N., & McLaughlin, M. (1996). "Old-fashioned, good teachers": African American parents' views of effective early instruction. *Learning Disabilities Research and Practice, 11*, 193–201.

Harry, B., & Anderson, M.G. (1994). The disproportionate placement of African American males in special education programs: A critique of the process. *Journal of Negro Education, 63*(4), 602–620.

Harry, B., Hart, J., & Klingner, J.K. (2005). African American families under fire: Ethnographic views of family strengths. *Remedial and Special Education, 26*(2), 101–112.

Harry, B., & Kalyanpur, M. (1994). Cultural underpinnings of special education: Implications for professional interactions with culturally diverse families. *Disability and Society, 9*(2), 145–165.

Harry, B., Kalyanpur, M., & Day, M. (1999). *Building cultural reciprocity with families: Case studies in special education.* Baltimore, MD: Paul H. Brookes Publishing Co.

Harry, B., & Klingner, J.K. (2006). *Why are so many minority students in special education? Understanding race and disability in schools.* New York, NY: Teachers College.

Harry, B., Rueda, R., & Kalyanpur, M. (1998). From normalization to ecocultural analysis: A sociocultural approach to responsive intervention with culturally diverse families of children with disabilities. *Exceptional Children , 66*(1), 123–136.

Hasnain, R., Sotnik, P., & Ghiloni, C. (2003). Person-centered planning: A gateway to improving vocational rehabilitation services for culturally diverse individuals with disabilities. *Journal of Rehabilitation, 69*(3), 10–17.

Hayden, D., Takemoto, C., Anderson, W., & Chitwood, S. (2008*). Negotiating the special education maze: A guide for parents and teachers* (4th ed.). Bethesda, MD: Woodbine House.

Heath, S.B. (1983). *Ways with words: Language, life, and work in communities and classrooms.* New York, NY: Cambridge University Press.

Heilman, E. (2004). Hoosiers, hicks, and hayseeds: The controversial place of marginalized ethnic whites in multicultural education. *Equity & Excellence in Education, 37*, 67–79.

Helander, B. (1995). Disability as incurable illness: Health, process, and personhood in Southern Somalia. In B. Ingstad & S.R. Whyte (Eds.), *Disability and culture* (pp. 73–93). Berkeley, CA: University of California Press.

Henze, R.C., & Vanett, L. (1993). To walk in two worlds—or more? Challenging a common metaphor of native education. *Anthropology and Education Quarterly, 24*(2), 116–134.

Heshusius, L. (1994). Freeing ourselves from objectivity: Managing subjectivity or turning toward a participatory mode of consciousness. *Educational Researcher, 23*(3), 15–22.

Hewes, J., & Chinn, S. (Producers), & Percival, D., & Crisp, M. (Directors). (2005). *Beyond the color line* [Motion picture.] United States of America: PBS.

Hines, P.M., & Boyd-Franklin, N. (2005). African American families. In M. McGoldrick, J. Giordano, & N. Garcia-Preto (Eds.), *Ethnicity and family therapy* (3rd ed., pp. 77–86). New York, NY: Guilford Press.

Hmong family prevents surgery on son. (1991, January). *Omaha World Herald,* p. 16.

Hodges, V.G., Burwell, Y., & Ortega, D. (2003). Empowering families. In L.M. Gutierrez, R.J. Parsons, & E.O. Cox (Eds.), *Empowerment in social work practice: A sourcebook* (2nd ed., pp. 146–162). Pacific Grove, CA: Brooks/Cole.

Holden, G.W. (2002). Perspectives on the effects of corporal punishment: Comment on Gershoff. *Psychological Bulletin, 28*(4), 590–595. doi:10.1037/0033-2909.128.4.590

Hollins, E. (2008). *Culture in school learning: Revealing the deep meaning.* New York, NY: Routledge.

Howard, W.L., Bicard, S.E., & Cavanaugh, R.A. (2007). Educational equality for students with disabilities. In J.A. Banks & C.A. McGee Banks (Eds.), *Multicultural education: Issues and perspectives* (pp. 329–359). Hoboken, NJ: John Wiley & Sons.

Hruby, G.G., & Hynd, G.W. (2006). Decoding Shaywitz: The modular brain and its discontents. *Reading Research Quarterly, 41*(4), 544–556.

Hun, T., Berkvens, J. & Kalyanpur, M. (2008, March). *Attitudes towards disability and inclusion among Cambodian families and adults with disabilities: Implications for professionals.* Paper presented at the Center for Khmer Studies International Conference on Cambodia and Mainland Southeast Asia at its Margins: Minority Groups and Borders, Siem Reap, Cambodia.

Illich, I. (1971). *Deschooling society.* New York, NY: Harper & Row.

Individuals with Disabilities Education Act Amendments of 1997, PL 105-17, 20 U.S.C. §§ 1400 *et seq.*

Individuals with Disabilities Education Act (IDEA) of 1990, PL 101-476, 20 U.S.C. §§ 1400 *et seq.*

Individuals with Disabilities Education Improvement Act of 2004, PL 108-446, 20 U.S.C. §§ 1400 *et seq.*

Ingstad, B. (1995). Mphoyamodimo—a gift from God: Perspectives on "attitudes" toward disabled persons. In B. Ingstad & S.R. Whyte (Eds.), *Disability and culture* (pp. 246–266). Berkeley, CA: University of California Press.

Ingstad, B., & Whyte, S.R. (Eds.). (2007). *Disability in local and global worlds.* Berkeley, CA: University of California Press.

Jacob, E. (1995). Reflective practice and anthropology in culturally diverse classrooms. *Elementary School Journal, 95,* 451–463.

Janko, S. (1994). *Vulnerable children, vulnerable families: The social construction of child abuse.* Thousand Oaks, CA: Sage Publications.

Joe, J.R. (1997). American Indian children with disabilities: The impact of culture on health and education services. *Families, Systems, and Health, 15,* 251–261.

Johnson, D. (Producer), & Wilcox, R. (Director and Producer). (2009). *Hope and redemption: The Lena Baker Story* [Motion picture]. United States of America: Laughing Crow Entertainment.

Kalyanpur, M. (1995, October). Developing cultural competence: Social skills training for classroom teachers of culturally diverse learners. *Social Skills Newsletter,* 2–5.

Kalyanpur, M. (1996). The influence of Western special education on community-based services in India. *Disability and Society, 11*(2), 249–270.

Kalyanpur, M. (1998). The challenge of cultural blindness: Implications for family-focused service delivery. *Journal of Child and Family Studies, 7*(3), 317–332.

Kalyanpur, M. (2005). *Secondary transition and cultural diversity [Online].* Lawrence, KS: University of Kansas, Department of Special Education. Retrieved from www.transitioncoalition.org

Kalyanpur, M. (2009). Cultural variations on the construct of self-advocacy in the Indian context. In M. Alur & V. Timmons (Eds.), *Inclusive education across cultures: Crossing boundaries, sharing ideas* (pp. 331–341). Thousand Oaks, CA: Sage Publications.

Kalyanpur, M. (2011). Paradigm and paradox: Education for all and the inclusion of children with disabilities in Cambodia. *International Journal on Inclusive Education,* 1–19. doi:10.1080/13603116.2011.555069

Kalyanpur, M., & Gowramma, I.P. (2007). Cultural barriers to South Indian families' access to services and educational goals for their children with disabilities. *Journal of the International Association of Special Education, 8*(1), 69–82.

Kalyanpur, M., & Harry, B. (1997). A posture of reciprocity: A practical approach to collaboration between professionals and parents of culturally diverse backgrounds. *Journal of Child and Family Studies, 6,* 487–509.

Kalyanpur, M., & Harry, B. (1999). *Culture in special education: Building reciprocal family-professional relationships.* Baltimore, MD: Paul H. Brookes Publishing Co.

Kalyanpur, M., Harry, B., & Skrtic, T., (2004). Equity and advocacy expectations of culturally diverse families' participation in special education. In D. Mitchell (Ed.), *Special educational needs and inclusive education: Major themes in education* (pp. 358–378). London, England: Routledge Falmer.

Kalyanpur, M., & Misra, A. (2011). Facing the challenge of inclusion in India. In K. Mazurek & M. Winzer (Eds.), *Special education in an international perspective* (pp. 193–216). Washington, DC: Gallaudet University Press.

Kalyanpur, M., & Rao, S.S. (1991). Empowering low-income black families of handicapped children. *American Journal of Orthopsychiatry, 61,* 523–532.

Katz, L.F., Lederman, C.S., & Osofsky, J.D. (2010). *Child-centered practices for the courtroom and community: A guide to working efficiently with young children and their families in the child welfare system.* Baltimore, MD: Paul H. Brookes Publishing Co.

Keller, H., Lamm, B., Abels, M., Yovsi, R., Borke, J., Jensen, H., et al. (2006). Cultural models, socialization goals, and parenting ethnotheories: A multicultural analysis. *Journal of Cross-Cultural Psychology, 37,* 155–172.

Killion, M.U. (2005). China's amended constitution: Quest for liberty and independent judicial review. *Washington University Global Studies Law Review, 4*(43), 43–80.

Kincaid, J. (1990). *Lucy.* New York, NY: Plume Books.

Kittler, M., Rygal, D., & McKinnon, A. (2011). Special review article: Beyond culture or beyond control? Reviewing the use of Hall's high-/low-context concept. *International Journal of Cross Cultural Management, 11*(1), 63–82.

Kleinman, A. (1980). *Patients and healers in the context of culture.* Berkeley, CA: University of California Press.

Klingner, J.K., Artiles, A.J., & Mendez-Barletta, L. (2006). English language learners who struggle with reading: Language acquisition or LD? *Journal of Learning Disabilities, 39,* 108–128.

Knotek, S. (2003). Bias in problem-solving and the social process of student study teams: A qualitative investigation. *The Journal of Special Education, 37*(1), 2–14.

Koch, H., Foner, N. (Producers), & Gyllenhaal, S. (Director). (1995). *Losing Isaiah* [Motion Picture]. United States of Amercia: Paramount.

Kremenitzer, J. (2005). The emotionally intelligent early childhood educator: Self-reflective journaling. *Early Childhood Education Journal, 33*(1), 3–9.

Kushner, M. & Ortiz, A. (2000). The preparation of early childhood education teachers to serve English language learners. In *National Institute on Early Childhood Development and Education, new teachers for a new century: The future of early childhood professional preparation* (pp. 123–154). Washington, DC: U.S. Department of Education.

Lai, Y., & Ishiyama, F.I. (2004). Involvement of immigrant Chinese-Canadian mothers of children with disabilities. *Exceptional Children, 71*, 97–108.

Langer, E., & Moldoveanu, M. (2000). The construct of mindfulness. *Journal of Social Issues, 56*(1), 1–9.

Lareau, A. (2003). *Unequal childhoods: Class, race, and family life.* Berkeley, CA: University of California Press.

Lareau, A., & Shumar, W. (1996). The problem of individualism in family–school policies. *Sociology of Education, 69*(Suppl.), 24–39.

LaSalle, B. (2003). *Finding Ben: A mother's journey through the maze of Asperger's.* Chicago, IL: Contemporary Books.

Lau, A.S. (2010). Physical discipline in Chinese American immigrant families: An adaptive culture perspective. *Cultural Diversity and Ethnic Minority Psychology, 16*(3), 313–322. doi:10.1037/a0018667

Lea, D. (2001). *An ethnographic study concerning the perceptions of adolescent mothers' of children with disabilities participation on their child's early intervention team.* (Unpublished dissertation). University of Maryland, College Park, MD.

Lea, D. (2006). 'You don't know me like that': Patterns of disconnect between adolescent mothers of children with disabilities and their early interventionists. *Journal of Early Intervention, 28*, 264–282. doi:10.1177/105381510602800403

Leary, J. (2005). *Posttraumatic slave syndrome: America's legacy of enduring injury and healing.* Milwaukee, WI: Uptone Press.

Leech, N.L., & Onwuegbuzie, A.J. (2007). An array of qualitative data analysis tools: A call for data analysis triangulation. *School Psychology Quarterly, 22*(4), 557–584.

Lehr, S., & Taylor, S.J. (1986). *Roots and wings: A manual about self-advocacy.* Boston, MA: Federation for Special Needs.

Leon, E. (1996, September 7). *Challenges and solutions for educating migrant students.* Lansing, MI: Michigan Department of Education. (ERIC Document Reproduction Service No. ED 393 615)

Leung, E.K. (1988, October). *Cultural and acculturational commonalities and diversities among Asian Americans: Identification and programming considerations.* Paper presented at the Ethnic and Multicultural Symposium, Dallas, TX. (ERIC Document Reproduction Service No. ED 298 780)

Levin, B. (2008). Curriculum policy and the politics of what should be learned in schools. In F.M. Connelly, M.F. He, & J. Phillion, (Eds.), *The SAGE handbook of curriculum and instruction* (pp. 7–24). Thousand Oaks, CA: Sage Publications.

Levin, H. (1990). At-risk students in a yuppie age. *Educational Policy, 4*, 284–285.

Levy, R.I. (1996). Essential contrasts: Differences in parental ideas about learners and teaching in Tahiti and Nepal. In S. Harkness & C.M. Super (Eds.), *Parents' cultural belief systems: Their origins, expressions, and consequences* (pp. 123–142). New York, NY: Guilford Press.

Lewis, J. (2009). Redefining qualitative methods: Believability in the fifth moment. *International Journal of Qualitative Methods, 8*(2), 1–14.

Lieberman, A.F. (1990). Infant–parent intervention with recent immigrants: Reflections on a study with Latino families. *Zero to Three, 10*(4), 8–11.

Livingston, S. (1997). *Rethinking the education of deaf students: Theory and practice from a teacher's perspective.* Portsmouth, NH: Heinemann.

Locust, C. (1988). Wounding the spirit: Discrimination and traditional American Indian belief systems. *Harvard Educational Review, 59*, 315–330.

Logan, S.L. (Ed.). (2001). *The black family: Building strength, self-help, and positive change* (2nd ed.). Boulder, CO: Westview Press.

Lynch, E.W., & Hanson, M.J. (1998). *Developing cross-cultural competence: A guide for working with young children and their families* (2nd ed.). Baltimore, MD: Paul H. Brookes Publishing Co.

Lynch, E.W., & Hanson, M.J. (2011). *Developing cross-cultural competence: A guide for working with children and their families* (4th ed.). Baltimore, MD: Paul H. Brookes Publishing Co.

Mallory, B.L. (1995). The role of social policy in life-cycle transitions. *Exceptional Children, 62,* 213–233.

Manuelito, K. (2005). The role of education in American Indian self-determination: Lessons from the Ramah Navajo Community School. *Anthropology and Education Quarterly, 36,* 73–87.

Mardiros, M. (1989). Conception of childhood disability among Mexican-American parents. *Medical Anthropology, 12,* 55–68.

Marion, R. (1979). Minority parent involvement in the IEP process: A systematic model approach. *Focus on Exceptional Children, 10*(8), 1–16.

Markey, U.A. (1997). Valuing all families. *Tapestry: Weaving Sustaining Threads, 1*(3), 1.

Marshall, C., Mitchell, D., & Wirt, F. (1989). *Culture and education policy in the American states.* New York, NY: Falmer Press.

McAdoo, H.P. (2002). *Black children: Social, educational and parental environments* (2nd ed.). Thousand Oaks, CA: Sage Publications.

McCall, N. (1995). *Makes me wanna holler: A young black man in America.* New York, NY: Random House Vintage Publishing.

McCall, Z., & Skrtic, T.M. (2009). Intersectional needs politics: A policy frame for the wicked problem of disproportionality. *Multiple Voices for Ethnically Diverse Exceptional Learners,* 113–123.

McCarthy, M.R., & Soodak, L.C. (2007). The politics of discipline: Balancing school safety and rights of students with disabilities. *Exceptional Children, 73*(4), 456–474.

McCray, C. (2007). Beyond Brown: Examining the perplexing plight of African American principals. *Journal of Instructional Psychology, 34*(4), 247–256.

McDermott, R., Goldman, S., & Varenne, H. (2006). The cultural work of learning disabilities. *Educational Researcher, 35*(6), 12–17.

McDonnell, L.M., McLaughlin, M.J., & Morison, P. (Eds.). (1997). *Educating one and all: Students with disabilities and standards-based reform.* Washington, DC: National Academy Press.

McGillicuddy-De Lisi, A.V., & Subramanian, S. (1996). How do children develop knowledge? Beliefs of Tanzanian and American mothers. In S. Harkness & C.M. Super (Eds.), *Parents' cultural belief systems: Their origins, expressions, and consequences* (pp. 143–168). New York, NY: Guilford Press.

McGoldrick, M., Giordano, J., & Garcia-Preto, N. (2005). *Ethnicity and family therapy* (3rd ed.). New York, NY: Guilford Press.

McGowan, B.G. (1988). Helping Puerto Rican families at risk: Responsive use of time, space, and relationships. In C. Jacobs & D.D. Bowles (Eds.), *Ethnicity and race: Critical concepts in social work* (pp. 48–70). Silver Spring, MD: National Association of Social Workers.

McHatton, P., & Correa, V. (2005). Stigma and discrimination: Perspectives from Mexican and Puerto Rican mothers of children with special needs. *Topics in Early Childhood Special Education, 25*(3), 131–142.

McIntosh, P. (1989). White privilege: Unpacking the invisible knapsack. *Peace and Freedom, 49*(4), 10–12.

McKenzie-Pollock, L. (1996). Cambodian families. In M. McGoldrick, J. Giordano, & N. Garcia-Preto (Eds.), *Ethnicity and family therapy* (2nd ed., pp. 307–315). New York, NY: Guilford Press.

McKenzie-Pollock, L. (2005). Cambodian families. In M. McGoldrick, J. Giordano, & J.K. Pearce (Eds.), *Ethnicity and family therapy* (3rd ed., pp. 290–301). New York, NY: Guilford Press.

McLeod, P., & Polowy, C.I. (2000). *Social workers and child abuse reporting: A review of state mandatory reporting requirements.* Washington, DC: National Association of Social Workers.

Mehan, H. (1993). Beneath the skin and between the ears: A case study in the politics of representation. In S. Chaiklin & J. Lave (Eds.), *Understanding practice: Perspectives on activity and context* (pp. 241–267). New York, NY: Cambridge University Press.

Mehan, H., Hartwick, A., & Miehls, J.L. (1986). *Handicapping the handicapped: Decision-making in students' educational careers.* Stanford, CA: Stanford University Press.

Mercer, C.D. (1997). *Students with learning disabilities.* Upper Saddle River, NJ: Merrill/Prentice-Hall.

Mercer, J. (1973). *Labeling the mentally retarded.* Berkeley, CA: University of California Press.

Meyers, C. (1992). Hmong children and their families: Consideration of cultural influences on assessment. *The American Journal of Occupational Therapy, 46,* 737–744.

Mezirow, J. (1997). Transformative learning: Theory to practice. *New Directions for Adult and Continuing Education, 74,* 5–12.

Miles, M. (2002). Community and individual responses to disablement in South Asian histories: Old traditions, new myths? *Asia Pacific Disability Rehabilitation Journal, 13*(2), 1–16.

Miles, M., & Miles, C. (1993). Education and disability in cross-cultural perspective: Pakistan. In S.J. Peters (Ed.), *Education and disability in cross-cultural perspective* (pp. 167–235). New York, NY: Garland.

Miller, A.B., & Keys, C.B. (1996). Awareness, action, and collaboration: How the self-advocacy movement is empowering for persons with developmental disabilities. *Mental Retardation, 34,* 312–319.

Mlawer, M.A. (1993). Who should fight? Parents and the advocacy expectation. *Journal of Disability Policy Studies, 4*(1), 105–115.

Monks, J., & Frankenberg, R. (1995). Being ill and being me: Self, body and time in multiple sclerosis narratives. In B. Ingstad & S.R. Whyte (Eds.), *Disability and culture* (pp. 107–136). Berkeley, CA: University of California Press.

Mont, D. (2002). *A different kind of boy: A father's memoir about raising a gifted child with autism.* Philadelphia, PA: Jessica Kingsley.

Moore, W. (2010). *The other Wes Moore: One name and two fates—A story of tragedy and hope.* New York, NY: Spiegel and Grau/Random House.

National Commission on Children. (1991). *Beyond rhetoric: A new American agenda for families.* Washington, DC: Author.

No Child Left Behind Act of 2001, PL 107-110, 115 Stat. 1425, 20 U.S.C. §§ 6301 *et seq.*

Officer, A., & Groce, N.E. (2009). Key concepts in disabilities. *The Lancet, 374*(9704), 1795–1796.

Ogbu, J.U., & Simons, H.D. (1998). Voluntary and involuntary minorities: A cultural-ecological theory of school performance with some implications for education. *Anthropology & Education Quarterly, 29*(2), 155–188. doi:10.1525/aeq.1998.29.2.155

Oswald, D.P., Coutinho, M.J., & Best, A.M. (2005). Community and school predictors of overrepresentation of minority children in special education. In D.J. Losen & G. Orfield (Eds.), *Racial inequity in special education* (pp. 1–13). Cambridge, MA: Harvard Education Press.

Ovesen, J., &Trankell, I-B. (2010). *Cambodians and their doctors: A medical anthropology of colonial and post-colonial Cambodia.* Singapore: NIAS Press.

Palmer, S.B., & Wehmeyer, M.L. (2002). Promoting self-determination in early elementary school: Teaching self-regulated problem-solving and goal-setting skills. *Remedial and Special Education, 24,* 115–126.

Parette, H.P., Meadan, H., & Doubet, S. (2010). Fathers of young children with disabilities in the United States: Current status and implications. *Childhood Education, 86*(6), 382–387.

Park, C.C. (1982). *The siege: The first eight years of an autistic child.* Boston, MA: Back Bay Books/ Little, Brown.

Park, C.C. (2001). *Exiting nirvana: A daughter's life with autism.* Boston, MA: Little, Brown.

Park, M.S. (2001). The factors of child physical abuse in Korean immigrant families. *Child Abuse and Neglect, 25*(7), 945–58.

Patterson, O. (2010). Inequality in America and what to do about it. *Nation, 291,* 18–20.

Payne, R.K. (2005). *A framework for understanding poverty.* Highlands, TX: aha! Process, Inc.

Pedersen, P.B. (1981). Alternative futures for cross-cultural counseling and psychotherapy. In A.J. Marsella & P.B. Pedersen (Eds.), *Cross-cultural counseling and psychotherapy* (pp. 312–337). New York, NY: Pergamon.

Peshkin, A. (1988). In search of subjectivity: One's own. *Educational Researcher, 17,* 17–22.

Pfaelzer, J. (2007). *Driven out: The forgotten war against Chinese Americans.* New York, NY: Random House.

Philips, S. (1983). *The invisible culture: Cultural democracy, bi-cognitive development, and education.* New York, NY: Academic Press.

Piestrup, A.M. (1973). *Black dialect interference and accommodations of reading instruction in first grade.* Berkeley, CA: University of California Press. (ERIC Document Reproduction Service No. ED 119 113)

Powers, L.E., Singer, G.H.S., & Sowers, J.A. (1996). Self-competence and disability. In L.E. Powers & G.H.S. Singer (Eds.), *On the road to autonomy: Promoting self-competence in children and youth with disabilities* (pp. 3–24). Baltimore, MD: Paul H. Brookes Publishing Co.

Provenzo, E., Renaud, J., & Provenzo, A. (2008). *Encyclopedia of the social and cultural foundations of education.* Thousand Oaks, CA: Sage Publications.

Raghavan, C.S., Harkness, S., & Super, C.M. (2010). Parental ethnotheories in the context of immigration: Asian Indian immigrant and Euro-American mothers and daughters in an American town. *Journal of Cross-Cultural Psychology, 41,* 617–632. doi:10.1177/0022022110362629

Ramírez, M., & Castañeda, A. (1974). *Cultural democracy, bi-cognitive development, and education.* New York, NY: Academic Press.

Rao, S.S. (1996). "A little inconvenience": Perspectives of Bengali families of children with disabilities on inclusion and disability. *Disability & Society, 16*(4), 531–548.

Rao, S., & Kalyanpur, M. (2002). Promoting home–school collaboration in positive behavior support. In J.M. Lucyshyn, G. Dunlap, & R.W. Albin (Eds.), *Families and positive behavior support: Addressing problem behavior in family contexts* (pp. 219–242). Baltimore, MD: Paul H. Brookes Publishing Co.

Rauscher, L., & McClintock, M. (1997). Ableism curriculum design. In M. Adams, L.A. Bell, & P. Griffin (Eds.), *Teaching diversity and social justice: A sourcebook* (pp. 198–230). New York, NY: Routledge.

Ravitch, D. (2010). *The death and life of the great American school system: How testing and choice are undermining education.* New York, NY: Basic Books.

Red Horse, J. (1980). American Indian elders: Unifiers of Indian families. *Social Casework, 61,* 490–493.

Renz-Beaulaurier, R. (2003). Empowering people with disabilities: The role of choice. In L.M. Gutierrez, R.J. Parsons, & E.O. Cox (Eds.), *Empowerment in social work practice: A sourcebook* (2nd ed., pp. 73–82). Pacific Grove, CA: Brooks/Cole.

Rhodes, R.L. (1996). Beyond our borders: Spanish-dominant migrant parents and the IEP process. *Rural Special Education Quarterly, 15*(2),19–22.

Rogers-Dulan, J., & Blacher, J. (1995). African American families, religion, and disability: A conceptual framework. *Mental Retardation, 33,* 226–238.

Rogoff, B. (2003). *The cultural nature of human development.* New York, NY: Oxford University Press.

Roseberry-McKibbin, C. (1995). Distinguishing language differences. *Multicultural Education, 2*(4), 12–16.

Ross-Sheriff, F., & Chaudhari, S. (2004). Asian Indian children and families. In R. Fong (Ed.), *Culturally competent practice with immigrant and refugee children and families* (pp. 146–162). New York, NY: The Guilford Press.

Ross-Sheriff, F., & Husain, A. (2004). South Asian Muslim children and families. In R. Fong (Ed.), *Culturally competent practice with immigrant and refugee children and families* (pp. 163–182). New York, NY: The Guilford Press.

Rubin, K., & Chung, O.B. (Eds.). (2006). *Parenting beliefs, behaviors, and parent–child relations: A cross-cultural perspective.* London, England: Psychology Press.

Rueda, R., Monzo, L., Shapiro, J., Gomez, J., & Blacher, J. (2005). Cultural models of transition: Latina mothers of young adults with developmental disabilities. *Exceptional Children, 71*(4), 401–414.

Sánchez, S.Y., & Thorp, E.K. (2008). Teaching to transform: Infusing cultural and linguistic diversity. In P.J. Winton, J.A. McCollum, & C. Catlett (Eds.), *Practical approaches to early childhood professional development: Evidence, strategies, and resources* (pp. 81–97). Washington, DC: Zero to Three Press.

Scarlett, W.G. (2005, March/April). Building relationships with young children. *Child Care Information Exchange,* 38–40.

Schalock, R.L., Luckasson, R.A., & Shogren, K.A. (2007). The renaming of mental retardation: Understanding the change to the term intellectual disability. *Intellectual and Developmental Disabilities, 45*(2), 116–124.

Scheer, J., & Groce, N. (1988). Impairment as a human constant: Crosscultural and historical perspectives on variation. *Journal of Social Issues, 44,* 23–37.

Scherzer, A.L. (2009). Experience in Cambodia with the use of a culturally relevant developmental milestone chart for children in low- and middle-income countries. *Journal of Policy and Practice in Intellectual Disabilities, 6*(4), 287–292.

Schön, D.A. (1983). *The reflective practitioner: How professionals think in action.* New York, NY: Basic Books.

Schum, T.R., McAuliffe, T.L., Simms, M.D., Walter, J.A., Lewis, M., & Pupp, R. (2001). Factors associated with toilet training in the 1990s. *Ambulatory Pediatrics, 1*(2), 79–86.

Schweder, R.A., Mahapatra, M., & Miller, J.G. (1990). Culture and moral development. In J.W. Stigler, R.A. Schweder, & G. Herdt (Eds.), *Cultural psychology: Essays on comparative human development* (pp. 134–203). Cambridge, England: Cambridge University Press.

Serpell, R. (1994). The cultural construction of intelligence. In W.J. Lonner & R.S. Malpass (Eds.), *Readings in psychology and culture* (pp. 157–163). Needham Heights, MA: Allyn & Bacon.

Serpell, R. (1997). Critical issues, literacy connections between school and home: How should we evaluate them? *Journal of Literacy Research, 29*, 587–616.

Serpell, R., Mariga, K., & Harvey, K. (1993). Mental retardation in African countries: Conceptualization, services, and research. *International Review of Research in Mental Retardation, 19*, 1–39.

Shafer, M.S., & Rangasamy, R. (1995). Transition and Native American youth: A follow-up study of school-leavers on the Fort Apache Indian Reservation. *Journal of Rehabilitation, 61*(1), 60–65.

Shapiro, J.P. (2003). No pity: People with disabilities forging a new civil rights movement. In S. Plous (Ed.), *Understanding prejudice and discrimination* (pp. 36–48). Boston, MA: McGraw Hill.

Shapiro, J., & Simonsen, D. (1994). Educational/support group for Latino families of children with Down syndrome. *Mental Retardation, 32*, 403–415.

Shaywitz, S.E., & Shaywitz, B.A. (2004). Neurobiologic basis for reading and reading disability. In P. McCardle & V. Chhabra (Eds.), *The voice of evidence in reading research* (pp. 417–442). Baltimore, MD: Paul H. Brookes Publishing Co.

Shaywitz, S., & Shaywitz, B. (2009). Functional brain imaging in studies of reading and dyslexia. *Encyclopedia of language and literacy development.* Retrieved from http://literacyency clopedia.ca/index.php?fa=items.show&topicId=281

Silverstein, R. (2000). Emerging disability policy framework: A guidepost for analyzing public policy. *Iowa Law Review, 85*(5), 1757–1784.

Skiba, R., Simmons, A., Ritter, S., Kohler, K., Henderson, M., & Wu, T. (2006). The context of minority disproportionality: Practitioner perspectives on special education referral. *Teachers College Record, 108*(7), 1424–1459.

Skinner, D.G., Correa, V., Skinner, M., & Bailey, D.B. (2001). Role of religion in the lives of Latino families of young children with developmental delays. *American Journal on Mental Retardation, 106*(4), 297–313.

Skinner, D., & Weisner, T.S. (2007). Sociocultural studies of families of children with intellectual disabilities. *Mental Retardation and Developmental Disabilities Research Reviews, 13*, 302–312.

Skrtic, T.M. (1991). *Behind special education: A critical analysis of professional culture and school organization.* Denver, CO: Love Publishing.

Skrtic, T.M. (1995a). The crisis in professional knowledge. In E.L. Meyen & T.M. Skrtic (Eds.), *Special education and student disability: An introduction. Traditional, emerging, and alternative perspectives* (4th ed., pp. 567–608). Denver, CO: Love Publishing.

Skrtic, T.M. (1995b). Deconstructing/reconstructing the professions. In T.M. Skrtic (Ed.), *Disability and democracy: Reconstructing (special) education for postmodernity* (pp. 3–62). New York, NY: Teachers College Press.

Skrtic, T.M. (2004). The crisis in special education knowledge: A perspective on perspective. In S. Danforth & S. Taft (Eds.), *Crucial readings in special education* (pp. 80–95). Englewood Cliffs, NJ: Prentice Hall.

Skrtic, T.M. (2005). A political economy of learning disabilities. *Learning Disability Quarterly, 28*(2), 149–155.

Skrtic, T.M., & McCall, Z. (2010). Ideology, institutions, and equity: Comments on Christine Sleeter's "Why Is there learning disabilities." *Disability Studies Quarterly, 30*(2). Retrieved from http://dsq-sds.org/article/view/1230/1277

Sleeter, C. (1986). Learning disabilities: The social construction of a special education category. *Exceptional Children, 53*, 46–54.

Sleeter, C.E. (1998). Yes, learning disabilities is political; what isn't? *Learning Disability Quarterly, 21*(4), 289–296.

Sleeter, C.E. (2001). Preparing teachers for culturally diverse schools: Research and the overwhelming presence of whiteness. *Journal of Teacher Education, 52*(4), 94–106.

Sleeter, C.E. (2010). Why is there learning disabilities? A critical analysis of the birth of the field in its social context. Reprinted from T.S. Popkewitz (Ed.), *The formation of school subjects: The struggle for creating an American institution* (pp. 210–237). London, England: Palmer Press, in *Disability Studies Quarterly 30*(2).

Smart, J.F., & Smart, D.W. (1991). Acceptance of disability and the Mexican American culture. *Rehabilitation Counseling Bulletin, 34*, 357–367.

Smith, M.J., & Ryan, A.S. (1987). Chinese-American families of children with developmental disabilities: An exploratory study of reactions to service providers. *Mental Retardation, 25*, 345–350.

Smith, P., & Routel, C. (2010). Transition failure: The cultural bias of self-determination and the journey to adulthood for people with disabilities. *Disability Studies Quarterly, 30*(1). Retrieved from http://www.dsq-sds.org/article/view/1012/1224

Sohng, S.S.L., & Song, K-H. (2004). Korean children and families. In R. Fong (Ed.) *Culturally competent practice with immigrant and refugee children and families.* (pp. 81–99). New York, NY: The Guilford Press.

Souljah, S. (2000). *Coldest winter ever.* New York, NY: Pocket Book Publishers.

Sparrow, S.S., Cicchetti, D.V., & Balla, D.A. (2005). *The Vineland Adaptive Behavior Scales—Second Edition.* London, England: Pearson Assessment.

Spindler, F., & Spindler, L. (1990). *The American cultural dialogue and its transmission.* London, England: Falmer Press.

Stanovich, K.E., & Stanovich, P.J. (1996). Rethinking the concept of learning disabilities: The demise of aptitude/achievement discrepancy. In D.R. & N. Torrance (Eds.), *The handbook of education and human development: New models of learning, teaching and schooling* (pp. 117–147). Malden, MA: Blackwell Publishing.

Stein, D.B. (2002). A new and circumspect strategy to reify ADD/ADHD? *Ethical Human Sciences and Services, 4*(3), 235–237.

Sternberg, R.J. (1996). *Successful intelligence.* New York, NY: Simon & Schuster.

Sugai, G., & Horner, R.H. (2002). The evolution of discipline practices: School-wide positive behavior supports. *Child and Family Behavior Therapy, 24*, 23–50.

Sullivan, A. (2011). Disproportionality in special education identification and placement of English Language Learners. *Exceptional Children, 77*(3), 317–334.

Sutton, C.T., & Broken Nose, M.A. (2005). American Indian families: An overview. In M. Mc-Goldrick, J. Giordano, & N. Garcia-Preto (Eds.), *Ethnicity and family therapy* (3rd ed., pp. 43–54). New York, NY: Guilford Press.

Swick, K.J. (1997). Involving families in the professional preparation of educators. *The Clearing House, 70*, 265–268.

Tajima, E.A., & Harachi, T.W. (2010). Parenting beliefs and physical discipline practices among Southeast Asian immigrants: Parenting in the context of cultural adaptation to the United States. *Journal of Cross-Cultural Psychology, 41*(2), 212–235. doi:10.1177/0022022109354469

Talle, A. (1995). A child is a child: Disability and equality among the Kenya Masai. In B. Ingstad & S.R. Whyte (Eds.), *Beyond culture* (pp. 56–72). Berkeley, CA: University of California Press.

Taylor, R.J., Chatters, L.M., Hardison, C.B., & Riley, A. (2001). Informal social support networks and subjective well-being among African Americans. *Journal of Black Psychology, 27*(4), 439–463. doi:10.1177/0095798401027004004

Taylor, S.J. (2001). Caught in the continuum: A critical analysis of the principle of the least restrictive environment. In D. Fisher & D.L. Ryndak (Eds.), *The foundations of inclusive education: A compendium of articles on effective strategies to achieve inclusive education originally published in JASH* (pp. 13–25). Baltimore, MD: TASH (reprinted from *JASH, 13*[1], 41–53).

Test, D.W., Fowler, C.H., Brewer, D.M., & Wood, W.M. (2005). A content and methodological review of self-advocacy intervention studies. *Exceptional Children, 72*(1), 101–125.

Test, D.W., Fowler, C.H., Wood, W.M., Brewer, D.M., & Eddy, S. (2005). A conceptual framework of self-advocacy for students with disabilities. *Remedial and Special Education, 26*(10), 43–54.

Thomson, P., & Gunter, H. (2011). Inside, outside, upside down: The fluidity of academic researcher "identity" in working with/in school. *International Journal of Research & Method in Education, 34*(1), 17–30.

Thorp, E.K. (2009). *Selected dilemma strategies.* Crosswalks Talk. Retrieved from http://www.fpg.unc.edu/~scpp/crosswalks/pages/presentations.cfm#remindme

Thorp, E., & Sánchez, S. (1998). The use of discontinuity in preparing early educators of culturally, linguistically and ability-diverse young children and their families. *Zero to Three, 18*, 27–33.

Thressiakutty, A.T., & Govinda Rao, L. (2001). *Transition of persons with mental retardation from school to work.* Secunderabad, India: National Institute for the Mentally Handicapped.

Tillman, L. (2006). Researching and writing from an African-American perspective: Reflective notes on three research studies. *International Journal of Qualitative Studies in Education (QSE), 19*(3), 265–287.

Ting-Toomey, S., & Chung, L.C. (2007). *Understanding intercultural communication.* New York, NY: Oxford University Press.

Tobin, J.J., Hsueh, Y., & Karasawa, M. (2009). *Preschool in three cultures revisited: Japan, China, and the United States.* Chicago, IL: Chicago University Press.

Traustadottir, R. (1995). A mother's work is never done: Constructing a "normal" family life. In S.J. Taylor, R. Bogdan, & Z.M. Lutfiyya (Eds.), *The variety of community experience: Qualitative studies of family and community life* (pp. 47–66). Baltimore, MD: Paul H. Brookes Publishing Co.

Trawick-Smith, J. (1997). *Early childhood development: A multicultural perspective.* Upper Saddle River, NJ: Merrill.

Turnbull, A.P., & Ruef, M.B. (1996). Family perspectives on problem behavior. *Mental Retardation, 34,* 280–293.

Turnbull, A.P., Turnbull, H.R., Erwin, E.J., Soodak, L.C., & Shogren, K.A. (2011). *Families, professionals, and exceptionality: Positive outcomes through partnerships and trust* (6th ed.). Upper Saddle River, NJ: Pearson.

Turnbull, H.R., & Stowe, M.J. (2001). A taxonomy for organizing the core concepts according to their underlying principles. *Journal of Disability Policy Studies, 12,* 177–197.

Turnbull, H.R., Turnbull, A.P., Stowe, M.J., & Huerta, N.E. (2007). *Free appropriate public education: The law and children with disabilities* (7th ed., revised printing). Denver, CO: Love.

Turner, J.H. (2003). *Human institutions: A theory of societal evolution.* Lanham, MD: Rowman & Littlefield.

Tyack, D.B. (1993). Constructing difference: Historical reflections on schooling and social diversity. *Teachers College Record, 95,* 8–34.

Tyack, D.B., & Hansot, E. (1982). *Managers of virtue: Public school leadership in America, 1820-1980.* New York, NY: Basic Books.

U.S. Department of Education. (2007). *26th annual report to congress on the implementation of the Individuals with Disabilities in Education Act 2004, Vol 2.* Washington, DC: Author.

U.S. Department of Education. (2009). *The 29th annual report to congress on the implementation of the Individuals with Disabilities Education Act 2004.* Washington, DC: Author.

U.S. Department of Education, Institute for Education Sciences, National Center for Education Statistics. (2003). *National Assessment of Adult Literacy.* Retrieved from http://nces.ed.gov/naal/framework.asp

U.S. Department of Labor. (1965). *The Negro family: The case for national action.* Washington, DC: U.S. Government Printing Office.

Valdés, G. (1996). *Con respeto: Bridging the distances between culturally diverse families and schools: An ethnographic portrait.* New York, NY: Teachers College Press.

Valsiner, J. (1989). Organization of children's social development in polygamic families. In J. Valsiner (Ed.), *Child development in cultural context* (pp. 67–86). Toronto, Ontario, Canada: Hogrefe and Huber.

Valsiner, J. (2008, June). *Culture within development: Similarities behind differences.* Paper presented at Da Xia Forum Lecture, Shanghai, China.

Vanleit, B., Channa, S., & Prum, R. (2007). Children with disabilities in rural Cambodia: An examination of functional status and implications for service delivery. *Asia Pacific Disability Rehabilitation Journal, 18*(2), 53–68.

Vygotsky, L. (1978). *Mind in society: The development of higher psychological processes.* M. Cole, V. John-Steiner, S. Scribner, & E. Sounerman (Eds. and Trans.). Cambridge, MA: Harvard University Press.

Walker, S. (1986). Attitudes toward the disabled as reflected in social mores in Africa. In K. Marfo, S. Walker, & B. Charles (Eds.), *Childhood disability in developing countries: Issues in habilitation and special education* (pp. 239–249). New York, NY: Praeger.

Ware, L.P. (1994). Contextual barriers to collaboration. *Journal of Educational and Psychological Consultation, 5,* 339–357.

Wechsler, D. (1991). *The Wechsler Intelligence Scale for Children* (3rd ed.). London, England: Pearson Assessment.

Wechsler, D. (2004). *The Wechsler Intelligence Scale for Children* (4th ed.). London, England: Pearson Assessment.

Weisner, T.S. (2002). Ecocultural understanding of children's developmental pathways. *Human Development, 45,* 275–281.

Weiss, B.D., & Coyne, C. (1997). Communicating with patients who cannot read. *The New England Journal of Medicine, 337*(4), 272–274.

Welles-Nyström, B. (1996). Scenes from a marriage: Equality ideology in Swedish family policy, maternal ethnotherapies, and practice. In S. Harkness & C.M. Super (Eds.), *Disability and culture* (pp. 3–35). Berkeley, CA: University of California Press.

Wheelock, J., Oughton, E.A., & Baines, S. (2003). Getting by with a little help from your family: Toward a policy-relevant model of the household. *Feminist Economics, 9*(1), 19–45.

Whyte, S.R., & Ingstad, B. (1995). Disability and culture: An overview. In B. Ingstad & S.R. Whyte (Eds.), *Disability and culture* (pp. 3–35). Berkeley, CA: University of California Press.

Wilder, L.K., Jackson, A.P., & Smith T. (2001). Secondary transition of multicultural learners: Lessons from the Navajo Native American experience. *Preventing School Failure, 45*(3), 119–124.

Wisconsin v. Yoder, 406 U.S. (1972).

Wolfensberger, W. (1972). *Normalisation: The principle of normalisation in human services.* Toronto, Ontario, Canada: National Institute on Mental Retardation.

Wolfram, W. (2007). Sociolinguistic myths in the study of African American English. *Linguistic and Language Compass, 2,* 292–313.

Wong, M.-H. (1989). Kohlberg's "just community" and the development of moral reasoning: A Chinese perspective. In J. Valsiner (Ed.), *Child development in cultural context* (pp. 87–110). Toronto, Ontario, Canada: Hogrefe and Huber.

Ysseldyke, J.E., Algozzine, B., &Thurlow, M.L. (1992). *Critical issues in special education* (2nd ed.). Boston, MA: Houghton Mifflin.

Zhang, D., Wehmeyer, M.L., & Chen, L-J. (2005). Parent and teacher engagement in fostering the self-determination of students with disabilities: A comparison between the United States and the Republic of China. *Remedial and Special Education, 26*(1), 55–64.

Zola, I.K. (1986). The medicalization of American society. In P. Conrad & R. Kern (Eds.), *The sociology of health and illness: Critical perspectives* (2nd ed., pp. 378–394). New York, NY: St. Martin's Press.

Index

Page references to tables, figures, and boxes are indicated by *t, f,* and *b,* respectively.

Independence
  as cornerstone of special education,
    104–106
  culturally defined, 81
  interpretations of for student service's, 28
  literacy and, 28–29
  meanings of, 29, 104
  policies reflecting value of, 36
  satisficing perspective, 108–109
  see also Anglo-American families; United
    States culture
Indian families
  communication, 75
  community identity and, 93
  goals and, 104
  immutable characteristics in, 42
  self-advocacy and, 107b
  spiritual causes of disabilities, 51
  value inequality, 43
  work, 111b
Individuality
  contrasting cultural traditions in, 40–42
  as a cornerstone of special education,
    106–109
  under Individuals with Disabilities Educa-
    tion Act (IDEA), 37–38
  reflecting on, 22
  value of, 24, 36
  see also Anglo-American families; United
    States culture
Individualized education program (IEP),
    28–29, 72, 75–78
Individualized family service plan (IFSP), 37
Individuals with Disabilities Education
    Act (IDEA) Amendments of 1997
    (PL 105-17), 35
Individuals with Disabilities Education Act
    (IDEA) of 1990 (PL 101-476), 35, 36–40
Individuals with Disabilities Education
    Improvement Act (IDEA) of 2004
    (PL 108-446)
  parent participation and, 23–24, 65–66,
    72–75
  Part C, 82
  values in, 23–24, 35
Induction, process of, 64
Industrialization, 7
Instantiation, 93–94, 95
Institutional transitions, 104, 105
Integration (acculturation pattern), 5
Intellectual disability (ID), 11–12, 46
Interactions, parent–professional, 84–85
  see also Communication
Intercultural communication (ICC)
  competence in, 160–162
  integrating cultural reciprocity into,
    162–165
  overview of, 160

  as a pedagogical tool, 165–166
  teacher preparation in, 158, 159f
Interdependence
  in adulthood, 106
  goals and, 104
  parental ethnotheories and, 88
  reflecting on, 22
  self-advocacy and, 108, 108b
International Labor Organization, 95

Jamaican families, 41
Jargon, 3–4, 57–58, 60, 61b
  see also Language; Medicalizing;
    Terminology
Jewish families, 51, 103
Journaling, 122–124, 152–153
Judgment categories, 46
Juice (Dickerson, 1992), 131

Kin-corporate families, 89
Know What I Mean? (Dyson, 2007), 131
Knowledge
  contrasting types of, 68–69
  expert, 59–60
  intercultural communication (ICC) and,
    161, 163–164
  parental, 71
  of self and rights, 107b
Korean families, 41, 43

Labeling
  backlash from, 62
  under Individuals with Disabilities Educa-
    tion Act (IDEA), 35
  idiosyncratic nature of, 46
  of parents, 70, 70b, 140
  reifying tendency of, 60
  stigmatizing effect of, 64–65
Language, 3–4, 57–58
  see also Jargon
Latino families
  community identity and, 93
  family interactions, 91
  family structure, 89
  interdependence, 106
  meaningful work and, 110–111
Least restrictive environment (LRE), 36, 39
Lens, cultural, 149, 160, 167
The Life of Rayful Edmond: The Rise and Fall
    (Fraser, 2005), 131
Literacy, 28–29, 73–74
  see also Reading
Litigation, 38
Logistical factors, 77
Losing Isaiah (Koch & Foner, 1995), 130